Solutions that Work

Solutions that Work
Fighting Poverty in Winnipeg

edited by
Jim Silver

Published by
Canadian Centre for Policy Alternatives–Manitoba
and Fernwood Publishing

Copyright © 2000 by the authors.
All rights reserved. No part of this book may be reproduced or transmitted in any form or by any means, electronic or mechanical, including photocopying, or by any information storage or retrieval system, without permission in writing from the authors.

Canadian Cataloguing in Publication Data

Main entry under title:
Solutions that work
(Basics from Fernwood Publishing)
ISBN 1-55266-021-4
1. Poverty--Manitoba--Winnipeg. 2. Poor--Services for--Manitoba--Winnipeg. I. Silver, James, 1946- II. Series.

RC118.S64 2000   362.5'0912743   C00-950047-2

Printed and published in Canada

Canadian Centre for Policy Alternatives–Manitoba
309-323 Portage Ave.
Winnipeg, MB
R3B 2C1
tel: 204-943-9962
fax: 204-943-9978
email: ccpamb@mb.sympatico.ca
http://www.policyalternatives.ca

Fernwood Publishing
P.O. Box 9409, Stn. A.
Halifax, NS
B3K 5S3
tel: 902-422-3302
fax: 902-422-3179
http://home.istar.ca/~fernwood

Table of Contents

Contributors i

Preface iii

Chapter 1
Persistent Poverty in Canada
By Jim Silver 1

Chapter 2
High and Rising: The Growth of Poverty in Winnipeg
By Darren Lezubski, Jim Silver, and Errol Black 26

Chapter 3
Workfare in Manitoba
By Shauna MacKinnon 52

Chapter 4
The Case for a Strong Minimum Wage Policy
By Errol Black and Lisa Shaw 70

Chapter 5
Aboriginal Economic Development In Winnipeg
by John Loxley 84

Chapter 6
In the Face of Poverty: What a Community School Can Do
By Heather Hunter 111

Chapter 7
Solutions that Work: Fighting Poverty in Winnipeg's Inner City
By Jim Silver 126

Editor's Acknowledgements

For their many and varied contributions to this book I am grateful to Wayne Antony, Errol Black, Gilbert Dong, Ed Finn, Kerri-Anne Finn, Heather Hunter, Darren Lezubski, John Loxley, Shauna MacKinnon, Jim Mulvale, Todd Scarth, Lisa Shaw, and Harold Shuster. I am especially happy to acknowledge the contribution, by way of continued love and support, made by my wife and daughter, Loa Henry and Zoe Silver.

Contributors

Errol Black is a professor of economics at Brandon University, and a board member of the Canadian Centre for Policy Alternatives-Manitoba.

Heather Hunter is the Assistant Superintendent of Student Services in the River East School Division, and was until recently the Principal of William Whyte Community School in Winnipeg.

John Loxley is a professor of economics at the University of Manitoba, and a board member of the Canadian Centre for Policy Alternatives-Manitoba.

Darren Lezubski is the Senior Researcher at the Social Planning Council of Winnipeg.

Shauna MacKinnon is an anti-poverty activist in Winnipeg, and a board member of the Canadian Centre for Policy Alternatives-Manitoba. Her academic work has concentrated on Canadian social policy.

Lisa Shaw is a researcher with the Canadian Centre for Policy Alternatives-Manitoba.

Jim Silver is a professor of political science at the University of Winnipeg, and Chair of the Board of the Canadian Centre for Policy Alternatives-Manitoba.

Preface

This is a book about poverty in Winnipeg, but not just Winnipeg. It is true that poverty is higher in Winnipeg than in most Canadian cities, and that the high levels of poverty affecting Aboriginal people is a greater problem in Winnipeg than in most—not all—large Canadian centres. But the patterns of poverty identified here and the solutions that are advanced are not at all unique to Winnipeg. The trends in the incidence of poverty over the past twenty years and the relationship of poverty to household types, to changes in the structure of the labour market and to the nature of the political response to poverty, including reductions in levels of social assistance, are patterns that are familiar to all Canadian urban centres.

There is, however, a distinct advantage in looking at poverty by means of a case study of one particular city. The authors in this volume look at poverty from several different perspectives, producing a more richly layered and textured analysis than might otherwise be possible. The closer attention to detail that is made possible by this method is especially important in considering solutions to poverty, which is the purpose of this book.

A wide variety of solutions to poverty have been tried in Winnipeg, as in the rest of Canada. The neo-liberal response instituted in recent years by federal and provincial governments, featuring a reliance on the forces of the "free" market, has failed. "Trickle-down" economic policies and dramatic cuts to government transfer payments have not reduced the level of poverty in Canada. While it is true that poverty is a complex and multi-faceted phenomenon for which there is no single solution, it is nevertheless the case that community-based initiatives are a *necessary* feature of any real and lasting attempt to eradicate poverty in Canada. Winnipeg's rich experience with community-based solutions to poverty is evidence of that truth and may be a model for other cities throughout Canada and beyond.

While the purpose of this book is to reflect on local community-based solutions to poverty, it is of course the case that developments beyond the local level play a crucial role in any attempt to develop solutions to poverty. For example, improvements at the provincial and national levels in income security and labour market policies are desperately needed in the fight against poverty. One can imagine a range of such policy changes, the result of which would be the creation of a climate in which the community-based solutions discussed in this volume would flourish and proliferate. Similarly, although they are discussed only briefly here, in the opening chapter, developments in the global political economy in recent decades run directly counter to the initiatives described in this book. Indeed, at least some of the community-based strategies discussed in this volume—local hiring and procurement; incentives for local economic development in preference to corporate incursions, for example—are likely to contravene specific provisions of the various trade agreements to which Canada is now bound. The global affects the local; inner-city efforts in Winnipeg to build an indigenous economy that meets local peoples' needs are not at all unrelated to mass protests in late 1999 in Seattle.

The focus of this book, however, is very much on the local. What may be said is that the crisis of poverty in Winnipeg and the many innovative and imaginative community-based responses to that crisis being put into practice in Winnipeg are solutions that can be and are being applied right across the country and beyond. Local community-based solutions can and do have national and even global applications.

The first chapter, "Persistent Poverty in Canada," places Winnipeg in a national context by identifying the patterns of poverty in Canada as a whole over the past twenty years. The risk of poverty is shown to be related to household type, as well as to gender, age, and the number and age of children in a family. These factors, in turn, are largely a function of differing relationships to the labour market. The rapidly changing character of the labour market, in particular the growth of part-time and low wage jobs and of self-employment, plus declining real wage levels, have been important factors in keeping poverty levels in Canada persistently high these past two decades. This trend has been added to by the dramatic cuts in various forms of social assistance. Poverty levels have remained high even as unemployment levels have declined since 1993. Since poverty levels have historically declined when unemployment has declined, this apparent severing of the connection between employment and poverty is a particularly worrisome trend.

Chapter Two, "High and Rising: The Growth of Poverty in Winnipeg," documents the steady, indeed dramatic, growth of poverty in Winnipeg, and especially in Winnipeg's inner city, since 1981—a process which mirrors the Canadian trends identified in the first chapter. The high incidence and rapid growth of poverty in Winnipeg's inner city are associated with high and growing rates of unemployment, low and declining rates of labour force participation, and low and declining real income levels. This is especially the case for single parents and Aboriginal people, and especially Aboriginal youth, in the inner city. Contrary to popular belief, however, there are more poor people beyond than within Winnipeg's inner city, and while most single parents and most Aboriginal people are poor, most poor people are neither Aboriginal nor single parents. From these observations the authors draw two conclusions. First, the high incidence of poverty in the inner city, and among single parents and Aboriginal people, is a particularly acute problem. Second, it would be a serious mistake to assume that poverty in Winnipeg is confined to particular parts of the city or to particular parts of the population. Indeed, the authors argue that the problem of poverty in Winnipeg as a whole has reached crisis proportions. The crisis of poverty in Winnipeg demands an immediate and dramatic response. A major part of the response, the authors contend, has to be the community-based solutions that are a major theme of this book.

Chapter Three, "Workfare in Manitoba," examines the welfare "reforms" instituted in the 1990s by the former Conservative government of Manitoba, culminating in the introduction of workfare in 1996—another Canada-wide trend. Workfare is a deeply flawed response to the problem of poverty. It is based on the false assumption that people on welfare are lazy, dishonest and undeserving. There is no evidence to sustain this assumption. Moreover, workfare is coercive, although coercion is neither necessary nor appropriate. Workfare does not create a long-term solution to poverty, nor to unemployment. There is no evidence that workfare programs—despite their frequently high costs—are successful in moving people out of the welfare system. Instead, social assistance recipients are shuffled through a series of temporary jobs, in some cases involving subsidies to private sector employers. Rarely do the jobs become permanent once the subsidy has expired. In other cases, welfare recipients are forced to work on a "voluntary" basis with community organizations. There is a dark irony at work in a government policy which forces the poor to work for free for agencies which are no longer able—because of funding cuts by that same government—to provide them with effective support. The author concludes that the most successful programs are voluntary, community-based programs that provide supports to people to enable them to improve their own circumstances.

Chapter Four, "The Case For a Strong Minimum Wage Policy in Manitoba," begins by detailing the significant decline in recent years in Manitoba's minimum wage, in real and in relative terms—a decline which is not peculiar to Manitoba but is Canada-wide. The chapter then sets out the cases both for and against a higher minimum wage. The argument *against* higher minimum wages—that a high minimum wage results in job loss, thus hurting the very people it was intended to benefit—is shown to be inconsistent with the bulk of recent empirical evidence. The evidence is that a higher minimum wage has, at worst, a modest effect on the availability of jobs and may even result in more jobs being created than lost. A higher minimum wage results in a reduction of the incidence of low incomes, and thus of poverty, and a reduction in the degree of inequality in the distribution of income. Thus a higher minimum wage is an important part of an effective anti-poverty strategy. It is also likely that a higher minimum wage will increase aggregate levels of economic activity and of employment, thus benefitting the economy as a whole. The authors conclude by calling not only for a higher minimum wage, but also for the indexation of the minimum wage to the Consumer Price Index for Manitoba, in order to ensure that its value is not eroded in real terms as the result of inflation.

Chapter Five, "Aboriginal People in the Winnipeg Economy," describes the particularly difficult circumstances faced by a significant proportion of Winnipeg's rapidly growing Aboriginal community. Although this issue is more significant in Winnipeg than in most Canadian cities, it is by no means peculiar to Winnipeg. As measured by most economic indicators—unemployment and labour force participation rates, average income levels, adequacy of housing, rates of mobility and incidence of poverty—Aboriginal people in Winnipeg are, on average, less well off than Winnipeg's non-Aboriginal population. This is so despite clear evidence of a desire to secure paid employment and despite active participation in a wide range of informal sector activities. Complicating these problems is the fact that most Aboriginal political organizations lack the institutional and financial capacity for economic planning and development. Yet, some of the most innovative and promising community-based solutions to poverty have arisen from the efforts of Aboriginal people working in Winnipeg's inner city. This chapter lays the foundations of the community-based anti-poverty initiatives that are the "solutions that work" referred to in the title of this volume.

The way in which a community-based solution has been applied at an inner city school in one of Winnipeg's lowest-income neighbourhoods is the subject of Chapter Six, "In The Face of Poverty: What a Community School Can Do." By using its resources to purchase locally and to hire locally, the school has contributed to local economic development and local employment, thus strengthening and stabilizing families in the surrounding community. In addition, Heather Hunter, author and former Principal of the school, describes how the community has been brought into the school's decision-making process, creating opportunities for people who live in poverty to be the actors—the ones who shape and create their world—rather than the acted upon. The premise is that this, too, will strengthen and stabilize families and community. This is absolutely essential because stronger and more stable families and communities are the key to better school performance by children in poverty. The example described in this chapter is evidence, applicable to all Canadian settings, of the important part that local schools can play—and, by extension, that other such institutions *could* play—in advancing the community-based solutions to poverty that are the focus of this book.

Chapter Seven, "Solutions that Work: Fighting Poverty in Winnipeg's Inner City," provides a range of evidence drawn from recent authoritative reports that poverty in Winnipeg has reached crisis proportions. The costs—both to those growing numbers who live in poverty and in a variety of ways to society as a whole—are far too high. Those solutions tried in the past—both free-market, "trickle-down" economics and top-down programs conceived and delivered by government officials to, rather than with, those who are poor—have not worked. The solutions that work are community-based solutions which actively involve and support those who are living in poverty in solving their own problems. Using the voices of inner city residents and anti-poverty activists, many examples of exciting and innovative community-based initiatives by which people in poverty work to solve their own problems and meet their own needs are described. Adequate funding of such community-based initiatives, together with a range of supportive government policies—the provision of adequate and affordable child care facilities, the enactment of a strong minimum wage policy, investment in early childhood education initiatives, for example—constitute the basis of a strategy by which poverty in Winnipeg, and in other Canadian urban centres, could be overcome. All that is needed is the political will to act.

Chapter 1
Persistent Poverty in Canada
By Jim Silver

For the past two decades, poverty rates in Canada* have remained persistently high. Rates are higher now than twenty years ago: 17.2 percent in 1997, as compared with 13.1 percent in 1979 (National Council of Welfare (NCW), 1987, p. 2; NCW, 1997). Until very recently, poverty rates moved in lock-step with broad economic trends, rising slightly during the recession of the early 1980s, from 15.3 percent in 1980 to 18.2 percent in 1983, declining during the ensuing economic recovery to 13.6 percent in 1989, then rising again during the early 1990s recession to 17.4 percent in 1993. However, rates have *not* declined significantly with the recovery of the mid-1990s, but have remained relatively flat, at 17 percent-plus (Table One). The failure of Canadian poverty rates to decline in the mid-1990s as economic growth resumed and unemployment rates dropped represents a significant and worrisome break with traditional patterns.

Although international comparisons are difficult, by some measures Canada's overall poverty rate is higher than other liberal democratic industrialized countries, with the exception of the United States. By other measures Canada ranks in about the middle of industrialized countries. With respect to particular populations within countries, Canada has the second highest rate of child poverty, after the U.S., and the third highest rate of single-parent poverty, after the U.S. and Australia (Canadian Council on Social Development (CCSD), 1994, pp. 1 and 5). The United Nations Human Poverty Index, 1999, ranks Canada ninth from the top among seventeen industrialized countries in its treatment of the poor. Taking into account the percentage of the population not expected to live to age sixty, the level of functional illiteracy, the incidence of income poverty, and the incidence of long-term unemployment, the United Nations Development Program (UNDP) concludes that eight industrialized countries ranked higher than Canada in their treatment of the poor (UNDP, 1999, pp. 130-31 and 149). The lower rates of poverty in other industrialized countries suggest that the high rates in Canada are not inevitable, and could be lowered with different policy decisions.

People at Risk of Poverty

While rates of poverty for all persons in Canada have been persistently high throughout the 1980s and 1990s, particular populations in Canada are more likely than others to be poor. One important determinant of the risk of poverty is family type. Single-parent mothers and unattached individuals are much more likely to

* The Statistics Canada Low Income Cut Offs (LICO) are used to determine poverty rates. Please see the Appendix, "The Debate About Poverty Lines," in Chapter Two.

Acknowledgements

For their contributions to earlier versions of this chapter I am grateful to Wayne Antony, Shauna MacKinnon, Todd Scarth and Lisa Shaw.

Table 1: Poverty Trends, All Persons (1980-1997)

Year	Poor Persons	All Persons	Poverty Rate
1980	3,624,000	23,626,000	15.3%
1981	3,643,000	23,814,000	15.3%
1982	3,951,000	24,021,000	16.4%
1983	4,406,000	24,229,000	18.2%
1984	4,397,000	24,348,000	18.1%
1985	4,170,000	24,535,000	17.0%
1986	3,976,000	24,807,000	16.0%
1987	3,912,000	25,075,000	15.6%
1988	3,744,000	25,348,000	14.8%
1989	3,487,000	25,729,000	13.6%
1990	3,821,000	26,099,000	14.6%
1991	4,227,000	26,495,000	16.0%
1992	4,320,000	26,901,000	16.1%
1993	4,775,000	27,398,000	17.4%
1994	4,795,000	28,867,000	16.6%
1995	5,070,000	29,193,000	17.4%
1996	5,190,000	29,542,000	17.6%
1997	5,121,000	29,846,000	17.2%

SOURCE: National Council of Welfare, Poverty Profile 1997. Table 2.

be poor than are couples. Figure One reveals that, in 1997, 57.1 percent of single mothers had incomes below the poverty line. Unattached individuals experienced poverty rates ranging from 27.2 percent to 42.0 percent, depending upon the sex and age of the individuals. Rates for couples, by contrast, ranged from 7.0 percent to 11.9 percent.

Women are more likely than men to be poor. Since 1980, poverty rates for women have consistently been one-third again as high as poverty rates for men (NCW, 1996, p. 86). In all age categories, the incidence of poverty is higher for women than for men, and the spread by gender is especially wide for older (65+ years) and younger (18-24 years) women (NCW, 1997, p. 37).

Young people, both women and men, also have a relatively high incidence of poverty. This is the case for all family types. For single-parent mothers, couples with children, childless couples, unattached women, and unattached men, those under the age of twenty-five years have a much higher incidence of poverty than those twenty-five years of age and over. The rate of poverty for the relatively small number of single mothers under the age of twenty-five, for instance, is an astonishing 93.3 percent (NCW, 1999, Graph P-1, p. 39).

In addition to correlating with gender and age, poverty also correlates with the number and age of children. As shown in Figures Two and Three, the greater the number and the younger the age of children in a family, whether a two-parent or a single-parent family, the greater is the likelihood of poverty.

Both the growth of poverty and the relationship of children to poverty are reflected also in food bank usage in Canada. In March 1999, 790,344 people in Canada used food banks—more than the total population of Winnipeg, and more than double the 378,000 who had used food banks a decade earlier in March 1989. More than 40 percent of those who used food banks in 1999 were children under the age of eighteen, although children under the age of eighteen comprise only

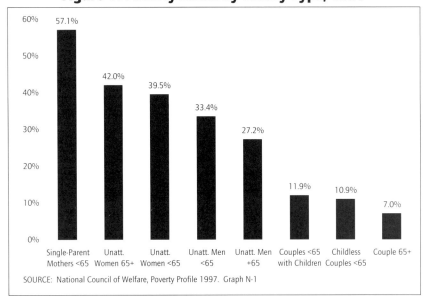

Figure 1: Poverty Rates by Family Type, 1997

SOURCE: National Council of Welfare, Poverty Profile 1997. Graph N-1

26.5 percent of Canada's population (Canadian Association of Food Banks, 1999, pp. 1 and 3).

Poverty and the Labour Market

The fact that the incidence of poverty varies by family type is likely attributable in large part to varying relationships to the labour market. For example, that two-parent families and couples without children are the family types with the lowest incidence of poverty is largely attributable to the greater likelihood that they will have a second wage-earner in the family, an option not available, by definition, to unattached individuals. That single-parent families have the highest rate of poverty is largely attributable to the much greater likelihood that they will have no wage earners in the family. That the incidence of poverty among single-parent families is higher for those with children under seven years of age is attributable to the greater difficulty of working in the paid labour force when children are not yet in school.

This is evidence that a person's relationship to the paid labour force is the most important determinant of poverty. As the Ecumenical Coalition for Economic Justice puts it: "Unemployment is the single most reliable predictor of poverty for those aged 18 to 65" (Ecumenical Coalition for Economic Justice, 1996, p. 9). Conversely, as the National Council of Welfare observes: "... a good job is the best insurance against poverty for Canadians under the age of 65" (NCW, 1996, p. 37). This can be seen clearly in Figure Four, which correlates the incidence of poverty with the number of weeks worked in 1997. The more weeks of work that a family put in, the less likely they were to be poor.

The number of weeks worked by working poor families has declined dramatically since the 1970s. For those with earned incomes in the lowest 10 percent of working families, the average number of weeks worked per year has been cut almost in half, from 43.3 to 23.5 (Yalnizyan, 1998, pp. 41 and 46).

4 Solutions That Work

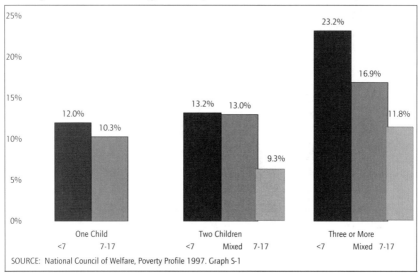

Figure 2: Poverty Rates for Two-Parent Familes under 65, by Number and Age Group of Children under 18, 1997

SOURCE: National Council of Welfare, Poverty Profile 1997. Graph S-1

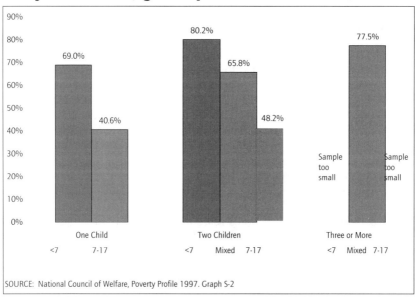

Figure 3: Poverty Rates for Single-Parent Mothers Under 65, by Number and Age Group of Children under 18, 1997

SOURCE: National Council of Welfare, Poverty Profile 1997. Graph S-2

The incidence of poverty can also be correlated with the *type* of work one does, as shown in Table Two. The incidence of poverty is particularly high for those in primary industries and in the service and retail sectors.

Table Two also reveals that being in the paid labour force and earning wages is no guarantee against poverty. An important category of people in poverty are the working poor. Recall the National Council of Welfare's observation about the correlation between employment and poverty: "… a *good* (my emphasis) job is the best insurance against poverty …." However, growing numbers of jobs are either part-time or pay low wages, or both, so that even though people are working, their earnings may be so low that they are still below the poverty line. Figure Five shows that in 1997 less than one-half—44 percent—of heads of all poor families under 65 years of age had no employment, while 35 percent worked part-time and 21 percent—just over one in five—worked full-time. In short, the majority of heads of poor families, 56 percent, were in the paid labour force. For unattached individuals under 65 years of age, the situation was similar: 55 percent of those who were poor in 1997 were among the working poor. Most of the poor are members of the "working poor."

Part-Time and Low-Wage Jobs

These data reflect two important trends in the Canadian economy: the growth of part-time work and self-employment; and the growth of low-wage jobs.

The proportion of jobs that are part-time has grown steadily from under 5 percent in the 1950s, to over 18 percent in 1998 (Table Three).

As economist Jim Stanford (1996, pp. 132-33) has observed: "Fully one-half of the new jobs created in Canada during the 1980s were non-standard: that is, jobs that were not full-time, were not year round, or involved working for more than a single employer." As a result, "Part-time jobs make up almost 1 in 5 (job) opportunities now, compared to 1 in 10 in the mid-1970s" (Yalnizyan, 1998, p. 26). In clerical, sales and service occupations, 6 of every 10 workers are part-time, a fact which contributes to the relatively high proportion of people in those occupations who have incomes below the poverty line, as shown in Table Two.

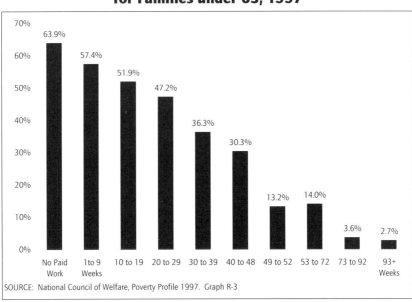

Figure 4: Poverty Rates by Weeks of Work for Families under 65, 1997

SOURCE: National Council of Welfare, Poverty Profile 1997. Graph R-3

Further, part-time workers are more likely than full-time workers to be paid low wages. In 1995, 43 percent of part-time workers earned less than $7.50 per hour, while fewer than 10 percent of full-time workers earned less than $7.50 per hour. And while 60-70 percent of full-time workers had access to benefits packages—pensions, medical/dental, paid sick leave—fewer than 20 percent of part-time workers had such benefits. Thus the growth of part-time jobs as a proportion of the total number of jobs in Canada is an important factor in explaining the persistently high rates of poverty in the 1980s and 1990s. It is perhaps not surprising to learn that the percentage of part-time workers who wanted but could not find full-time jobs tripled between 1975 and 1994, from 11 to 35 percent (Schellenberg, 1997, p. 39):

> ... the number of part-time workers has been growing in comparison to full-time workers. It appears that the polarization of the work force—with one group of workers receiving good wages, benefits and job security, and another group, including most part-time workers, receiving poor wages, no benefits and little security—is worsening (Schellenberg, 1997, p. 2).

Similarly, the numbers and proportion of Canadians who are self-employed has grown significantly in the last two decades (Table Four). This is almost certainly a consequence of changes in the structure of the Canadian economy and changes in government economic policy.

From 1977 to 1998 the number of self-employed Canadians doubled, from 1.3 million to 2.5 million, and their share of the total numbers employed grew from one in eight (12.8 percent) to more than one in six (17.6 percent). Growth in the numbers and proportion of self-employed has been more rapid in the 1990s than in the 1980s. In the 1980s self-employment grew at an annual average rate of 2.4 percent, compared to a 1.9 percent average annual growth rate for all employment. In the 1990s the average annual growth rates were: self-employment, 3.3 percent; total employment, 0.2 percent (Statistics Canada, 1997, p. 7). "Of the million plus jobs added to the labour market this decade, over half have come from

Table 2: Poverty Rates By Occupation, 1997

Occupational Group	Family Heads	Unattached Individuals
Managerial	3.5%	10.6%
Processing and Machining	6.1%	10.5%
Professional	8.0%	17.1%
Transport	8.5%	20.1%
Construction	8.9%	27.8%
Product Fabrication	9.5%	18.5%
Farming, Fishing, Forestry	10.8%	33.5%
Sales	11.2%	28.5%
Clerical	14.5%	24.6%
Services	19.4%	41.6%

SOURCE: National Council of Welfare, Poverty Profile, 1997, Table 9

Figure 5: Work Activity by Family Heads under 65, 1997

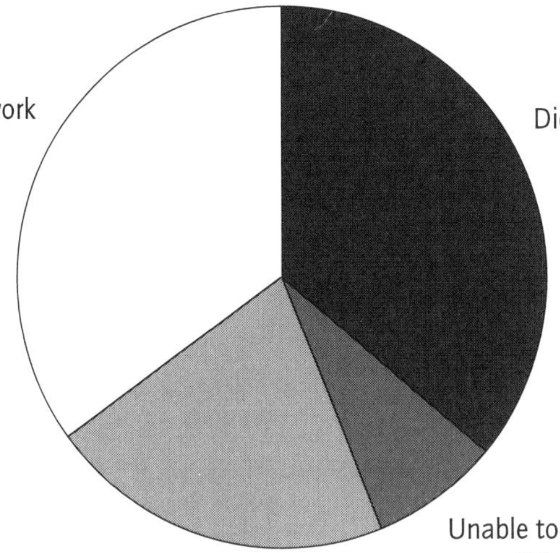

- Part time work 35%
- Did not work 36%
- Unable to work 8%
- Full time work 21%

SOURCE: National Council of Welfare, *Poverty Profile 1997*, Graph AG-1

Table 3: Growth in Part-Time Work as a Percentage of Total Employment, Canada (1976-1998)

Year	Part-Time Employed	Total Employed	Part-Time Employed as a Percentage of Total Employed
	(In Thousands of Persons)		
1976	1,217	9,776	12.4%
1980	1,591	11,082	14.4%
1985	1,997	11,742	17.0%
1986	2,049	12,095	16.9%
1987	2,068	12,422	16.6%
1988	2,152	12,819	16.8%
1989	2,169	13,086	16.6%
1990	2,236	13,165	17.0%
1991	2,343	12,916	18.1%
1992	2,375	12,842	18.5%
1993	2,480	13,015	19.1%
1994	2,493	13,292	18.8%
1995	2,509	13,506	18.6%
1996	2,589	13,676	18.9%
1997	2,649	13,941	19.0%
1998	2,684	14,326	18.7%

SOURCES: Statistics Canada, *Canadian Economic Observer* (11-210), Table 8

Table 4: Self-Employment in Canada (1977-1998)

Year	Number of Self-Employed	Total Number Employed	Self-Employed as percent of Total Employed
1977	1,280,000	9,978,000	12.8%
1978	1,360,000	10,320,000	13.2%
1979	1,423,000	10,761,000	13.2%
1980	1,462,000	11,082,000	13.2%
1981	1,522,000	11,398,000	13.4%
1982	1,537,000	11,035,000	13.9%
1983	1,594,000	11,106,000	14.4%
1984	1,629,000	11,402,000	14.3%
1985	1,677,000	11,742,000	14.3%
1986	1,682,000	12,095,000	13.9%
1987	1,746,000	12,422,000	14.1%
1988	1,821,000	12,819,000	14.2%
1989	1,809,000	13,086,000	13.8%
1990	1,889,000	13,165,000	14.3%
1991	1,920,000	12,916,000	14.9%
1992	1,936,000	12,842,000	15.1%
1993	2,056,000	13,015,000	15.8%
1994	2,111,000	13,292,000	15.9%
1995	2,136,000	13,506,000	15.8%
1996	2,267,000	13,676,000	16.6%
1997	2,488,000	13,941,000	17.8%
1998	2,525,000	14,326,000	17.6%

SOURCE: Statitistics Canada, *Canadian Economic Observer* (11-210), Historical Supplement, 1998/99, Table 8, P. 33.

self-employment—accounting for 76 percent of the job growth in 1996 and 83 percent in 1997" (Yalnizyan, 1998, p. 29). The self-employed comprise a much higher proportion of total employment in Canada than in other industrial countries, including the U.S., where only 10 percent of workers are self-employed. By 1995, "... self-employment exceeded total employment in the public sector of the economy for the first time in Canada's post-war history" (Stanford, 1999, p. 131).

This dramatic growth in self-employment is almost certainly the result of changes in the Canadian economy. Downsizing of large corporations, cutbacks in government spending and the numbers of government employees, and high rates of unemployment more generally make self-employment an option/necessity for more people. Especially in the 1990s, the years when self-employment grew most strongly appear to correlate with years when paid employment grew least strongly, and vice versa (Stanford, 1999, p. 133).

On average, self-employed workers earn less than paid employees. This is especially the case for what Statistics Canada calls "own-account" self-employment—that is, when the self-employed person works on his or her own and has no employees. In the 1990s, 90 percent of the growth in self-employment was "own-account" self-employment; and "own-account" self-employment now accounts for approximately 60 percent of the total self-employed. In 1995 the average earnings of own-account self-employed persons was $22,900, or two-thirds the average for paid employees (Stanford, 1999, p. 132; see also Yalnizyan, 1998, p. 30). It is true that some self-employed persons earn a great deal, but a higher proportion of the self-employed have low earnings: "... almost 5 percent of the self-employed

Table 5: Unemployment Rates and Poverty Rates, 1980-1997

Year	Unemployment Rate	Poverty Rate
1980	7.5%	15.3%
1981	7.6%	15.3%
1982	11.0%	16.4%
1983	11.9%	18.2%
1984	11.3%	18.1%
1985	10.5%	17.0%
1986	9.6%	16.0%
1987	8.9%	15.6%
1988	7.8%	14.8%
1989	7.5%	13.6%
1990	8.1%	14.6%
1991	10.4%	16.0%
1992	11.3%	16.1%
1993	11.2%	17.4%
1994	10.4%	16.6%
1995	9.5%	17.4%
1996	9.7%	17.6%
1997	9.2%	17.2%

SOURCES: Statistics Canada, *Canadian Economic Observer* (11-210), Historical Supplement, 1998/99 Table 8, P. 36 and National Council of Welfare, Poverty Profile 1997. Table 2.

earned over $100,000 in 1995, versus just 1 percent of paid employees. At the bottom end, over 35 percent of all self-employed individuals earned less than $15,000 the same year, compared to just 17 percent of paid workers" (Stanford, 1999, p. 132). And in fact it is likely that the average earnings of the self-employed are even lower than these numbers suggest, since "these averages exclude individuals with negative income from self-employment, and those who have been operating their businesses for less than 16 months" (Stanford, 1999, p. 421, fn. #6).

Low wages are also an important contributing factor in explaining the persistently high rates of poverty in Canada. This appears to be particularly so on the Prairies, where poor families were more likely to be fully employed than in other regions, "… indicating that low wages were a major contributor to their market poverty" (Schellenberg and Ross, 1997, p. 38). In the twenty-year period from 1976 to 1995, the annual earnings of a full-year, full-time worker employed at the minimum wage declined by 25-30 percent in almost every Canadian province (Battle, April 1999, p. 4; see also Black and Shaw, Chapter Four).

As one recent study put it:

> … the main cause of persistent poverty is Canada's precarious labour market … . The economy of the 1990s is creating an abundance of "non-standard" jobs which pay low wages, offer few if any benefits and are often part-time or unstable (Battle, 1996, p. 1).

This combination of an increasing proportion of part-time jobs and a drop in the real value of minimum (and near-minimum) wages is almost certainly a significant part of the explanation for the troubling trend observed in Canada in recent years—the break in the long-term correlation between rates of poverty and of unemployment. It has historically been the case that when unemployment has declined, the rate of poverty has declined; when unemployment has risen, the rate of poverty has risen. However, the drop in official rates of unemployment since 1992/93 has *not* been accompanied by a significant decline in poverty rates. On the contrary, poverty rates have remained virtually constant even while official unemployment rates have been declining.

A close examination of the numbers in Table Five shows that: the rate of unemployment rose in 1982 and again in 1983, and the poverty rate rose in each of those years; the unemployment rate declined in each year from 1984 to 1989, and the poverty rate declined in each of those years; the unemployment rate rose in 1990, 1991, and 1992, and so did the poverty rate. However, in 1993 the unemployment rate nudged slightly downward, yet the poverty rate rose significantly. In 1995 the unemployment rate dropped almost a full percentage point, but the poverty rate rose by almost a full percentage point and has remained at approximately that 17 percent-plus level since. The same trend has been observed in the U.S.:

> Economic growth—long one of the most effective and politically attractive anti-poverty tools available—has not been effective in reducing poverty in the United States over the past fifteen years.

> Further, official U.S. statistics for 1993

> … showed a historically unprecedented result: in 1993, when the rate of economic growth (after inflation) was 3 percent—a very healthy growth rate indeed—the proportion of Americans who were poor in that year actually *rose* at the same time as the aggregate economy was expanding. Behind these dry statistics lies one of the most discouraging facts for American social policy: an expanding economy no longer guarantees a decline in poverty (Blank, 1997, p. 54).

This is largely attributable to the fact that "Among the least-skilled men, wages have fallen more than 20 percent in the last 15 years" (Blank, 1997, p. 60).

This trend may also be attributable, in part, to the potentially misleading character of *official* rates of unemployment. Official unemployment rates do not take account of "discouraged" workers—those who have given up actively looking for work. One might hypothesize that more people would give up actively looking for work—would become "discouraged" workers—when jobs are scarce and/or when *good* jobs are scarce, ie., when a high proportion of jobs are part-time and/or low-wage. Labour force participation rates may yield some insight into this phenomenon. Labour force participation rates represent the proportion of persons aged eighteen to sixty-five who are either working or actively looking for work. Labour force participation rates in Canada have been declining, from 67.3 percent in 1990 to 64.9 percent in 1996. What this means can be ascertained from the observation that "… if the participation rate had remained constant—at 67.3 percent—

another 570,000 individuals would have been in the labour market in 1996" (Black, 1998, p. 84).

"Official" unemployment rates also do not tell us what percentage of those who are working are part-time workers who want but cannot find full-time employment—ie, the "underemployed." However, Statistics Canada does gather such data, and when these and data on discouraged workers are taken into account, the *real* unemployment rate is much higher than the official rate:

> In 1995, the real unemployment rate—which includes people who have given up actively searching for work and part-time workers who want full-time jobs—was 15.2 percent or 60 percent higher than the 9.5 percent official rate (Battle, 1996, p. 1).

It is for these reasons—together with the enormous amounts of money taken out of social programs, especially since the 1995 federal budget, as will be described in a later section of this chapter—that recent declines in unemployment rates have not been reflected in significant declines in poverty rates. On the contrary, recent economic growth has dramatically widened the gap between rich and poor in Canada:

> In 1973, the top 10 percent of families with children under 18 earned an average income 21 times higher than those at the bottom ($107,000 compared to $5200 in 1996 dollars) …. By 1996 … the top 10 percent made 314 times as much as the families in the bottom 10 percent (an average $137,000 compared to an average annual market income of less than 1997) (Yalnizyan, 1998, p. 45).

Young people, those under thirty-five years of age, appear to have suffered most from the economic restructuring that has taken place since the early 1980s. As Yalnizyan observes:

> People under 35 years of age are evidently worth less than workers of the same age before the recession of 1981-82. But it is the young men whose hourly rates of pay have been most sharply and consistently eroded over the past 15 years. Virtually every data source, from Census to special surveys, documents this same trend. Study after study shows that we are devaluing our young. (Yalnizyan, 1998, p. 24).

Child Poverty

A particularly troubling aspect of the persistently high level of poverty in Canada is the growth of child poverty. In 1980, 984,000 children under eighteen years of age were living in poverty—a poverty rate of 14.9 percent. By 1997, the number of children under eighteen living in poverty had grown to 1,384, 000, an increase of almost half a million children, and the poverty rate had risen by almost five full percentage points, to 19.6 percent (Table Six).

By 1989, the number and proportion of children under eighteen living in poverty was lower than in 1980. The real and dramatic growth in child poverty occurred in the 1990s. Given that this book examines poverty in Winnipeg, it is espe-

Table 6: Poverty Trends, Children under 18 Years of Age (1980-1997)

Year	Poor Children	All Children	Poverty Rate
1980	984,000	6,619,000	14.9%
1981	998,000	6,552,000	15.2%
1982	1,155,000	6,476,000	17.8%
1983	1,221,000	6,437,000	19.0%
1984	1,253,000	6,377,000	19.6%
1985	1,165,000	6,361,000	18.3%
1986	1,086,000	6,390,000	17.0%
1987	1,057,000	6,380,000	16.6%
1988	987,000	6,395,000	15.4%
1989	934,000	6,438,000	14.5%
1990	1,105,000	6,522,000	16.9%
1991	1,210,000	6,606,000	18.3%
1992	1,218,000	6,704,000	18.2%
1993	1,415,000	6,799,000	20.8%
1994	1,334,000	6,997,000	19.1%
1995	1,441,000	7,011,000	20.5%
1996	1,481,000	7,093,000	20.9%
1997	1,384,000	7,053,000	19.6%

SOURCE: National Council of Welfare, Poverty Profile 1997. Table 3.

Table 7: Children under 18 Living in Poverty, By Province, 1997

Province	Poor Children, in All Family Types		Poor Children of Two-Parent Families Under 65		Poor Children of Single-Parent Mothers Under 65	
	Number of Children	Poverty Rate	Number of Children	Poverty Rate	Number of Children	Poverty Rate
Newfoundland	30,000	23.3%	20,000	17.7%	8,000	75.2%
PEI	5,000	14.5%	2,000	7.9%	3,000	63.4%
Nova Scotia	46,000	21.2%	20,000	11.6%	23,000	69.7%
New Brunswick	34,000	20.2%	19,000	13.4%	12,000	58.5%
Quebec	343,000	20.9%	175,000	13.3%	148,000	61.1%
Ontario	537,000	19.8%	304,000	13.6%	207,000	60.6%
Manitoba	58,000	21.5%	28,000	12.6%	28,000	70.2%
Saskatchewan	48,000	18.6%	15,000	7.5%	30,000	65.6%
Alberta	116,000	15.8%	61,000	9.9%	51,000	58.2%
British Columbia	166,000	18.7%	90,000	12.6%	61,000	51.5%
Canada	1,384,000	19.6%	735,000	12.7%	571,000	60.4%

SOURCE: National Council of Welfare, Poverty Profile 1997. Table 20.

cially notable that in 1997, Manitoba had the second highest rate of child poverty among Canadian provinces (Table Seven).

There is an important sense in which the notion of "child poverty" is misleading since, as the National Council of Welfare (1996, p. 13) quite rightly observes, "Children are poor because their parents are poor." However, there is strong evidence that growing up in a poor family adversely affects a child's life chances.

David p. Ross and Paul Roberts examined the correlation between family income and twenty-seven separate elements of child development—indicators pertaining to a child's family, community, behaviour, health, cultural and recreational participation, and education. They found that for each of the variables:

> ... children living in families with lower incomes are found to be at a greater risk of experiencing negative outcomes and poor living conditions than those in higher-income families. It is also evident from these data that child outcomes and living conditions improve gradually as family incomes rise (Ross and Roberts, 1999, p. 3).

Some of these correlations are quite striking. For example, delayed vocabulary development occurs more than four times as frequently among children from low-income families as it does among children from high-income families; and "... about one in six teens from low-income families is neither employed nor in school, compared to only one teen in twenty-five from middle-and high-income families." The result is what Ross and Roberts call "poverty of opportunity"—children who grow up in poor families are, on average, less likely to do well in life than children who grow up in non-poor families (Ross and Roberts, 1999, pp. 8, 25, 34 and 36). A similar study by Bernard Schissel, in this case focusing on Saskatchewan youth, reaches similar conclusions:
... living in poverty reduces the emotional well-being of children and youth, places their physical and emotional health at risk, and impairs their satisfaction with and success in the educational system (Schissel, 1997, p. 1).

Campaign 2000, which describes itself as "... a national movement to build awareness and support for the 1989 all-party House of Commons resolution 'to seek to achieve the goal of eliminating poverty among Canadian children by the year 2000,'" describes the lasting effects of child poverty as follows:

> ... child poverty is associated with poor health and hygiene, a lack of a nutritious diet, absenteeism from school and low scholastic achievement, behavioural and mental problems, low housing standards, and in later years, few employment opportunities and a persistently low economic status (CCSD, 1994, p. 1).

A quarter century ago, in their 1975 study *Poor Kids*, the National Council of Welfare argued the same:

> To be born poor is to face a lesser likelihood that you will finish high school, lesser still that you will attend university. To be born poor is to face a greater likelihood that you will be judged a delinquent in adolescence and, if so, a greater likelihood that you will be sent to a 'correctional institution.' To be born poor is to have the deck stacked against you at birth, to find life an uphill struggle ever after (NCW, 1975, p. 1).

In short, children who grow up in poor families are more likely to end up as the adult heads of poor families—and so poverty reproduces itself. A crucial factor in the reproduction of poverty is the relationship between poverty and educational attainment. The lower the level of educational attainment, the higher is the risk of poverty, as shown in Figure Six.

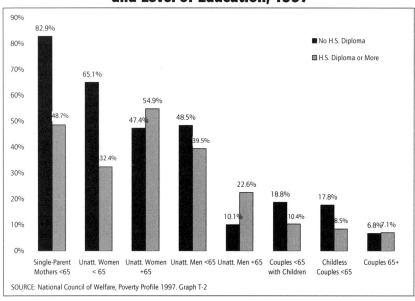

Figure 6: Poverty Rates by Family Type and Level of Education, 1997

SOURCE: National Council of Welfare, Poverty Profile 1997. Graph T-2

A vicious cycle is therefore created: poor children are less likely to do well in school; those who do less well in school are more likely to experience poverty as adults. The likelihood is increased that their children, in turn, will do less well in school, and so poverty is reproduced. It is for this reason that the growth of child poverty is a particularly serious aspect of a serious Canadian problem—our persistently high overall rates of poverty.

The Economy

The persistently high levels of poverty throughout the 1980s and 1990s are associated with the relatively weak economy during this period. As measured by almost any indicator, the Canadian economy—like virtually all economies in the industrialized world—was much weaker in the 1980s and 1990s than it had been during the long, post-war economic boom. As shown in Table Eight, the average annual rate of growth in both GDP and employment from 1950 to 1980 was approximately double the rate from 1981 to 1997, and approximately triple the rate from 1990 to 1997. Unemployment rates from 1981 to 1997 were almost double the rates from 1950 to 1980, while real earnings declined from 1981 to 1997, compared to an average annual growth rate of 2.3 percent in the earlier period. Real short-term interest rates were six times higher, and real long-term rates four times higher, in the 1981 to 1997 period, than they had been in the earlier period. This combination of relative economic stagnation and high real interest rates was reflected in the emergence of annual deficits and a build-up of accumulated debt (Table Eight).

Why has the Canadian economy experienced such a decline in the past twenty-five years? The first part of the answer has to do with the character of the global economy of which Canada is a part. Capitalism—the economic system which now prevails in Canada and in most of the world—has certain intrinsic features. Chief among these is the constant, competitive drive of individual capitalist firms to earn profits. This relentless drive for ever more profits has certain inevitable results. These include: a constant revolutionizing of the means of production, leading to rapid technological change, as firms relentlessly innovate in an attempt to find ways to produce goods and services less expensively, and thus gain an advantage over their competitors; and a constant drive to expand, which results both in ever-larger firms and in geographic expansion, as transnational corporations scour the globe in search of lower wages, bigger markets and cheaper raw materials, in order to maximize their profits. These two phenomena, globalization and the constant revolutionizing of the means of production, are important parts of the explanation for the economic downturn of the past twenty-five years.

While it is true that economic activity has become much more global in the past quarter century, globalization is best thought of not as a *new* phenomenon, but rather as an accentuation of the drive to expand that is intrinsic to capitalism. In the past quarter century, trade between nations and investment across national borders have increased dramatically. Companies no longer confine their production to their home nations—they may, and do, set up production facilities anywhere in the world, choosing to locate wherever they are most likely to be able to maximize profits.

> As transnational entities, corporations can play one nation off against another by moving to where the concessions and incentives are greatest, the relative labour costs lowest ... and environmental standards the most limited (Teeple, 1995, p. 85).

This often means locating production where labour costs are lowest and/or where government regulations of their activities are weakest. This trend has been accelerated by international trade agreements, such as the Canada-US Free Trade Agreement and the North American Free Trade Agreement. The distinguishing feature of these international treaties is that they significantly reduce the capacity of elected governments to interfere with the profit-seeking activities of transnational corporations (TNCs). They free these corporations from many of the obstacles placed in their way by governments—obstacles such as environmental regulations and labour standards. This increases the freedom of TNCs to search the globe for the most profitable production sites, making it more likely that TNCs will set up shop wherever they can maximize their profits. For many industries—especially heavily unionized, relatively high wage, mass production industries—this has meant the relocation of production facilities to jurisdictions where government regulations are weaker and wages are lower. The result has been massive job loss and the downward pressure on wage levels—especially the wage levels of relatively unskilled workers—that was described in the last section of this chapter. "The effects of this emerging global labour market began to become visible from the early 1970s on with a general downward pressure on wages in the industrial world" (Teeple, 1995, p. 67).

In the face of the intensified competition created by globalization, companies have sought not only to reduce wage levels, but also to create what the corporate sector calls more "flexible" workforces. Corporations have sought to move away from the relatively fixed and permanent high-wage regime characteristic of the

Table 8: Economic Performance Indicators, 1950-1997

	The "Golden Age"	The Age of "Permanent Reccession"	
	1950-1980	1981-1997	1990-1997
Average Annual Growth Real GDP	4.7%	2.4%	1.8%
Average Annual Growth Real GDP per capita	2.8%	1.1%	0.5%
Average Annual Growth Total Employment	2.6%	1.4%	0.8%
Average Unemployment Rate	5.4%	9.8%	10.0%
Average Annual Growth Real Earnings	2.3%	-0.5%	0.3%
Real Short-Term Interest Rates	0.9%	5.6%	5.1%
Real Long-Term Interest Rates	1.6%	6.5%	6.8%
Changes in Government Program Spending (as a % of GDP)	+ 16.3 points	+1.1 points	-2.5 points

	1950 - 1980	1981-1996
Annual Federal Deficit	0.0%	4.2%
Closing Federal Debt (as a % of GDP)	23.0%	73.0%

SOURCES: Stanford, Paper Boom, Table 9-2: and Stanford, "Deficit-Mania, Table 2.

mass production industries of the 1950s and 1960s—sometimes referred to as "Fordism," after the mass production, relatively high-wage system introduced early in the century by Henry Ford—to a more flexible labour force, increasingly characterized by the use of part-time and lower-waged work. The resultant increase in part-time work and decrease in wages at the lower end of the income scale has been a significant factor in creating the high levels of poverty in the 1980s and 1990s, and is an important part of the reason that poverty levels have not significantly declined as unemployment levels have dropped since 1993.

This increased degree of globalization, and the problems it creates for many working people, especially those with relatively little formal education and relatively few skills, has been facilitated by the particularly rapid technological change associated with the microelectronics revolution and more particularly the widespread use of computers. By the mid-1970s, computers were beginning to be widely employed in industry. The results have been dramatic. Not only has their use facilitated the increased globalization of economic activity, including, in particular, an acceleration of the ease and rapidity by which finance capital can be moved around the globe, but also their use in industry—in both factories and offices—has resulted in massive job loss, which has also exerted downward pressure on wage levels at the lower end of the wage scale, and contributed to the growth of (generally low-paid) self-employment. Most of the jobs which relatively unskilled school-leavers could look forward to walking into in the 1950s and 1960s, jobs with which a family could be supported, are now gone. Such jobs have re-located elsewhere or have been eliminated by technology, only to be replaced by low-wage and often part-time work in the service sector.

The increased extent of globalization, together with the revolutionizing of the means of production effected by the widespread application in industry of the computer, have had a significant economic impact in the past twenty-five years. They have been major causes of the growth of part-time employment and self-employment, and the downward pressure on wage levels, which in turn have been major factors in pushing poverty levels up to, and keeping them at, the levels of the 1980s and 1990s.

Government policy is also an important part of the explanation for the economic downturn of the past twenty-five years. Of particular importance was the shift to monetarism and high real interest rates. As shown in Table Eight, real interest rates in Canada were dramatically higher in the two decades after 1980 than they had been in the three decades before. These high real interest rates not only added to the size of annual deficits, which led to reductions in government spending—about which more in the next section of this chapter—but also they contributed to a reduction in private investment. In the 1970s, total private investment in Canada was 19.1 percent of GDP; from 1990 to 1998 it was 15.7 percent of GDP (Stanford, 1999, Table Seven-2, page 154).

The ostensible purpose of the high interest rate policy was to reduce inflation; the more important purpose was to keep levels of unemployment from falling too low—this happens because higher real interest rates impede borrowing for productive investment, with the result that fewer jobs are created. The reasoning behind this perverse policy—a policy clearly articulated and aggressively carried out by the Bank of Canada—has been that when unemployment is low, workers feel emboldened to demand higher wages, and higher wages impinge upon corporate profits and contribute to inflation. By contrast, when unemployment is higher, and especially when social benefits for those not employed are weak, then the fear and insecurity created by the risk of job loss reduces the upward pressure on wage levels and on inflation. The fear and insecurity created by higher levels of unemployment and reduced social benefits are therefore functional in a capitalist economy.

Thus the structural factors contributing to the weakness of the Canadian economy during the 1980s and 1990s and to the growth in part-time and self-employment, have been added to by the economic policies of Canadian governments. Together, these factors fueled the growth of unemployment and the downward pressure on wages.

Social Policy

A second major contributant to the persistently high poverty levels of the 1980s and 1990s has been the dismantling, during that period, of the many social policy mechanisms put in place during the post-war boom as the means by which to protect individuals from the hazards of the inevitable ups and downs of the capitalist economy. Overall government spending, and particularly government spending on social programs, has been dramatically reduced during the 1980s and 1990s. Unemployment insurance has been restructured to the disadvantage of unemployed workers, universality of social programs has been largely abandoned, and the social safety net has been significantly weakened.

These changes in social policy were directly related to the dramatic changes in the economy. The social policy initiatives of the 1950s and 1960s and the early 1970s were funded out of the proceeds of the long post-war economic boom. Sustained economic growth and relatively low levels of unemployment generated the government revenue, the "fiscal dividend," needed to pay for new social programs. With the end of the post-war boom in the early 1970s and its replacement with a long period of relative economic stagnation, the fiscal dividend disappeared and was replaced by government deficits and the build-up of accumulated debt (see Table Eight).

It is important to note that social spending did not *cause* the deficit/debt problem; the economic stagnation and the associated high interest rate/high unemployment strategy did. However, most governments chose to respond to the problem by cutting social spending. It is likely that social spending was targeted, in large part, because it was too effective in reducing the fear and anxiety that forces workers to reduce their wage demands and to accept jobs of lesser quality—and in an increasingly competitive global economy and global labour market, it was seen to be necessary to create a more "flexible" labour force. As early as 1975 concerns were being expressed by advocates of unfettered free enterprise about the perceived consequences of the redistributive character of the welfare state in advanced capitalist economies. The various elements of the welfare state, by placing a floor under the incomes of citizens, were removing the fear of unemployment and of poverty that made people anxious to work at whatever wages and under whatever conditions were on offer. For profitability to be restored, the relative security created by the welfare state had to be eroded. As the 1975 Trilateral Commission put it, there was too much democracy, an "excess" of democracy, and the solution was to attack "big government" (Crozier et al, 1975).

In Canada, as in most other advanced capitalist economies, these concerns found expression in cuts to government spending. This can be seen when government spending is measured as a share of GDp. Federal program spending as a share of GDP began to decline after 1975. By 1995, even before Finance Minister Paul Martin had announced massive spending cuts in that year's federal budget, "… government in Canada was already smaller as a share of our economy than it had been two decades earlier" (Stanford, 1998, p. 31). Federal program spending in the 1996/97 fiscal year was 13 percent of GDP, the lowest level as a share of the Canadian economy since 1950/51 (Yalnizyan, 1998, p. 64). Since the big cuts to federal spending in the 1995 budget, government spending in Canada has dropped rapidly by international standards:

> In 1995 Canada ranked in the middle of the seven largest industrialized economies (often known as the "G7" economies) in terms of the size of government programs relative to GDp. Since then, we have fallen to second-last in the G7 as a result of huge spending cuts by the federal and provincial governments, and now we rank ahead only of the United State (Stanford, 1998, p. 32).

And even relative to the United States, government spending in Canada is shrinking: "… in 1992 total government program spending as a share of GDP was two-thirds higher in Canada than in the U.S., but by 1998 this 'social advantage' would shrink to barely one-quarter." As Stanford (1998, p. 45) observed, given this dramatic decline in public spending: "It is hard to imagine how Canada's reputation as a 'kinder, gentler' society will be sustained."

A good deal of the government spending cuts were targeted at what might broadly be called social programs. This initially took the form of reductions in the rate of increase of federal government spending on transfer payments to the provinces for health, education and social assistance, and the abandonment, in 1977, of the federal government's open-ended commitment to pay 50 percent of whatever provincial governments might spend on health and post-secondary education. Federal government contributions to what was called Established Programs Financing (EPF)—the 1977 program by which federal funds were transferred to the provinces for health and post-secondary education—were tied to the rate of growth of per capita GNP, and from the early to mid 1980s, and especially subsequent to the 1984 election of the Conservative government of Brian Mulroney, the rate of growth in federal transfers was further reduced, primarily by limiting the growth of federal transfers to a rate *less than* the rate of growth in the GNP:

> Ottawa's contribution to the EPF was limited to an annual growth rate of 2 percent below the rate of GNP growth in 1985/86, then 3 percent below the rate of GNP growth in 1989, and then zero in 1990 and again in the 1991 budget, through to 1995 (Silver, 1992, p. 233).

The results of these seemingly innocuous changes, often called "de-indexing," were dramatic, saving the federal government—and making unavailable to provincial governments for social spending—an estimated $150 billion over a fifteen-year period (Silver, 1992, p. 234). Provincial governments had to either make up these costs, or, as was generally the case, cut their spending on these services. In addition, in 1991, Bill C-69 placed a 5 percent limit on the growth in federal contributions to Ontario, Alberta and B.C. under the Canada Assistance Plan (CAP)—the cost-shared, federal-provincial program by which welfare and social assistance services were financed—even though the costs to these provinces under CAP were increasing at the time at approximately 7 percent per annum (Silver, 1992, p. 234).

The biggest change to, and the biggest reduction in, the federal transfer payment system came five years later, in 1996. The EPF and CAP were rolled into a new program, called the Canadian Health and Social Transfer (CHST). In its first two years of operation, 1996/97 and 1997/98, the CHST transferred to the provinces for health, post-secondary education and social assistance an amount that was $7 billion *less* than what would have been the case under the previous transfer payment arrangements (Pilkingham and Ternowetsky, 1999, p. 93; Yalnizyan, 1998, p. 56). Further, the CHST is a block transfer, which means that the provinces get a single amount for health, education and social assistance, and it is up to each province to determine the allocation of funds to these various purposes. This is contrary to the previous system, under which the federal government transferred to the provinces a *specific* amount for social assistance by means of the CAp. The result has been that:

> … dollars that were traditionally spent on the safety net, are now in direct competition with the spending needs of health and education. If we compare the political clout of the health and education sectors with that of social assistance, there are grounds for assuming that welfare dollars will be further squeezed as the competition for scarce resources heats up (Pulkingham and Ternowetsky, 1999, p. 93).

In other words, middle-class Canadians demanding more spending on health and education are almost certain to have more success than social assistance recipients calling for greater spending for their needs.

Making matters worse for social assistance recipients is the fact that under the CHST, the standards that existed under the CAP are now eliminated. Under CAP, the provinces were required—in order to receive federal funds for social assistance—to ensure: that all people judged to be in need received funding; that benefit levels met basic needs; that an appeal procedure existed enabling people to challenge welfare decisions; and that no work requirement was imposed as a condition of receiving social assistance. The removal of these standards almost certainly will result in reduced levels of social assistance. The net result is that the CHST "opens the way for jurisdictions to provide little or no assistance to those in need" (CCSD, 1996), because these forms of assistance "… are no longer mandated by legislation or directly supported by cost-shared transfers" (Pulkingham and Ternowetsky, 1999, p. 94). This is precisely what appears to have happened: "… since 1995 the provinces of British Columbia, Alberta, Manitoba, Ontario, Quebec, Nova Scotia, Prince Edward Island and Newfoundland have cut back their benefit rates, eligibility to programs of assistance and/or shelter allowances" (Yalnizyan, 1998, p. 57). In Ontario, for example, welfare rates were cut by 21.6 percent in 1995. In addition, the removal of these standards opens the door for provincial workfare programs, which have already been introduced in many provinces (MacKinnon, Chapter 3). The net result is that social assistance recipients now experience a greater degree of financial insecurity and are subject to a variety of forces pushing them to enter the paid labour force, usually at the low-wage end of the job market.

The desire to push people on social assistance into the paid work force has driven other recent social policy changes. The Family Allowance was partially de-indexed—that is, annual increases were pegged at a level less than the rate of increase in the cost of living—in 1985. In 1989 the Family Allowance benefits of those above a certain income threshold were clawed back, thus changing what had been a universal social program to an income contingent program. The abandonment of the principle of universality is especially significant, since universal benefits are more likely to enjoy broadly based support—and the support of middl-class recipients—than are income contingent benefits, which are more likely to be supported only by that lower income segment of the population which receives the benefits. In 1992 the Family Allowance was abandoned entirely, and replaced with the Child Tax Benefit, the stated purpose of the change being to better target low-income families with children. "With this action, the government made absolutely clear its rejection of the principle of universality …" (Pulkingham and Ternowetsky, 1999, p. 88). Particularly significant is the fact that, by means of the Working Income Supplement, only parents who were in the paid labour force were eligible for additional benefits as a result of the shift to the Child Tax Benefit; low-income parents on welfare and Employment Insurance received the same benefits as they previously had. The effect, and the intent, was to push social assistance recipients into the paid labour force.

This policy had the perverse effect of reinforcing—in the same way that workfare will—one of the primary structural mechanisms keeping the rate of poverty persistently high—namely low wages.

> … because of these policies, low wages became more attractive even if remuneration levels were unable to meet basic needs. In this context the

Table 9: Percentage of Unemployed Persons Receiving Employment Insurance Benefits, Canada, 1976-1998

Year	Regular Beneficiary Without Earnings	Total Number of Unemployed	Percentage of Unemployed Collecting Employment Insurance (EI)
1976	585,663	754,000	77.7%
1980	558,217	900,000	62.0%
1985	925,107	1,381,000	67.0%
1986	857,420	1,283,000	66.8%
1987	800,793	1,208,000	66.3%
1988	781,622	1,082,000	72.2%
1989	785,067	1,065,000	73.7%
1990	855,731	1,164,000	73.5%
1991	1,023,678	1,492,000	68.6%
1992	1,004,912	1,640,000	61.3%
1993	929,234	1,649,000	56.4%
1994	771,341	1,541,000	50.1%
1995	633,264	1,422,000	44.5%
1996	606,246	1,469,000	41.3%
1997	507,420	1,414,000	35.9%
1998	480,185	1,305,000	36.8%
Monthly Data for 1999			
Jan	454,180	1,371,000	33.1%
Feb	463,000	1,341,000	34.5%
Mar	460,870	1,302,000	35.4%
Apr	455,710	1,309,000	34.8%
May	457,740	1,309,000	35.0%

SOURCES: Statistics Canada, CANSIM D736544 and *Canadian Economic Observer (11-210)*, Hitorical Supplement, 1998/99. Table 8

> Working Income Supplement acted as a low-wage subsidy, making low-wage jobs more tolerable, enlarging the pool of people willing to take up low-wage jobs, and thereby intensifying a downward pressure on wages (Pulkingham and Ternowetsky, 1999, p. 89).

Such policies are consistent with the desire to respond to a more competitive global economy by creating a more "flexible," more "competitive" labour force.

In 1997/98 the Child Tax Benefit was replaced by the new National Child Benefit (NCB). The result was an increase in federal child benefits paid to all low-income families—both the working poor and those on social assistance. However, the provinces are encouraged by the federal government to clawback a portion of the NCB from social assistance recipients. Two provinces, New Brunswick and Newfoundland, have chosen not to do so, but rather to leave the money in the hands of families on social assistance. All other provinces reduce their payments to social assistance recipients, and reinvest the "savings" in programs and services for all low-income families with children. These new programs and services are combined with the Canada Child Tax Benefit to create the new National Child

Benefit. The result is that in all but two provinces, the working poor receive the entire NCB in cash; those on social assistance do not.

There is considerable debate about the merits of this new initiative. There are some, like social policy analyst Ken Battle of the Caledon Institute, who believe that, whatever its current limitations, the National Child Benefit has the *potential* to be "... the most important social policy innovation since medicare," and to be the basis on which governments could "... wage a real war on family poverty"— although as of now it is "... only a down payment ... .much work remains to be done"(Battle, 1999, pp. 38 and 60). The National Council of Welfare is more guarded, calling the new National Child Benefit "promising," and "a small step forward" (NCW, 1997, p. 12), while a study by the Canadian Policy Research Network observes that while the NCB "... is an important new program and might be a useful anti-poverty measure, it will only be truly effective if the amount of the benefit is increased significantly (Jenson and Stroick, 1999, p. 22). Others are hostile, pointing to a variety of perceived weaknesses, including: the absence of national standards for the provincial reinvestment programs; the fear that the provinces may use the money simply to offset costs they would have incurred anyway; and the fact that the program is only partially indexed. What is more, the National Child Benefit claws back a portion of the benefits of those low-income families on social assistance, but *not* those low-income families who are working for wages (Pulkingham and Ternowetsky, 1999, P, 90). The purpose, again, is "to improve work incentives"; the danger is that provinces might use the National Child Benefit as justification for pushing social assistance recipients into workfare programs (Battle, 1999, p. 53). This concern is not without foundation, since it is the determination to push people into the paid labour force, irrespective of the fact that growing numbers of jobs are part-time and low-wage and will not drive workers' incomes above the poverty line, that characterizes so many of the social policy changes of the 1980s and 1990s.

That is certainly the case with Unemployment Insurance. In 1989/90 Unemployment Insurance was effectively privatized. As the result of Bill C-21, the federal government withdrew from its previous role as financial contributor to Unemployment Insurance, leaving the financing of this crucial program completely in the hands of employees and employers. There followed a series of changes to UI in the early to mid 1990s, each making the provision of UI more restrictive: stricter qualifying requirements and reductions in the level and duration of benefits, for example (Pulkingham and Ternowetsky, 1999, p. 86). These trends were intensified with the introduction in 1996 of Bill C-12, creating the new Employment Insurance (EI) system. The more restrictive provisions applying to EI have served to accelerate the downward trend in the proportion of unemployed Canadians receiving EI benefits. As shown in Table Nine, just over one-third of unemployed Canadians were collecting Employment Insurance benefits in 1998.

The effect of these changes to Employment Insurance over the past decade has been to make employment more precarious, with the result that wage demands are reduced. This is no accident, since the purpose is to:

... harmonize Canada's labour market outcomes with those of our trading partners (especially the U.S.). The reforms aim to enhance the international competitiveness of Canada's economy on a low-wage basis; this goal is achieved by deliberately increasing the economic insecurity facing

Canadian workers, hence moderating their wage demands and disciplining their behaviour in the workplace (Stanford, 1996, p. 144).

This purpose is, as shown, consistent with many of the changes made to Canadian social programs throughout the 1980s and especially the 1990s.

The cuts to and re-design of social programs in Canada during the past two decades were not necessary for fiscal reasons. Social spending did not cause the deficit/accumulated debt problem (Mimoto and Cross, 1991), and necessary though it was to bring recurrent deficits under control, social spending did not have to be cut to solve the problem. This has been demonstrated repeatedly in the Alternative Federal Budgets prepared annually since 1995 by Cho!ces and the Canadian Centre for Policy Alternatives. As Stanford observes:

> Just as it was high interest rates and slow growth that lit the fuse on Canada's fiscal explosion earlier in the 1980s and 1990s, it was the post-1995 decline in interest rates and improving economic growth prospects that laid the foundation for the recovery of public-sector finances. Spending cuts accelerated the elimination of deficits; *but those deficits would have disappeared anyway,* at a slower pace, thanks to lower interest rates and stronger economic growth (Stanford, 1998, p. 46-47).

That social spending has been cut and programs re-designed as they have throughout the 1980s and 1990s has been the result of conscious government policy. These social policy changes were, at least in part, an attempt to create a more flexible, more competitive labour force in Canada in response to the increased global competitiveness arising from the economic changes described in the previous section. The result of these economic changes, together with the cuts to and changes in social policy, has been the persistently high poverty levels described in the first section of this chapter.

It is widely acknowledged that there is no single solution to the problem of poverty. Any effective response will have to be multi-faceted. What follows from the argument in this chapter is that an effective anti-poverty strategy would have to include the creation of more good jobs and the construction of a stronger set of social policies. Additional measures would include: higher minimum wages (Black and Shaw, Chapter 4); a stronger social housing policy (Skelton, 1998); strengthened trade unions; adequate and affordable childcare; early education initiatives. Each of these implies a more activist state governing directly in the interests of those at the lower end of the income scale.

However, the emphasis in this book is not primarily on such activist state intervention. Rather it is on the collective efforts of people in poverty to solve, with appropriate supports, their own problems. There is a strong community economic development orientation to the chapters in this book. This orientation is predicated on the two-fold observation that the free market, neoliberal economic strategies of the past two decades have not "trickled down" to the benefit of those in poverty, but neither are top-down government programs, which are delivered *to* and *for* low-income Canadians, a lasting solution to poverty. The solutions that work are community-based solutions which provide the supports to enable those in poverty to begin to solve their own problems.

References

Antony, Wayne and Les Samuelson. *Power and Resistance: Critical Thinking about Canadian Social Issues, Second Edition* (Halifax: Fernwood Publishing, 1998).

Battle, Ken. *Precarious Labour Market Fuels Rising Poverty* (Ottawa: Caledon Institute, December 1996).

———. *Persistent Poverty* (Ottawa: Caledon Institute, December 1997).

———. "Poverty and the Welfare State," in Antony and Samuelson, 1998, pp. 53-75.

———. *Poverty Eases Slightly* (Ottawa: Caledon Institute, April 1999).

———. "The National Child Benefit: Best Thing Since Medicare or New Poor Law," in Durst (ed.), 1999, pp. 38-60.

Black, Errol. "The 'New' Crisis of Unemployment: Restoring Profits and Controlling Labour," in Antony and Samuelson, 1998, pp. 76-94.

———. and Jim Silver. *A Flawed Economic Experiment: The New Political Economy of Manitoba* (Winnipeg: Canadian Centre for Policy Alternatives-Manitoba, 1999).

Blank, Rebecca. *It Takes a Nation: A New Agenda For Fighting Poverty* (Princeton: Princeton University Press, 1997).

Broad, Dave, and Wayne Antony (eds.). *Citizens or Consumers? Social Policy in a Market Society* (Halifax: Fernwood Publishing, 1999).

Canadian Association of Food Banks. *HungerCount 1999* (Toronto: Canadian Association of Food Banks, September 1999).

Canadian Council on Social Development (CCSD). *Countdown '92: Campaign 2000 Child Poverty Indicator Report* (Ottawa: CCSD, November 1992).

———. *Countdown '94: Campaign 2000 Child Poverty Indicator Report* (Ottawa: CCSD, November 1994).

———. *Maintaining a National Social Safety Net: Recommendations on the Canada Health and Social Transfer, Position Statement* (Ottawa: CCSD, 1996).

———. *The Progress of Canada's Children 1998* (Ottawa: CCSD, 1998).

Cho!ces and Canadian Centre for Policy Alternatives. *Alternative Federal Budget Papers 1998* (Ottawa: CCPA and Cho!ces, 1998).

Clarke, Tony. *Silent Coup: Confronting The Big Business Takeover of Canada* (Ottawa and Toronto: CCPA and Lorimer, 1997).

Crozier, M., S. p. Huntington, and J. Watanuki. *The Crisis of Democracy, Report on the Governability of Democracies to the Trilateral Commission* (New York: New York University Press, 1975).

Durst, Douglas (ed.). *Canada's National Child Benefit: Phoenix or Fizzle?* (Halifax: Fernwood Publishing, 1999).

Ecumenical Coalition for Economic Justice. *Promises To Keep, Miles To Go: An Examination of Canada's Record in the International Year for the Eradication of Poverty (1996)* (Toronto: Ecumenical Coalition for Economic Justice, 1996).

Jenson, Jane, and Sharon M. Stroick. "A Policy Blueprint For Canada's Children," *Reflexion*, Canadian Policy Research Network, October 1999.

McBride, Stephen, and John Shields. *Dismantling a Nation: The Transition to Corporate Rule in Canada* (Halifax: Fernwood Publishing, 1997).

Mimoto, H. and p. Cross. "The Growth of the Federal Debt," *Canadian Economic Observer*, pp. 3.1-3.17, June 1991.

National Council of Welfare (NCW). *Poor Kids: A Report By The National Council of Welfare on Children in Poverty in Canada* (Ottawa: National Council of Welfare, 1975).

———. *Progress Against Poverty, Revised Edition* (Ottawa: NCW, 1987).

———. *Poverty Profile 1996* (Ottawa: National Council of Welfare, 1998).

———. *Poverty Profile 1997* (Ottawa: National Council of Welfare, 1999).

———. *Child Benefits: A Small Step Forward* (Ottawa: National Council of Welfare, 1997)

Pulkingham, Jane, and Gordon Ternowetsky. *Remaking Canadian Social Policy: Social Security in the Late 1990s* (Halifax: Fernwood Publishing, 1996).

———. "Neoliberalism and Retrenchment: Employment, Universality, Safety-Net Provisions and a Collapsing Canadian Welfare State," in Broad and Antony (eds.), 1999, pp. 84-98.

Ross, David, and Paul Roberts. *Income and Child Well-Being: A New Perspective on the Poverty Debate* (Ottawa: CCSD, May 1999).

Schellenberg, Grant. *The Changing Nature of Part-Time Work* (Ottawa: CCSD, 1997).

———, and David Ross. *Left Poor by the Market: A Look At Family Poverty And Earnings* (Ottawa: CCSD, 1997).

Schissel, Bernard. *The Roots of Disadvantage: The Differential Effects of Poverty on Rural and Urban Youth* (Prepared for The Centre For Rural Studies and Enrichment, St. Peter's College, Muenster, Saskatchewan, November 1997).

Silver, Jim. "Constitutional Change, Ideological Conflict and the Redistributive State," in James N. McCrorie and Martha MacDonald (eds), *The Constitutional Future of the Prairie and Atlantic Regions of Canada* (Regina: Canadian Plains Research Centre, 1992).

Skelton, Ian. *The Shelter Shortage: New Directions for Low-Cost Housing Policy in Canada* (Winnipeg: CCPA-MB, 1998).

Stanford, Jim. "Discipline, Insecurity and Productivity: The Economics Behind Labour Market 'Productivity,'" in Pulkingham and Ternowetsky, 1996, pp. 130-150.

———. "The Rise and Fall of Deficit-Mania: Public Sector Finances and the Attack on Social Canada," in Antony and Samuelson, 1998, pp. 29-52).

———. *Paper Boom: Why Real Prosperity Requires a New Approach to Canada's Economy* (Ottawa and Toronto: CCPA and Lorimer, 1999).

Statistics Canada. *Labour Force Update*, (71-005-XPB), Autumn 1997.

———. *Canadian Economic Observer, Historical Supplement* (11-210-XPB), 1998/99.

Teeple, Gary. *Globalization and the Decline of Social Reform* (Toronto: Garamond Press, 1995).

United Nations Development Programme. *Human Development Report 1999* (New York: Oxford University Press, 1999).

Yalnizyan, Armine. *The Growing Gap: A Report on Growing Inequality Between Rich and Poor in Canada* (Toronto: The Centre For Social Justice, 1998).

Chapter 2
High and Rising
The Growth of Poverty in Winnipeg
By Darren Lezubski, Jim Silver, and Errol Black

In this chapter, we attempt to identify trends in the socio-economic circumstances of people living in Winnipeg's inner city. In particular, we attempt to identify, for both Winnipeg's inner city and the city as a whole, changes in population, household formation, labour force characteristics, income levels, educational attainment and poverty rates. It is the growing incidence of poverty which is our particular concern. In some cases, we examine data relating specifically to the circumstances of Aboriginal people, youth and single-parent households.

Our review of these quantitative indicators leads us to the view that Winnipeg's inner city is at a critical juncture. Although levels of educational attainment are improving in Winnipeg, including the inner city, in all other respects the socio-economic circumstances of those living in Winnipeg's inner city continue to deteriorate. The population of the inner city continues to decline, as do labour force participation rates and average income levels, while unemployment rates, the proportion of single-parent households and poverty rates continue to grow.

Indeed, the incidence of poverty has reached what we consider to be catastrophic levels. By 1996, more than half of all inner city households had incomes below the poverty line, while an astonishing four of every five Aboriginal households were below the poverty line.

We believe that what we have documented is the continued growth in our midst of what might reasonably be thought of as "third world" living conditions. Growing numbers of people in Winnipeg's inner city, and in Winnipeg as a whole, are struggling to make do in these inadequate and steadily worsening conditions. Poverty is now so high as to be far beyond anything that ought to be considered acceptable in our community. It constitutes an emergency, and demands immediate attention.

Methodological Issues

The majority of data cited in this study are from customized census data purchased from Statistics Canada by a Census Data Consortium headed by the Social Planning Council of Winnipeg. This source makes it possible to assemble data for unique geographical areas such as Winnipeg's inner city. Additional historical census materials are drawn from public data published regularly in various Statistics Canada sources.

Acknowledgements

The authors are grateful to the Social Planning Council of Winnipeg for making available to us their customized census Canada data. We also wish to thank John Hofley, Lisa Shaw and one anonymous referee for their contributions to earlier drafts of this chapter.

There is no universally accepted definition of the inner city. The inner city boundary used here and shown in Figure One corresponds to the area defined by the Census Data Consortium and is the sum of thirty-three individual neighbourhoods*. In Table One we show adjusted inner city population trends, using both the early and current inner city boundary.

Population: Inner City Decline-Suburban Growth

Winnipeg's overall population is growing, albeit slowly, while Winnipeg's inner city population continues to decline as shown in Table One. The population of Winnipeg's CMA has grown from 540,265 in 1971 to 667,210 in 1996, an increase of 23.5 percent over 25 years. This represents an annual growth rate of roughly 1 percent. This rate of growth is slow by comparison with other Canadian cities, as shown in Table Two.

For the same period the population in Winnipeg's inner city dropped from 142,150 to 108,695, a decline of 23.5 percent, or 1 percent per year. The inner city's share of Winnipeg's population has dropped from 28.7 percent in 1966 to 16.3 percent in 1996 (Table Three).

The inner city has been losing people to the suburbs and the exurbs. This is a process long underway. In his 1979 study of Winnipeg's Core Area Johnston found that:

> The inner city has been steadily losing population since 1941 .... For the period from 1941 to 1976 the overall loss was 29 percent. In contrast, the outer areas of Winnipeg have been showing a steady increase in population. Movement recently encouraged by new construction in the suburbs has resulted in a population increase of greater than 200 percent ... between 1941 and 1976 (Johnston, 1979: 39-49).

The trend—inner city population decline, suburban population growth—is shown in Tables Three and Four. Despite a slight change between 1981 and 1986,

---

*Early inner city boundaries consisted of twenty-seven Statistics Canada census tracts. Those census tracts were: 11 – 17, 21 – 29, 33 – 36, 42- 45, 48, and 116 – 117. Since 1986 a revised, larger inner city boundary based on custom neighbourhood boundaries rather than census tracts has been utilized.

The current inner city boundary includes all of the twenty-seven census tracts which comprised the earlier inner city plus four additional census tracts: 18, 46 – 47, and 49. In an effort to allow for historical compatibility, original Statistics Canada data sources by census tract for 1966, 1971, 1976 and 1981 were consulted and inner city totals based on the current boundary were calculated. Random rounding and slight incongruities in geographical boundaries do not allow for a precise match; however, the recalculated figures provide a close match to the inner city boundaries now in use.

Where possible, data are presented for the Winnipeg Census Metropolitan Area (CMA) and the inner city. In some instances, historical data for the CMA are not available. In such cases data for the Winnipeg Census Division (CD) have been substituted. The Winnipeg CMA includes the Winnipeg Census Division together with adjacent urban and rural areas (known as the urban and rural fringes) that have a high degree of social and economic integration with the census division.

Figure 1: Winnipeg's Inner City

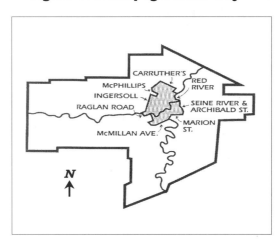

Table 1: Early & Current Inner City Populations, 1966-1996

Year	Early Boundary	Current Boundary
1966	132,395	145,910
1971	125,575	142,150
1976	109,540	124,100
1981	98,865	111,760
1986	102,365	115,150
1991	100,085	113,865
1996	96,160	108,695

Source: Dominion Bureau of Statistics, & Statistics Canada Census 2A Profiles. various years.

the process of inner city population decline and suburban population growth continues.

The real story behind the substantial decline in inner city population is the growth of Winnipeg's suburbs. An examination of the ten fastest-growing neighbourhoods in Winnipeg since 1971 reveals that all ten are located outside of the inner city. By contrast, of the ten Winnipeg neighbourhoods with the greatest population *declines* from 1971 to 1996, six are located in the inner city* (Special Tabulations of 1971 & 1996 Census).

---

*The ten fastest-growing neighbourhoods, 1971-1996, were: The Maples, Tyndall Park, River Park South, Valley Gardens, River East, Dakota Crossing, Linden Woods, Fort Richmond, Meadowood and Richmond West. The six inner city neighbourhoods among the ten with the greatest population declines were: William Whyte, St. John's, West Alexander, Wolseley, Central St. Boniface and Spence.

We conclude that what has been happening for many years in Winnipeg is that a large proportion of those who can afford to do so have been leaving the inner city for the suburbs. This sets in motion a process that has been described as "inner city decay" (Leo and Shaw, 1998; Harris and Scarth, 1999). As people leave for the suburbs, businesses follow. The tax base in the inner city is eroded. Services decline. Housing prices drop. Low housing prices attract those with low incomes. A non-virtuous circular process is set in motion: higher income families leave the inner city and are replaced by lower income families entering the inner city. The result, as will be shown, is an inner city population with much lower levels of labour force participation and much higher levels of unemployment and poverty than is the case for the city as a whole. These problems become concentrated in the inner city and left unchecked, generate their own downward momentum. The recent (fall and winter 1999) epidemic of arson in Winnipeg's inner city is but the most recent manifestation of this process.

Population: Growth in the Proportion of Youth in the Inner City

Historically, Winnipeg's inner city has had a lower proportion of young people than the Winnipeg CMA. This was almost certainly the result of families with young children moving to the suburbs throughout the post-war period. The inner city continues to have a lower proportion of young, but the proportion of the inner city's population that is under 15 years of age has been growing since 1981, as shown in Table Five. The proportion of inner city children under six years of age has been growing most rapidly.

The growth in the proportion of children and especially very young children, is especially significant because of the very high and rapidly growing rate of poverty in the inner city, and because of the relationship between poverty and educational attainment. As will be described later, where rates of poverty are high, educational attainment is likely to be reduced. Where educational attainment is low, poverty tends to be reproduced. Thus the rapidly growing proportion of very young children in Winnipeg's inner city suggests that, if left unattended, poverty in the inner city will continue to grow, and the rate of growth may even accelerate.

Households & Families

Another significant characteristic of Winnipeg's inner city is the high and growing proportion of single-parent households, seven of every eight of which are female-headed. More than one in every four inner city households in 1996 were single parents, compared to approximately one in every six or seven in the Winnipeg CMA. The proportion of single parents in Winnipeg's inner city is almost double the proportion in the Winnipeg CMA—27.1 percent compared to 15.8 percent in 1996—and the proportion has grown significantly since 1976, from 17.5 percent to 27.1 percent (Table Six).

However, when we examine the actual numbers, as opposed to percentages, we find that the number of single-parent families is much greater *outside* the inner city than in the inner city. In 1996, for example, there were 6,400 single-parent families in the inner city, and 21,590 (27,990 – 6,400) elsewhere in Winnipeg. This has long been the case (Table Six). Single-parent families are more concentrated in the inner city, but there are more of them beyond than within the inner city.

Table 2: Canadian CMA's Ranked by Growth Rates, 1971-1996

CMA	1971 population	1996 population	% change 71-96
Calgary	400,154	821,628	105.30%
Oshawa	135,196 (1976)	268,773	98.9% (76-96)
Edmonton	490,811	862,597	75.70%
Saskatoon	125,079	219,056	75.10%
Vancouver	1,071,081	1,831,665	71.00%
Kitchener	224,390	382,940	70.70%
Ottawa-Hull	596,176	1,010,498	69.50%
Toronto	2,609,638	4,263,757	63.40%
Victoria	193,512	304,287	57.20%
Halifax	220,350	332,518	50.90%
London	264,469	398,616	50.70%
Quebec City	476,232	671,889	41.10%
Regina	138,956	193,652	39.40%
St. John's	129,304	174,051	34.60%
Trois-Riveres	106,031 (1976)	139,956	32.0% (76-96)
Hamilton	495,864	624,360	25.90%
St. Catharines	301,108	372,406	23.70%
Winnipeg	540,265	667,209	23.50%
Montreal	2,720,413	3,326,510	22.30%
Chicoutimi-Jonquiere	131,924	160,454	21.60%
Saint John	105,227	125,705	19.50%
Sherbrooke	125,183 (1981)	147,384	17.7% (81-96)
Windsor	245,167	278,685	13.70%
Thunder Bay	111,492	125,562	12.60%
Sudbury	153,959	160,488	4.20%

Source: Statistics Canada Census, various years. Calculations prepared by authors.

Table 3: Winnipeg CMA & Inner City Population 1941-2001

Year	Winnipeg CMA	Early Inner city boundary	Inner city as % of CMA	Current Inner City boundary	Inner city as % of CMA
1941	300,000	153,700	51.20%	n/a	n/a
1951	354,100	147,700	41.70%	n/a	n/a
1961	476,000	143,500	30.10%	n/a	n/a
1966	508,760	132,395	26.00%	145,910	28.70%
1971	540,265	125,575	23.20%	142,150	26.30%
1976	578,215	109,540	18.90%	124,100	21.50%
1981	584,845	98,865	16.90%	111,760	19.10%
1986	625,355	102,355	16.40%	115,150	18.40%
1991	652,355	100,085	15.30%	113,865	17.50%
1996	667,210	96,160	14.40%	108,695	16.30%
2001 *	674,000	93,800	13.90%	103,800	15.40%

* Projected by authors.
Source: Adapted from table 3.1, Johnston, 1979: 40, Statistics Canada Census various years & Special Tabulations various years.

Table 4: Population Change, Winnipeg & Inner City, 1966-1996

Period	% change Winnipeg CMA	% change Current Inner City
1966 – 1971	6.20%	-2.60%
1971 – 1976	7.00%	-12.70%
1976 – 1981	1.10%	-9.90%
1981 – 1986	6.90%	3.00%
1986 – 1991	4.30%	-1.10%
1991 – 1996	2.30%	-4.50%
1966 – 1996	31.10%	-25.50%

Source: Calculations performed by authors.

Changes in family type over time are also revealing. In the Winnipeg CMA, the total numbers of families, two-parent families, and single-parent families, are growing. In fact, single-parent families are growing especially rapidly. In the inner city, by contrast, the total number of families and of two-parent families is *declining*. Only the number of single-parent families is growing (Table Six).

By way of summary, we can say the following: the number of single-parent families is growing rapidly in Winnipeg as a whole; their proportion of the total families in the inner city is growing not only because of the growth in their numbers, but also because of the decline in the number of two-parent inner city families. This is a process long underway.

As a result of these trends, greater numbers of children are growing up in single-parent families. This is shown in Table Seven. In 1996, 21.9 percent of all children in Winnipeg—just over one in five—were growing up in a single-parent family, up from 13.0 percent in 1981. In the inner city, more than a third, 37.5 percent of all children, were living in single-parent families, up from 20.2 percent in 1981 (Table Seven).

If we examine actual numbers in Table Seven, we find that from 1981 to 1996, the number of children in single-parent families in Winnipeg grew rapidly, by 120.7 percent (from 19,145 to 42,250), while the number in the inner city grew slightly less rapidly, by 106.8 percent (from 5,020 to 10,385). The number of children in two-parent families in Winnipeg grew less quickly during that period, by 17.8 percent (from 127,755 to 150,525), while the number of children in two-parent families in the inner city actually declined, by 12.8 percent (from 19,830 to 17,290). In short, the number of children in single-parent families is growing rapidly, both in Winnipeg generally and in the inner city, but in the inner city this growth is magnified by a significant decline in the number of children in two-parent families.

The growth in the numbers and proportions of single-parent families and of children in single-parent families is significant. While it is important to acknowledge that many single-parent families are doing well, it is nevertheless the case, as will be shown shortly, that there is a higher probability that single-parent families and especially inner city single-parent families will have incomes below the poverty line. This contributes to the growing numbers of children growing up poor in Winnipeg. On the other hand, it would be a mistake to over-estimate the impor-

Table 5: Proportion of Children by Age, 1976-1996*

Year	WINNIPEG CMA		INNER CITY	
	under 6	6 - 14	under 6	14-Jun
1976	24.50%	40.30%	25.70%	36.90%
1981	23.90%	37.60%	26.60%	34.30%
1986	24.90%	36.20%	29.80%	33.20%
1991	26.30%	36.30%	32.50%	33.80%
1996	24.90%	37.20%	31.40%	35.60%

* Percentages for children 15 years of age and over not shown.
Source: Statistics Canada Census & Special Tabulations of 1971, 1981, 1986, 1991 & 1996 census. Calculations performed by authors.

Table 6: Census Families by Type, 1976-1996

Winnipeg CMA					
Year	Total Families	Husband-wife	% of total	Single Parent	% of total
1976	145,915	129,645	88.80%	16,270	11.20%
1981	152,145	132,710	87.20%	19,435	12.80%
1986	164,855	141,910	86.10%	22,950	13.90%
1991	172,375	146,830	85.20%	25,540	14.80%
1996	176,945	148,955	84.20%	27,990	15.80%

Inner city					
Year	Total Families	Husband-wife	% of total	Single Parent	% of total
1976	27,235	22,460	82.50%	4,760	17.50%
1981	23,915	19,000	79.40%	4,890	20.40%
1986	25,850	20,055	77.60%	5,785	22.40%
1991	24,700	18,500	74.90%	6,200	25.10%
1996	23,650	17,250	72.90%	6,400	27.10%

Source: Statistics Canada Census & Special Tabulations of 1976, 1981, 1986, 1991 & 1996 census. Calculations performed by authors.

tance of single parenthood to the growing levels of poverty in Winnipeg. As will be shown, while a very high proportion of single parents have incomes below the poverty line, most of those who are poor are not single parents.

Labour Force Characteristics

Paid employment is a key determinant of economic well-being (see Chapter One). The relative absence of paid employment in Winnipeg's inner city is a glaring problem. The data reveal that the unemployment rate is much higher in the inner city than the Winnipeg CMA—15.4 percent in the inner city, 7.9 percent in Winnipeg as a whole—and it has been increasing, although the increase has been minimal since 1991. The labour force participation rate is significantly lower in the

Table 7: Number of Children by Family Type, 1981, 1991 & 1996

Winnipeg CD	1981	%	1991	%	1996	%
All children	146,905	100.0%	189,615	100.0%	192,775	100.0%
Husband-wife	127,755	87.0%	150,160	79.2%	150,525	78.1%
Single parent	19,145	13.0%	39,455	20.8%	42,250	21.9%

Inner City	1981	%	1991	%	1996	%
All children	24,850	100.0%	28,100	100.0%	27,675	100.0%
Husband-wife	19,830	79.8%	17,900	63.7%	17,290	62.5%
Single parent	5,020	20.2%	10,200	36.3%	10,385	37.5%

Source: Statistics Canada Census & Special Tabulations of 1981, 1986, 1991 & 1996 census. Calculations performed by authors.

inner city than the Winnipeg CMA and has been declining steadily in the inner city, while remaining constant in the CMA. In 1981 the participation rate in the inner city was approximately 3 percentage points lower than in the Winnipeg CMA. By 1996 the gap had widened to approximately 9 percentage points. Participation rates are now very low in the inner city—58.4 percent in 1996, down from 63.5 percent in 1981—suggesting that large numbers of people in the inner city have given up looking for work. The combination of high and rising rates of unemployment and exceptionally low and still declining rates of labour force participation is particularly disturbing. It makes clear that a massive job creation strategy, aimed at creating well-paying jobs, has to be a central element in any serious anti-poverty effort.

If we examine these labour force characteristics by gender, we see that male unemployment rates are somewhat higher than female unemployment rates, especially in the inner city, and that the gap is widening. But it is the female labour force participation rates that are particularly notable. They are exceptionally low in the inner city. In the inner city in 1996 only 50.9 percent, or approximately one-half, of working age women were employed or looking for work (Table Eight). It is likely that this very low participation rate is linked to the high rate of single-parenthood and to the high and growing proportion of very young children in the inner city. Women continue to bear the bulk of the responsibility for child-rearing.

If we examine the labour force characteristics of single parents, seven of eight of whom are female, we find that the participation rates in the inner city and in Winnipeg as a whole are roughly comparable to the participation rates of all females. However, the unemployment rates of single parents are almost double the unemployment rates of all females in the labour force, both for the inner city and for Winnipeg as a whole, and unemployment rates have been growing extremely rapidly. From 1981 to 1996, single-parent unemployment rates almost doubled in Winnipeg, from 6.9 to 13.2 percent, while in the inner city they have more than doubled, from 11.6 to 24.3 percent .

We are not certain what accounts for this trend, although a partial explanation may lie in the declining real value of social assistance rates. From 1986 to 1996, the real value of social assistance for a single-parent with one child in Manitoba declined by almost 10 percent (National Council of Welfare, 1996). These rates were already very low. It is possible that social assistance rates are so low that single

Table 8: Adult Unemployment & Labour Force Participation Rates by Gender, 1986-1996

Year	Winnipeg CMA		Inner city	
	Unemployment rate % Males	Participation rate % Males	Unemployment rate % Males	Participation rate % Males
1986	7.5%	78.5%	14.0%	71.1%
1991	9.2%	76.1%	17.3%	67.0%
1996	8.5%	74.0%	17.8%	66.3%
	Unemployment rate % Females	Participation rate % Females	Unemployment rate % Females	Participation rate % Females
1986	8.1%	59.3%	10.5%	53.6%
1991	8.0%	61.4%	12.4%	52.0%
1996	7.3%	60.9%	12.4%	50.9%

Source: Statistics Canada Census & Special Tabulations of 1986, 1991 & 1996 census. Calculations performed by authors.

parents are being forced into the labour market to search for paid employment—a search which, according to the data, is frequently unsuccessful. It is also possible that there has been increased pressure on single parents to search for paid employment (See MacKinnon, Chapter 3; and Silver, Chapter 7). Given the high and rapidly growing proportion of children, and especially very young children, in the inner city, these rapidly growing rates of unemployment for single parents are troubling.

The labour force characteristics of inner city youth are also of concern. Young people aged 15 – 24 are less likely to be in the labour force, and if in the labour force, more likely to be unemployed, than is the case for the population generally (Table Nine). This is especially so for youth in the inner city. Almost one in five inner city youth were unemployed in 1996. Worse, the participation rate has plummeted since 1981, by more than 17 percentage points—a remarkable decline—so that by 1996 less than 60 percent of inner city youth were working or looking for work. This means that a very large proportion of this generation of inner city young people are not getting their foot in the door with a first employment opportunity. And the high and growing proportion of very young children in the inner city suggests that, if left unattended, the problem will continue to worsen.

If we separate out Aboriginal youth, these trends are accentuated and are even more alarming. In Winnipeg as a whole the labour force participation rate for Aboriginal youth has declined to 50.6 percent in 1996—only one-half of Aboriginal youth are working or looking for work. The unemployment rate is almost one in four—24.6 percent. In the inner city the numbers are worse still. A mere 40.1 percent of Aboriginal youth in the inner city are in the labour force; of these more than one-third, 35.1 percent, are unemployed (Table Ten). These figures are shocking and cause for alarm.

The high and rising rates of unemployment and low and declining labour force participation rates in Winnipeg's inner city are an important factor in explaining the central concern of this study—the high and growing incidence of poverty in Winnipeg's inner city. The particularly high rates of unemployment

Table 9: Youth (15-24) Labour Force Trends, 1981-1996

Year	Winnipeg CD		Inner city	
	Unemployment rate %	Participation rate %	Unemployment rate %	Participation rate %
1981	14.5%	76.7%	17.0%	76.6%
1986	13.4%	72.8%	17.2%	71.0%
1991	14.2%	70.1%	19.7%	64.6%
1996	14.3%	67.6%	18.9%	59.3%
	Unemployment rate % Males	Participation rate % Males	Unemployment rate % Males	Participation rate % Males
1986	14.7%	74.6%	19.7%	74.8%
1991	16.5%	71.4%	24.0%	66.6%
1996	15.4%	69.2%	21.8%	61.5%
	Unemployment rate % Females	Participation rate % Females	Unemployment rate % Females	Participation rate % Females
1986	12.1%	70.1%	14.8%	67.5%
1991	11.8%	68.9%	15.4%	62.6%
1996	13.2%	66.0%	16.2%	57.2%

Source: Special Tabulation of 1981, 1986, 1991 & 1996 Census

and low rates of labour force participation among inner city single parents, among youth aged fifteen to twenty-four, and even more, among Aboriginal youth aged fifteen to twenty-four, make clear that if left unattended, the problem will grow steadily worse.

Income Levels

Another important and related factor in understanding the high and growing incidence of poverty in Winnipeg's inner city is the low and declining income levels of inner city households, relative to all Winnipeg households. First, a much higher proportion of inner city households are concentrated at the lower income ranges. In 1996, for example, the proportion of inner city households who had incomes below $20,000 was almost twice as high as for all Winnipeg households: 47.2 percent in the inner city; 24.7 percent in Winnipeg as a whole. This means that almost one-half of all inner city residents had incomes in 1996 that were below $20,000 per annum. By contrast, the proportion of all Winnipeg households who had incomes of $50,000 or more in 1996 was more than double the proportion of inner city households: 36.4 percent in Winnipeg; 16.0 percent in the inner city (Special Tabulation of 1991 & 1996 Census).

Further, when inflation is taken into account, the already very low real incomes in the inner city declined more rapidly since 1986 than real incomes in the city as a whole. Specifically, from 1986 to 1996, real incomes in the inner city declined by 7.6 percent, as compared with a decline of 2.6 percent for Winnipeg.

This combination—a concentration of inner city households in the lower income ranges, coupled with the declining real value of inner city incomes relative to the city as a whole—is clearly linked to the high levels of unemployment and low levels of labour force participation shown in the previous section, and both

Table 10: Aboriginal Youth (15-24) Labour Force Characteristics, 1986-1996

Year	Winnipeg CMA		Inner city	
	Unemployment rate %	Participation rate %	Unemployment rate %	Participation rate %
1986	30.80%	55.30%	37.80%	49.10%
1991	28.90%	50.20%	37.70%	41.30%
1996	24.60%	50.60%	35.10%	40.10%

Source: Special Tabulation of 1986, 1991 & 1996 Census

are linked to the very high and growing rates of poverty identified in a later section.

Educational Attainment

Levels of educational attainment in the inner city are improving. The proportion of inner city adults with less than grade nine has been cut almost in half since 1981—from 26.8 percent to 15.2 percent—and the proportion with a university degree is more than one and a half times what it was in 1981—12.4 percent compared to 7.8 percent (Special Tabulation of 1981, 1986, 1991 & 1996 Census). This is a very positive development.

However, levels of educational attainment in the inner city continue to be consistently lower than those in the Winnipeg CMA. In 1996, 44 percent of inner city residents, compared to 35.3 percent of CMA residents, had not completed high school, while 15.2 percent of inner city residents compared to 9.1 percent of CMA residents had less than grade nine (Special Tabulation of 1981, 1986, 1991 & 1996 Census).

This is important because levels of educational attainment correlate positively with employment status, as shown in Table Eleven. In both Winnipeg and the inner city, those with less than grade twelve are more likely to be unemployed. This observation is consistent with the findings of earlier studies of Aboriginal populations in Manitoba: unemployment goes down and earnings go up for those Aboriginal people with higher levels of education (Hull, 1987; Loxley, 1996).

The positive correlation between educational attainment and subsequent employment status suggests that education is a way out of poverty. While this is true, the situation is complicated by the observation that the likelihood of a child's doing well in school correlates strongly with the socio-economic status of the child's parents and peers. This correlation was identified more than thirty years ago (Coleman, 1966) and has stood the test of time (Kelso, 1994, p. 53-56). The pattern is: low socio-economic status, low educational attainment; high socio – economic status, high educational attainment.

In short, a vicious circle is created: low socio-economic status correlates with low educational attainment, and low educational attainment correlates with lower levels of employment and incomes. This problem is particularly severe in Winnipeg's inner city, as revealed by Table One2, derived from the Winnipeg School Division No. 1 School Demographics Report, 1997/98. Table Twelve shows that at each and every one of Winnipeg's 15 inner city elementary schools, more than 50

Table 11: Adult Unemployment Rates by Level of Education, 1986-1996

Year	Winnipeg CD			Inner City		
	Less than grade 12	High School	Some University	Less than grade 12	High School	Some University
1986	11.00%	7.70%	6.10%	16.40%	10.50%	9.00%
1991	12.80%	7.80%	6.70%	20.50%	13.90%	10.30%
1996	13.10%	7.00%	6.00%	23.30%	13.10%	9.30%

Source: Special Tabulation of 1986, 1991 & 1996 Census.

percent of families with children in the school's catchment area have incomes below the low income cut-offs (LICO). At thirteen of these fifteen inner city schools, the proportion of families with children who have incomes below the LICO is two-thirds or more. At an additional thirteen elementary schools in Winnipeg School Division No. 1—i.e., thirteen non-inner city schools—more than 50 percent of families with children had incomes below the LICO.

These levels of poverty amongst parents of inner city school children are shocking. They are evidence of the very high degree of concentration of poverty in the inner city. Such highly concentrated poverty dramatically increases the likelihood that children in these neighbourhoods will, on average, do less well in school than the children of more well-to-do parents (Hunter, Chapter Six).

This likelihood is increased still further by the very high rates of migrancy in the inner city. We can develop a broad picture of migrancy by examining data on "movers" and "non-movers." Movers are those who, in the 1996 Census, had a different address than at the time of the 1991 Census. Non-movers are those who were at the same address for both the 1991 and the 1996 Census. In 1996 approximately 58 percent of inner city families were movers, compared to approximately 43 percent in the Winnipeg CMA. The proportion of movers has declined in the Winnipeg CMA since 1981—from approximately 48 percent to approximately 43 percent—but has increased in the inner city since 1981—from 52 percent to approximately 58 percent (Special Tabulation of 1981, 1986, 1991 & 1996 Census). In other words, the gap between the inner city and the Winnipeg CMA is widening.

Amongst Aboriginal people, the rate of migrancy is even higher. Almost four in every five Aboriginal families identified in the 1996 Census were movers (Special Tabulation of 1986, 1991 & 1996 Census).

It is important to note that the census data hide much of the inner city mobility. The census data tell us only how many households moved and how many did not move between two census periods, which is a five-year interval. However, many inner city families move much more frequently. A 1995 study by Manitoba Health observed that:

> Migrancy (frequent movers) is a particular problem for inner city children ... Migrancy combined with poverty, single-parent families and other social difficulties further exacerbates the difficulty of school aged children. In a 1992 review of inner city schools, the lowest migrancy rate (proportion of children moving per year in the school population) was 40.6 percent. The highest rate was 84.7 percent .... Some children have

Table 12: Rates of Poverty Amongst Parents of Inner City Elementary School Students, 1996

School	Weighted % of families with children whose incomes are below the LICO *
David Livingston	82.1%
Dufferin	74.3%
Fort Rouge	77.8%
John M. King	66.9%
Machray	68.2%
Mulvey	72.9%
Niji Mahkwa	84.6%
Norquay	70.8%
Pinkham	59.2%
Sister MacNamera	80.0%
Strathcona	67.0%
Victoria - Albert	73.2%
Wellington	56.9%
William Whyte	79.0%

* Data for families with children with incomes below the LICO are based on Income Tax Returns of families in the Division with children younger than 18 years of age. The weighting is to account for the fact that students do not necessarily attend their neighbourhood school.

Source: Derived from Winnipeg School Division No. 1, School Demographics Report 1997/98, table 1, p. F2.

been in 13 schools by 11 years of age .... Seventy-five percent (of migrants) were from unemployed single parent families .... In a nine-month period in 1992/93, there were 3,058 single parent family moves out of a possible 3,553 (Manitoba Health, 1995: 107-108).

High rates of unemployment and poverty very likely contribute to the high degree of mobility, which in turn adversely affects educational attainment. Thus high rates of mobility in Winnipeg's inner city and amongst selected populations are yet another factor adding to the perpetuation of poverty.

The Incidence of Poverty*

In Winnipeg, overall poverty rates—although already high—grew relatively slowly from 1971 to 1986. Since 1986, and especially since 1991, poverty rates have grown rapidly (Table Thirteen). According to 1996 Census Canada data soon to be re-

---

*We use the Statistics Canada Low Income Cut Offs (LICO) as the 'poverty line'. Please see the Appendix, "The Debate About Poverty Lines".

leased by the Canadian Council on Social Development, Winnipeg had the fourth highest poverty rate among the 25 CMA's in Canada, although Winnipeg's poverty rate was a mere 0.3 and 0.4 percent lower than the CMA's which ranked third and second (Lee, 2000). Similarly, although poverty rates for single-parent families in Winnipeg were already very high in 1971, they too grew slowly to 1991 and have increased significantly since (Table Fourteen).

In the inner city the story is different. Poverty rates have been very high since 1971 and have grown steadily and even dramatically to the point that more than half—50.8 percent—of all inner city households had incomes below the Statistics Canada Low Income Cut Offs in 1996 (Table Thirteen). This is a shocking figure.

For single parents in the inner city—the vast majority of whom are women—the situation is even worse. The number and the proportion of inner city single parents has been growing, as noted earlier, and the proportion below the poverty line has been growing rapidly, especially since 1981. By 1996, more than two of every three single-parent households in Winnipeg's inner city—68.5 percent—had

Table 13: Household Poverty Rate Trends, 1971-1996

Year	Households in poverty - Winnipeg CD	Households in poverty - Inner City
1971	20.6%	32.6%
1981	21.3%	36.2%
1986	21.8%	39.5%
1991	23.9%	44.3%
1996	28.4%	50.8%

Source: Special Tabulation of 1971, 1981, 1986, 1991 & 1996 Census

incomes below the poverty line. In Winnipeg as a whole, almost one-half of single parents—48.4 percent—had incomes below the poverty line in 1996 (Table Fourteen).

For Aboriginal people in Winnipeg, and especially in Winnipeg's inner city, the incidence of poverty is even higher. Poverty rates for Aboriginal people living in Winnipeg, and especially in Winnipeg's inner city, are astonishingly high. They are so high, in fact, that they ought to bring shame not only to the City of Winnipeg but also to Manitoba and Canada. Almost two-thirds of all Aboriginal households in Winnipeg—64.7 percent—have incomes below the poverty line; more than four-fifths of Aboriginal households in Winnipeg's inner city—80.3 percent—are below the poverty line (Table One5). Any anti-poverty effort must take these striking facts into account.

However, poverty is not just an Aboriginal problem. As Table Sixteen reveals, just over one in five inner city households living in poverty are Aboriginal; almost four in five, therefore, are non-Aboriginal. In short, most inner city Aboriginal households are living in poverty (Table Fifteeen), but most inner city households in poverty are non-Aboriginal (Table Sixteen).

Similarly, single-parent households in poverty constitute a relatively small proportion of the total families in poverty in Winnipeg's inner city. As a result, while most inner city single parents are living in poverty, most inner city households in poverty are other than single parents (Table Seventeen).

Table 14: Poverty Rates by Household Type, 1971-1996

	Winnipeg CD				
Year	Husband-wife no children	Husband-wife with child(ren)	Single Parent	Multiple Family	Non Family
1971	15.7%	11.8%	43.0%	10.4%	36.8%
1981	11.0%	10.4%	42.2%	14.5%	35.5%
1986	10.0%	11.1%	42.4%	11.7%	36.5%
1991	12.5%	11.8%	43.9%	11.5%	37.9%
1996	12.1%	14.3%	48.4%	15.6%	46.0%

	Inner City				
Year	Husband-wife no children	Husband-wife with child(ren)	Single Parent	Multiple Family*	Non Family**
1971	23.2%	23.6%	53.7%	16.1%	38.4%
1981	19.7%	24.5%	54.1%	19.8%	43.8%
1986	20.0%	29.0%	62.8%	12.5%	46.0%
1991	26.3%	33.0%	64.1%	18.2%	50.1%
1996	24.0%	36.0%	68.5%	26.7%	59.7%

Source: Special Tabulation of 1971, 1981, 1986, 1991 & 1996 Census.
* More than one Census family living in a household.
** Men or women living alone, or with someone to whom they are not related by blood, marriage or adoption.

If Aboriginal and single-parent households, despite their high rates of poverty, constitute only a small proportion of those with incomes below the poverty line, then who are the majority of those who are poor? The answer can be found in Table Seventeen. More than one-half of all Winnipeg households living in poverty, and almost two of every three inner city households living in poverty, are "non-family" households. Non-family households are defined as men or women living alone or with someone to whom they are not related by blood, marriage or adoption. From Table Fourteen we can see that almost one-half of all non-family households in Winnipeg—46.0 percent—and more than one-half of all non-family households in the inner city—59.7 percent—are poor. Their numbers are roughly equally divided between men and women. Most of the poor in the inner city are non-

Table 15: Total & Aboriginal Household Poverty Rate, 1971-1996

Year	Households in poverty - Winnipeg CD	Aboriginal Households in poverty - Winnipeg	Aboriginal Households in poverty - Inner city
1971	20.6%	57.1% *	n/a
1981	21.3%	53.7% *	n/a
1986	21.8%	45.6% **	67.2%
1991	23.9%	55.5% **	74.6%
1996	28.4%	64.7% **	80.3%

* Based on CMA boundary ** Based on CD boundary
Source: Special Tabulation of 1971, 1981, 1986, 1991 & 1996 Census.

Table 16: Inner City Aboriginal Households 1991-1996

Year	Aboriginal households as % of all inner city households	Aboriginal households as % of inner city households in poverty
1986	10.0%	16.4%
1991	12.1%	20.3%
1996	13.9%	22.0%

Source: Special Tabulation of 1986, 1991 & 1996 Census.

family households; most non-family households in the inner city are poor. The rate of poverty among non-family households has grown rapidly since 1981, in both the Winnipeg CMA and the inner city (Table Fourteen).

It may be argued that the dramatic growth in the number and proportion of non-family households in the inner city living below the poverty line is attributable not only to the high rates of unemployment and low rates of labour force participation noted earlier, but also to the sharp decline in social assistance rates for single employable adults and a decline in real wages in most sectors of the economy from 1990 to 1995. Social assistance rates for single employable adults declined by $1,243 in real terms from 1992 to 1996. This represents a drop of 17 percent in purchasing power (National Council of Welfare, 1997, Table Five, p. 32). Real wages declined by approximately 4 percent from 1990 to 1995 (Manitoba Bureau of Statistics, *Manitoba Statistical Review*, various numbers).

Finally, it is particularly important to note that while poverty is highly concentrated in Winnipeg's inner city, poverty in Winnipeg is by no means confined to the inner city. Table Seventeen showed that in 1996 there were many more families in poverty outside the inner city than there were in the inner city: 25,790 households in the inner city; 44,120 households in the rest of Winnipeg. Not only that, the numbers of people in poverty are growing more rapidly in Winnipeg as a

Table 17: Number of Households in Poverty, 1971-1996

Winnipeg CD						
Year	Total	Husband-wife no children	Husband-wife with child(ren)	Single Parent	Multiple Family	Non Family
1971	34,220	5,975	9,015	5,640	230	13,360
1981	44,650	5,460	7,900	7,590	240	23,455
1986	49,600	5,320	8,710	8,940	215	26,415
1991	57,500	7,030	9,195	10,525	235	30,515
1996	69,910	6,605	11,145	12,545	370	39,250

Inner City						
Year	Total	Husband-wife no children	Husband-wife with child(ren)	Single Parent	Multiple Family	Non Family
1971	15,115	2,360	2,685	2,465	120	7,480
1981	17,955	1,900	2,325	2,525	100	11,110
1986	20,440	1,875	2,825	3,475	70	12,200
1991	22,815	2,345	2,875	3,780	100	13,710
1996	25,790	1,940	3,035	4,170	135	16,510

Source: Special Tabulation of 1971, 1981, 1986, 1991 & 1996 Census.

Table 18: Percentage Change in Total & Low Income Households, 1971-1996

Year	Winnipeg CD		Inner City	
	% change all households	% change low income households	% change all households	% change low income households
1971 - 1981	27.1%	30.5%	7.0%	18.8%
1981 - 1986	7.5%	11.1%	4.1%	13.8%
1986 - 1991	6.0%	15.9%	-0.4%	11.6%
1991 - 1996	2.6%	21.6%	-1.3%	13.0%
1971 - 1996	48.1%	104.3%	9.5%	70.6%

Source: Special Tabulation of 1971, 1981, 1986, 1991 & 1996 Census.

whole than in the inner city. This is a result, to a large extent, of the decrease in the absolute number of people living in the inner city. Table Eighteen reveals that since 1971, with the exception of the period 1981-1986, the number of people living in poverty has grown more rapidly in Winnipeg as a whole than it has in the inner city. The poverty rate, by contrast—ie., the proportion of people who are poor—has grown more rapidly in the inner city than in Winnipeg as a whole because the total population of the inner city is declining, as was shown in Table One. As a result, rather than the conventional wisdom of the inner city as an island of poverty surrounded by a sea of affluence, we see poverty conditions spreading geographically.

The high and rapidly growing levels of poverty and of child poverty are reflected in the dramatic growth in food bank usage since 1987. Between 1987 and 1997 there has been a nine-fold increase in the number of households making use of food banks supplied by Winnipeg Harvest. By contrast, for Canada as a whole, the number of persons making use of food banks "only" doubled between March 1989 and March 1999 (Canadian Association of Food Banks, 1999).

By way of summary, we can say the following about the incidence of poverty in Winnipeg and Winnipeg's inner city. Rates of poverty are very high and they are growing rapidly, both in Winnipeg and in the inner city. Poverty is increasingly becoming concentrated, both in the inner city and in particular populations—especially single parents and, even more, Aboriginal people. In the inner city, and amongst single parents and Aboriginal people, poverty rates are at shocking levels.

However, at the same time that poverty is, in these ways, becoming increasingly concentrated, it is also spreading. For example, poverty is not confined to the inner city. More people in poverty live outside the inner city than in the inner city. Similarly, most people in poverty are neither Aboriginal nor single parents. Although the incidence of poverty is shockingly high in the inner city and amongst single parents and Aboriginal people, poverty is a widespread problem in Winnipeg. This is a finding we had not anticipated.

Finally, large and growing numbers and proportions of Winnipeg's children are growing up in poverty. This is especially so amongst Aboriginal people and single parents, whose share of the total population is increasing rapidly. In the inner city in particular the proportion of children and especially very young children is growing rapidly. This creates a great many well-documented problems (Silver, Chapter Seven).

Conclusion

The incidence of poverty in Winnipeg's inner city is extremely high, and growing rapidly. By 1996 more than one-half of all inner city households had incomes below the poverty line. More than two-thirds of single-parent households in the inner city, and an astonishing four-fifths of Aboriginal households in the inner city, had incomes below the poverty line. The high incidence and rapid growth of inner city poverty are associated with high and growing rates of unemployment, low and declining rates of labour force participation, and low and declining real income levels. The high levels of unemployment and especially low levels of labour force participation among inner city youth, and particularly Aboriginal youth, and the growing proportion of very young children in the inner city suggest that if left unattended the problems will worsen. Doing nothing is fostering the kinds of conditions and problems that have been well-documented for the inner cities of large American urban centres (Wilson, 1987; Jencks and Peterson, 1991; Jargowsky, 1997).

Serious as the problem of poverty is in the inner city, where it is very highly concentrated, it is important to note that most of Winnipeg's poor do not live in the inner city. There are more people in poverty, and their numbers are growing more rapidly, outside of the inner city than within the inner city. Similarly, while almost one-half of single-parent families and most Aboriginal people have incomes below the poverty line, most of those who are poor are neither single parents nor Aboriginal.

From these observations, we draw two conclusions. First, the high incidence of poverty in the inner city and among single parents and Aboriginal people, is a particularly acute problem. Second, it would be a serious mistake to assume that poverty in Winnipeg is confined to particular parts of the city or particular parts of the population.

It is our conclusion that the problem of poverty in Winnipeg has reached crisis proportions. It is a massive problem that requires immediate and dramatic response. It is no longer acceptable, if it ever was, to ignore or to pay lip-service to the high incidence and rapid growth of poverty in Winnipeg and its accentuated concentration in the inner city.

For so many people to be suffering in the midst of plenty is simply wrong. It is morally unacceptable. Why should some people have so little that their lives and their childrens' lives are adversely affected, when others have so much? What can possibly justify such levels of poverty? We do not believe that there can be any justification for the poverty that we have described, and we expect that most Canadians would agree with our ethical concerns.

Further, poverty is costly. Poverty adds significantly, for example, to health care costs. A 1995 study by Manitoba Health reported that those in the poorest income groups are ten times more likely to be admitted to hospital than those in the highest income groups. The study added that "there is no determinant of health that impacts more on the health of individuals than poverty" (Manitoba Health, 1995, pp. 30 and 58). If we are serious about reducing health care costs, we have to reduce poverty. Poverty also adds significantly to the cost of child and family services, and to the cost of policing and of corrections. Poverty reduces the likelihood of educational success, which results in higher unemployment and lower incomes, both of which are costly to society as a whole. And poverty deprives us as a society of the skills and energy of vast numbers of people who would, if it were not for the effects of poverty, make useful contributions to their personal and our collective well-being. We all benefit if poverty is eliminated.

Two additional observations are warranted. First, as serious as the high and rapidly growing incidence of poverty in Winnipeg is, it is distinctly possible that the problem will get worse. It is worse in some inner cities in North America (Leo and Shaw, 1998, p. 7), and if left unattended, the likelihood is so high as to be virtually certain that it will become worse in Winnipeg. Action is necessary if this is to be prevented.

Second, while Winnipeg's inner city suffers from a high incidence of poverty and related problems, it is also home to a growing number of very exciting and innovative and hopeful community-based initiatives which are making a difference, as discussed in Chapters Five, Six, and Seven of this volume.

Any long-term solution to poverty in Winnipeg must build on the many, outstanding community-based initiatives which have emerged in recent years, particularly from within the inner city. An effective anti-poverty strategy must, in addition, include changes in government policy leading to increased public investment in people, in the inner city and beyond.

We recommend the following as the *principles* which ought to drive a Winnipeg inner city anti-poverty strategy.

1. There needs to be a recognition that there is a crisis of poverty in Winnipeg and a commitment arising from this recognition to make the alleviation of poverty a priority and to take immediate action consistent with this priority.

2. A commitment must be made to build on the success and the potential of community-based groups working in various ways to fight poverty in the inner city and elsewhere in Winnipeg. Any long-term solution to poverty in Winnipeg must be built on the understanding that the solutions that work are those that are genuinely community-based. Community-based organizations are those in which members of the community are involved on an on-going basis in making the decisions; which meet local needs as identified by the community; which hire locally; and which provide opportunities for local residents (Silver, Chapter 7).

3. There must be a commitment to significant public investment in efforts to eradicate poverty. The problem of poverty cannot be tackled without significant public investment. Some examples of the kinds of public investment and related policy changes that are needed as elements of an effective anti-poverty strategy are the following:

a) An inner city investment fund must be established and inner city residents must be well represented on its decision-making board. A major area for such public investment ought to be in the renovation of the existing housing stock, both to provide adequate housing for those in need, and to create well-paying jobs and the training for such jobs for inner city residents. All such efforts ought to be carried out by community-based organizations.

b) A wide range of educational opportunities must be provided. The correlation between educational attainment and future employment and income prospects is very strong. Investment is needed in early childhood education, which has been shown to be a productive public investment (Schweinhart et al, 1993), and in a variety of educational initiatives which are tailored to the needs of people living in poverty, in the inner city and beyond.

c) Additional child-care facilities are necessary. An improvement in the availability and accessibility of public childcare facilities would create enhanced opportunities for young parents, especially young women.

d) Well-paying jobs for inner city residents and others living in poverty must be created. There are a great many unmet needs in Winnipeg communities and especially in the inner city. Community-based organizations can identify and can meet those needs and can create good jobs in the process. Higher levels of employment, especially among young people, are an essential component of an anti-poverty strategy and are an investment in our future.

e) The minimum wage needs to be increased. The decline in the real value of the minimum and near-minimum wages has been a significant factor in the growth of poverty in Winnipeg, and the evidence is strong that higher minimum wages are an important part of an anti-poverty strategy (Black and Shaw, Chapter Four).

Appendix: The Debate About Poverty Lines

There is a debate in Canada today about how to measure and therefore to define poverty. The most commonly used measurement is the Statistics Canada low income cut-offs (LICO). Most social policy groups in Canada use the LICO as poverty lines. However, Statistics Canada does not itself consider the LICO to be a poverty line. They published a paper in 1989 describing some of the limitations of the LICO (Wolfson and Evans, 1989). And there have been recent objections to this "relative" approach to defining and measuring poverty, perhaps most notably by the Fraser Institute (Sarlo, 1996). The result has been an initiative begun in 1997 by the federal, provincial and territorial governments, to consider the merits of an alternative measurement of poverty based on the market costs of a "basket" of goods and services deemed to be "essential" (Human Resources Development Canada, 1998).

The LICO

The LICO is established by using Statistics Canada data on family expenditures to determine what proportion of its total income the average Canadian household spent on food, clothing and shelter, and then by determining—some would say arbitrarily—that any household whose expenditures on these necessities is twenty percentage points or more higher than the average household has, by definition, an income below the LICO. The reasoning is that any household spending such a high proportion of its income on these three essentials has too little money left for such other necessary expenditures as transport, personal care, household supplies, recreation, health, and insurance.

There are 35 separate LICO in Canada. These are the result of dividing the population into seven different household types, based on the size of household, and establishing five different types of geographic area, based on the size of the community in which people live (Table A-1). Thus a family of four in a large centre like Vancouver would have a different LICO than a single person in Portage la Prairie, who in turn would have a different LICO than a single-parent with two children in Kingston.

Those who object to the LICO as a poverty line advance several arguments. One is that choosing to establish a LICO at twenty percentage points above what the average household spends on food, clothing and shelter is arbitrary. As will be argued shortly, all poverty lines, including those based on absolute measures, have an arbitrary element to them. More importantly, those opposed to the LICO as a poverty line argue that it is a relative as opposed to an absolute measure. They argue that it measures not poverty, but income inequality, because the LICO is based on a given family's expenditures relative to an average Canadian figure. A more meaningful measurement, these critics argue, would be to determine the cost of the basic necessities of life for any Canadian household. The cost of a "basket" of such necessities then becomes the poverty line; those with incomes below that amount are below the poverty line. This is the argument advanced by Christopher Sarlo, whose work on poverty has been published and promoted by the Fraser Institute (Sarlo, 1996). However, this absolute approach, based on the cost of a basket of basic necessities, raises as many problems as it solves.

The Fraser Institute Approach

The main problem with the absolute approach is the difficulty of determining what ought to be included in the basket of basic necessities of life and what ought to be

Table A-1: Statistics Canada's Low Income Cut Offs (1986 Base) for 1996

Family Size	Community Size				
	Cities of 500,000+	100,000 - 499,999	30,000 - 99,999	Less than 30,000	Rural Areas
1	16,061	14,107	13,781	12,563	10,933
2	21,769	19,123	18,680	17,027	14,823
3	27,672	24,307	23,744	21,644	18,839
4	31,862	27,982	27,338	24,922	21,690
5	34,811	30,574	29,868	27,228	23,699
6	37,787	33,185	32,420	29,554	25,724
7+	40,640	35,696	34,872	31,789	27,668

Source: National Council of Welfare. Poverty Profile 1995. Spring 1997.

excluded. Reasonable people can legitimately differ about this, and therefore the determination of what is a basic necessity is, in part, arbitrary. Professor Sarlo defines basic necessities very narrowly. He argues, for example, that the cost of health services and products not covered by Medicare and the cost of newspapers are not to be included in a basket of basic necessities. They are what Professor Sarlo calls "social comforts," or "social amenities" (Sarlo, 1996, pp. xvii, 28 and 46). Basic necessities by his definition include only the physical necessities of life:

> People are poor if they cannot afford all basic physical necessities—items the absence of which is likely to compromise long term physical well-being (Sarlo, 1996, p. 196).

The result is that Professor Sarlo's poverty line is very low compared to all other Canadian-designed poverty lines (Ross et al, 1994, pp. 12-25), and therefore by his definition there are far fewer Canadians living in poverty than is the case when, for example, the LICO is used (Table A-2). Professor Sarlo found that one million Canadians were below his absolute poverty line in 1988, leading him to conclude that "poverty, as it has been traditionally understood, has been virtually eliminated. It is simply not a major problem in Canada" (Sarlo, 1996, p. 2).

A different but reasonable conclusion might be that the presence in Canada of one million people whose incomes are "… too low to afford all of the basic requirements of living" (Sarlo, 1996, p. 193), is indeed a problem. Professor Sarlo thinks otherwise, arguing that existing government programs are sufficient to lift all of these people above his poverty line, so that "everyone is able to acquire all the basic necessities of life" (Sarlo, 1996, p. 193). By this means, he makes poverty disappear entirely.

Professor Sarlo's absolute approach to poverty constructs a definition of poverty that some have called "mean-spirited" (National Council of Welfare, 1998/99, p. 27). A family is only categorized as poor if their income is so low that they cannot afford the cost of basic physical necessities. It has also been observed that a definition which has the result of reducing the number of those for whom some form of public expenditure might be required is consistent with the ideological orientation of the Fraser Institute, an organization strongly in favour of reduced government expenditures.

The National Council of Welfare's biggest complaint with the very low poverty lines supported by the Fraser Institute of British Columbia has been that the Institute's only apparent interest in poverty lines is to show that poverty is not a

Table A-2: Comparative Poverty Lines for a Family of Four, 1988

	LICO	Sarlo
Poverty line*	$22,371	$13,140
Poverty rate	10.1%	2.5%
Number of poor families	172,115	43,292

* Assumes a community of between 100,000 and 499,999 persons

Source: derived from Table 1-1, Sarlo, 1996, P.3.

problem in Canada and does not warrant action by government (NCW, 1998/99, p. 5).

This seems to be the implication of an editorial in the *Winnipeg Free Press* (September 17, 1999), written in response to the release of *High and Rising: The Growth of Poverty in Winnipeg*, in September 1999. The *Free Press* editorial, which made reference to the real poverty of people living in the third world, implied that the use of the LICO exaggerated the extent of poverty in Winnipeg. It asserted that families with incomes at the LICO are not "… poor by the common understanding of that condition." However, on average, poor families in Winnipeg have incomes *far* below the LICO. Average household size in Winnipeg is approximately three. The LICO for a household of three in Winnipeg is $27,672. Winnipeg households with incomes below the LICO had an average annual income of $13,717 in 1996 and $12,211 in the inner city—less than half the level of the LICO.

A strong case can be made that the Sarlo approach, and by extension that of the *Winnipeg Free Press*, is too narrow and that the basic necessities of life in a society such as Canada's include more than simply what is needed to avoid compromising long-term physical well-being. For example, why would health and dental costs that are excluded by Medicare not be included in a "basket" of necessities? What about school supplies and school outings for children? Are these not needed in today's Canada? Reasonable people may well disagree about what items to include in a market basket of necessities, but most, we believe, would conclude that it is not reasonable to keep the basket as small as Professor Sarlo does.

That is what was found in an innovative experiment in Winnipeg in 1997. The Social Planning Council of Winnipeg and Winnipeg Harvest recruited seven low-income Winnipegers to determine what would be included in a basket of goods and services sufficient to provide an acceptable living level—what they described as "a reasonable but not extravagant expectation of living costs." Using a hypothetical family of three that included a single mother who neither smoked nor owned a car, plus a girl under six and a boy of fifteen years, they concluded that the cost of a basket of goods and services necessary to produce an acceptable living level required an annual income of $26,945.60. This figure is very close to the LICO of $27,672. Interestingly, the cost of food, clothing and shelter came to 59.8 percent of the hypothetical family's overall budget, which is consistent with the Statistics Canada method for calculating the LICO (Social Planning Council of Winnipeg and Winnipeg Harvest, September 1997, p. iii). As the National Council of Welfare put it: "That led them to the view that the market basket and statistical approaches validate each other and make both approaches more credible" (National Council of Welfare, 1998/99, p. 37).

Human Resources Development Canada has also been attempting to develop market-basket measures of poverty. The HRDC market-basket method calculates costs for food, clothing and shelter, and then rather than itemize and cost each of those additional items which would have to be in a market basket, as the "acceptable living level" calculation did, the HRDC adds an "other" category equal to 60 percent of the cost of food and clothing (National Council of Welfare, 1998/99, p. 23). This is consistent with the observation made earlier that any measure of poverty must, of necessity, include assumptions that are relatively arbitrary.

The Statistics Canada LICO not only avoids many of these problems, but also has certain advantages. It is true that it is, in part, arbitrary, but so too is the basic necessities approach, since someone must determine what is a basic necessity and what is not. Furthermore, it is true that the LICO is a relative as opposed to an absolute measurement, but poverty itself is a phenomenon having much to do with one's relative position in society. For example, it may be true, as Professor Sarlo argues, that school supplies and money for school outings are not necessities of life. Their absence does not "compromise long term physical well-being." However, it is reasonable to argue that these are good examples of why poverty is best thought of in relative terms. In Canada today, most children live in families able to afford school supplies and money for school outings. The child whose family cannot afford to do these things is, in a very real sense, a child who is living in poverty. In other words, poverty in Canada has a social and psychological component, as well as simply a physical component. Professor Sarlo may say that "I am not at all offended by inequality. I have no problem with large variations of income and wealth. I do not regard it as unjust or unfair that Wayne Gretzky earns one hundred times as much as most men his age" (Sarlo, 1996, p. 3). But most Canadians, we believe, find it both unjust and unfair that some families cannot purchase school supplies or pay for school outings, while others earn six-figure incomes. In a society of material affluence, there is more to poverty than simply the absence of the material means to meet bare physical needs.

This case is made more strongly in a recent study by David p. Ross and Paul Roberts. Ross and Roberts asked: what if the poverty line were set at a level sufficient to give all children roughly equal chances of full development? They examined twenty-seven elements of child development—such variables as children's behaviour, health, learning outcomes and participation in sports and clubs. They found that for 80 percent of these twenty-seven variables, the risks of negative outcomes for children were noticeably higher in families with incomes below $30,000, and for 50 percent of these variables, children in families earning less than $40,000 did noticeably less well. They conclude that an appropriate child poverty line is between $30,000 and $40,000 for a family of four, and observe that: "If healthier child development is considered to be an important objective of our society, it seems that at the very least, the LICO is defensible as a measure of poverty"(Ross and Roberts, 1999, p. 37).

It is our view that, whatever its limitations may be as a measurement of poverty, the Statistics Canada LICO is a useful measurement for research purposes. It enables us to determine that poverty is higher in Winnipeg than in most other Canadian centres, is higher in Winnipeg's inner city than in Winnipeg as a whole, and has been growing steadily in Winnipeg's inner city for many years and rapidly in recent years. These, we maintain, are useful research findings made possible by the use of the Statistics Canada LICO. What is more, our findings using the LICO are confirmed by the many reports published by agencies that work in and/or have studied the phenomenon of poverty in Winnipeg's inner city (Silver, Chapter Seven). And they are confirmed by the fact that the Social Planning Council/Winnipeg Harvest market-basket approach established acceptable living levels roughly equivalent to the Statistics Canada LICO. Professor Sarlo's claim that poverty "is simply not a major problem" in Canada has a hollow ring about it when Winnipeg, and especially Winnipeg's inner city, are examine, and throws into question the merits of his alternative approach to the measurement of poverty.

References

Dominion Bureau of Statistics. *Advance Bulletin Census of Canada 1966. Catalogue # 92-625* (Minister of Trade & Commerce, August 1967).

_____. *Census of Canada 1966 Population. Catalogue # 92-611* (Minister of Trade & Commerce, January 1968).

Hammond, Barry, and Ken Gibbons. "Testing in Schools," in Canadian Centre for Policy Alternatives-Manitoba, *Quarterly Review of Social and Economic Trends*, Volume 1, Number 2, Spring 1999, pp. 3-4.

Harris, George, and Todd Scarth. *What's a Million? The Capital Budget and the Financial Health of the City of Winnipeg* (Winnipeg: Canadian Centre for Policy Alternatives-Manitoba, 1999).

Human Resources Development Canada. *Construction of a Preliminary Market Basket Measure of Poverty, Report by the Federal/Provincial/Territorial Working Group on Social Development Research and Information* (Ottawa: Human Resources Development Canada, 1998).

Jargowsky, Paul A. *Poverty and Place: Ghettoes, Barrios, and the American City* (New York: Russell Sage Foundation, 1997).

Jencks, Christopher, and Paul Peterson (eds). *The Urban Underclass* (Washington D.C.: The Brookings Institute, 1991).

Johnston, Frank. *Core Area Report: A Reassessment of Conditions in Inner City Winnipeg* (Winnipeg: Institute of Urban Studies, 1979).

Lee, Kevin. *Urban Poverty in Canada* (Ottawa: CCSD, 2000).

Leo, Christopher and Lisa Shaw. *Inner City Decay in Winnipeg: Causes and Remedies* (Winnipeg: Canadian Centre for Policy Alternatives-Manitoba, 1998).

Manitoba Health. *The Health of Manitoba's Children*, by Brian Postl (Winnipeg: Queen's Printer, 1995).

National Council of Welfare. *Poverty Profile 1995* (Ottawa: National Council of Welfare, 1996).

_____. *Welfare Incomes 1996* (Ottawa: National Council of Welfare, 1997).

Ross, David P., and Paul Roberts. *Income and Child Well-Being: A New Perspective on the Poverty Debate* (Ottawa: CCSD, 1999).

Sarlo, Christopher A. *Poverty in Canada, 2nd Edition* (Vancouver: Fraser Institute, 1996).

Schweinhart, Lawrence J., Helen V. Barnes and David P. Weikart. *Significant Benefits: The High/Scope Perry Pre-School Study through Age 27* (Ypsilanti, Michigan: The High/Scope Press, 1993).

Schillington, Richard. "Government's Plan to 'End' Poverty—By Redefining and Hiding It," *CCPA Monitor*, Volume 5, Number 10, April 1999.

_____., and Clarence Lochhead. *The Canadian Fact Book on Poverty—1994* (Ottawa: The Canadian Council on Social Development, 1994).

Social Planning Council of Winnipeg and Winnipeg Harvest. *Acceptable Living Level* (Winnipeg: Social Planning Council of Winnipeg, 1997).

Statistics Canada. *Preliminary Bulletin 1971 Census of Canada No. 5* (Ottawa: Minister of Industry, Trade & Commerce, December 1971).

_____. *Winnipeg Census Tracts. Selected Social and Economic Characteristics. 1981 Census of Canada. Catalogue # 95-981* (Ottawa: Minister of Supply & Services Canada, September 1983).

_____. *Winnipeg Census Tracts. Selected Characteristics. 1981 Census of Canada Catalogue # 95-940* (Ottawa: Minister of Supply & Services Canada, October 1983).

_____. *Winnipeg Profiles: Part 1. 1986 Census of Canada. Catalogue # 95-173* (Ottawa: Minister of Supply & Services Canada, January 1988a).

_____. *Winnipeg Census Tract Profiles: Part 2. 1986 Census of Canada. Catalogue # 95-174* (Ottawa: Minister of Supply & Services Canada, December 1988).

_____. *Profile of Census Tracts—Winnipeg Part A. 1991 Census of Canada. Catalogue # 95-360* (Ottawa: Minister of Industry, Science & Technology, February 1993).

Wilson, William Julius. *The Truly Disadvantaged: The Inner City, The Underclass and Public Policy* (Chicago and London: The University of Chicago Press, 1987).

Wolfson, M.C., and J.M. Evans. *Statistics Canada's Low Income Cut-Offs: Methodological Concerns and Possibilities* (Ottawa: Statistics Canada, 1989).

Chapter 3
Workfare in Manitoba
By Shauna MacKinnon

Manitoba's welfare poor have been put through the wringer throughout the 1990s. Government policies have done nothing to alleviate poverty. Instead, government has increasingly blamed the poor. A review of social policy measures throughout the past decade reveals two major concerns.
- There has been an ideologically motivated, deliberate and systematic withdrawal of support for individuals and families on social assistance.
- The government has "dealt" with Manitoba's shameful poverty statistics by creating a perception that the blame for poverty falls on those who are poor. The government's message has been that people on welfare need fixing.

The attack on Manitoba's poor began in earnest in the early 1990s. A series of social service cutbacks resulted in great hardship for many. Provincial measures combined with the abolition by the federal government of the Canada Assistance Plan and its national standards were part of a significant shift in how government intervenes in the lives of the poor.

Setting the Stage for Workfare

The most regressive amendments to the Social Allowances Act began in 1993. These policy changes —which the National Council of Welfare called an "attack on Manitoba's poor"—were a precursor to the introduction of workfare (NCW, 1997, p. 72).

The following list highlights the changes to social policy in Manitoba since 1993.

1993

In order to standardize provincial/municipal welfare rates, the province of Manitoba amended the Social Allowances Act with the following detrimental changes.
- Exemptions dropped from $240 a month to $130 for families and from $125 to $95 a month for single people. (Exemptions refers to the amount of money social assistance recipients are able to earn in addition to their assistance. Money earned beyond the exemption amount is deducted in full from the recipient's social assistance payment.)
- Families lost the $205 monthly exemption on any child support payments they were receiving during their first three months on welfare.

Acknowledgements

Thanks to Pete Hudson and Lawrie Deane for their help with this chapter. Special thanks to my mother, Cecile MacKinnon, whose struggle with poverty has inspired me to challenge the myths and to fight for progressive change.

- Income tax refunds aside from tax credits were no longer exempt income.
- Provincial income supplements of up to $30 a month per child in low income families and a provincial supplement of more than $100 every three months for people fifty-five and older were also dropped from the list of exempt income.

Supplemental health insurance coverage for welfare recipients was cut back. Covered medication and services were trimmed, major restorative dental services were subject to new dollar limits and new welfare recipients had a three-month waiting period imposed on them for non-emergency dental and vision care.

Special welfare programs for students ended, resulting in the return of over a thousand people to the municipal welfare rolls.

1994

Shelter allowances were cut by $14 a month for employable single people.

The $30 supplement received monthly by single people and childless couples was cut.

The income definition used to determine tax credits was broadened to include incomes previously exempt, including social assistance. In effect, tax credits for welfare recipients were reduced and therefore the supplement paid directly to social assistance recipients through Family Services was reduced.

Grants to welfare organizations, day care facilities and nurseries were cut.

Special needs policies which included newborn allowances, assistance to purchase appliances, moving expenses, school supplies, household start-up needs, bedding, beds and other extraordinary expenses were eliminated.

There were further cuts to the range of prescription medication covered by social assistance.

The province spent $50,000 advertising its welfare fraud line.

1995

Single mothers became the suggested target of future cuts and administrative controls with the inception of welfare reform programs such as Taking Charge!, Manitoba's largest welfare reform program.

The province passed legislation to enforce child support from non-custodial parents—one of the few potentially positive social policy initiatives during this period.

1996

On June 4, 1996, the then Minister of Family Services, Bonnie Mitchelson, introduced Bill 36, The Social Allowances Amendment and Consequential Amendments Act. The intent of the Bill was to amend the Social Allowances Act in three ways: to provide for a one-tier system in the City of Winnipeg which would transfer responsibility for City of Winnipeg welfare recipients to the provincial system; to provide direction for welfare reform; and to update the Act with regard to the elimination of the Canada Assistance Plan.

The name of the Act was amended to accommodate the fundamental change as defined by welfare reform. With the passing of Bill 36, the Social Allowances Act was changed to the Employment and Income Assistance Act. The words "Social Allowances" were purposely eliminated and replaced to reflect an emphasis on "work."

The national standards that were firmly entrenched within the Canada Assistance Plan died with the Act. The impact of this for Manitoba was realized with the passing of Bill 36. Section 5.4 of the Employment and Income Assistance Act gives the provincial government the power to implement work for welfare policies. With regard to obligations regarding employment, Section 5.4(1) states that "an applicant, recipient or dependent as specified in the regulations has an obligation to satisfy the director or the municipality, as the case may be, that he or she (a) has met the employment obligations set out in the regulations that he or she is required to meet and (b) has undertaken any employability enhancement measure as set out in the regulations that he or she is required to undertake." "Where employment obligations are not met " section 5.4(2) allows the director "… to deny, reduce, suspend or discontinue the income assistance, municipal assistance or general assistance otherwise payable, in accordance with the regulations." Individuals could now be refused assistance if they failed to "meet the employment obligations to the satisfaction of the director or municipality." Years of post-war struggle to ensure the right to financial assistance for all citizens was gone.

Other changes in 1996 included the following.

- Rates were reduced from $458 to $411 per month for single employable people and from $774 to $692 for childless couples.
- Benefits were cut from people who did not meet "reasonable" training or employment expectations. All new applicants were now required to sign personalized training and employability plans.
- Family heads could lose up to $100 a month if they did not meet work expectations.
- The 1996 budget cut 3.2 percent of government spending, including $23 million in welfare spending.[1]
- The exemption of provincial tax credits paid to about 18,500 people on welfare in Winnipeg was reduced.
- The City of Winnipeg reduced its enhanced social assistance rates for children in 1996. They eliminated Christmas allowances for municipal welfare recipients and instead donated $135,000 to the Christmas Cheer Board.
- Municipal rates for children were reduced to provincial rates in 1997.

1999

An attempt to broaden the coercive nature of Bill 36 was introduced through Bill 40 in July 1999. This Bill expanded on Section 5.4 to allow the government to deny financial assistance to individuals who refused to participate in addiction treatment when ordered to do so. Recipients would also be obligated to attend parenting programs and training. The community would be given an increased role in the policing of welfare recipients as those individuals not in other programs would be expected to "volunteer" thirty-five hours per week in exchange for their benefits.

Shortly after being elected in September 1999, the NDP government announced that Bill 40 would not be implemented. The new government indicated a desire to implement policies that support and encourage rather than punish and browbeat the poor. Although this appears to be a step in the right direction, it was the contents of Bill 36 that opened the door to workfare and those fundamental changes are now legislation. The power to implement work for welfare policies is entrenched within the Employment and Income Assistance Act. As a result workfare remains a concern in Manitoba.

Origins of Workfare

The premise of workfare is that government-delivered income support is conditional upon the recipient participating in activities as prescribed by the government. The official rationale for this model is the claim that it will lead participants quickly back to employment.

The concept of work for welfare dates back to the Elizabethan poor laws of 1601. Providing work for the able-bodied unemployed was a central concern and obligation of the parish under Elizabethan poor laws. The able-bodied poor were sent to workhouses as it was felt that they would learn good work habits and earn their keep (Guest, 1997, p. 12).

At the end of the nineteenth century, the workhouse concept lost its popularity; "outdoor relief" became the chosen method of providing for the poor. This meant that any assistance available to the poor was provided on an emergency basis through municipalities and private charities. The principles of the poor laws remained.

This mechanism remained popular until the First World War, during which time attitudes toward the poor changed very little, in Canada as elsewhere. The poor were viewed as lazy, immoral, or incompetent—all of which was used as justification for limiting income assistance to very low levels. For example, the concept of "less eligibility"—the idea that assistance must be less than that which the lowest-paid labourer could earn—was a central tenet. The *beginnings* of a new approach were faintly visible after the war, with the inauguration of the "mothers' allowance" in British Columbia and Ontario and occasional statements from policy-makers and politicians that widowed and deserted mothers deserved a "pension" from the state for the socially necessary work of raising the next generation of citizens.

The Great Depression of the 1930s led to the idea that unemployment was beyond individual control; the notion that unemployed people were lazy was challenged. Unemployment was so widespread that it was no longer possible to blame the impoverished for their fate.

The Second World War brought an end to the catastrophic conditions of the Depression. Production and employment grew. So did demand for a public social safety net to avoid a return to Depression conditions.

The welfare state began to take shape with the passing of the Unemployment Insurance Act in 1940. The expansion of public assistance in Britain prompted the Canadian government to follow suit. The Report on Social Security for Canada (a report by Leonard Marsh in 1943, known as the Marsh Report) provided the basis for the development of a publicly administered welfare system, fashioned at least in part after the British model, that evolved through to the 1970s. Although the system was less than perfect and retained traces of the residual model of the poor laws, citizens' rights to assistance were more firmly entrenched through the national standards embodied in the Canada Assistance Plan (CAP), enacted in 1966.

The power of the welfare state peaked in the 1970s and then began to decline. By the 1990s the national standards of CAP had been completely abolished with the implementation of the Canada Health and Social Transfer (CHST). This new mechanism for the delivery of social services became policy in 1996. The National Council of Welfare has called the Canada Health and Social Transfer "the worst social policy initiative undertaken by the federal government in more than a generation" (National Council of Welfare, 1995). It is this fundamental change, in particular the loss of national standards, that has allowed workfare to re-emerge as the contemporary successor to the workhouse of the poor law era.

The Current Socio-political Environment

Increasingly, the right not to have to work in order to be entitled to receive welfare benefits is a thing of the past. But it is not just government policies that have changed. Perhaps more disturbing is the apparent change in public sentiment that has resulted in growing support for policies which penalize, demean and point a finger at the poor. How did we, as a society, move from public support for a fundamental right to government assistance for those in need to public contempt for the poor?

Discussion of welfare reform twenty years ago focussed on making the welfare state increasingly progressive. The idea of a guaranteed annual income was even floated on occasion—although it never came close to implementation, and as advanced by the Macdonald Royal Commission was a recipe for guaranteed annual poverty. Ideas of making the welfare state more progressive are now miles away. Stereotypes of the poor as lazy, undeserving and in need of punishment have been nurtured by governments to justify a return to pre-Second World War welfare measures. Even those individuals who contribute to society by caring for their children have been unable to escape the wrath of punitive policy-makers.

The former Government of Manitoba was at the forefront of the attack on the poor by systematically chipping away at welfare programs and suggesting that welfare recipients are lazy and dishonest. They implemented a welfare fraud line, implying, irresponsibly, that welfare cheats are running rampant. The welfare fraud line was not based on good empirical evidence at the time of its inception, and since then has failed to demonstrate any pervasive abuse of the welfare system. Instead, it contributed to a false perception of welfare fraud that allowed government to implement a series of regressive policy measures.

In fact, research indicates that "welfare fraud represents 2 to 3 percent of a total annual welfare bill of $15 billion. By way of comparison, an Ekos Research study in the summer of 1995 reported that two out of five people surveyed admitted that they cheated on their income taxes, and three out of four said they would cheat if they knew they would not get caught" (NCW, 1997, p. 117). Nonetheless, a lack of understanding of the issues has led to some public support for the draconian policy measures that have emerged.

The Manitoba Welfare Reform Model

Manitoba's Employment and Income Assistance Program was implemented in May of 1996. It was described by the former Government of Manitoba as the "Program of last resort for people who need help to meet basic personal and family needs" (Gorlick and Brethour, 1998). It is aimed at "helping people find a job or get back to work." Recipients must "maintain an active job search." Also known as "Welfare Reform," the Government's model consists of a variety of workfare/learnfare (mandatory job training) initiatives administered through the Department of Family Services and the Department of Education and Training. The stated goal is to provide training to "help people prepare for job searches and subsequent employment." Employment-based programs and services are also delivered through Community Partnerships and Employment Connections under the umbrella of Employment First. Participation in Employment First is mandatory for all income assistance recipients. Those who do not comply are punished with budget reductions. Single parents with a child under six years or a dependent child requiring extensive care, people with disabilities, the elderly and people in authorized crisis facilities are exempt.

The former Government of Manitoba maintained that the program would not displace workers or volunteers in the local economy. All Employment and Income Assistance applicants are expected to attend orientation programs where available. They must complete an employment plan and are to report their progress to a worker on a regular basis.

A 1998 national inventory of welfare-to-work programs reports that senior government officials have indicated that a more comprehensive evaluation would be forthcoming—one which measures cost effectiveness, evaluates outcome data collected on participants, and measures participant satisfaction (Gorlick and Brethour, 1998). There is no indication that such an evaluation is forthcoming; government officials contacted are unaware of it. However they did indicate that there has been an evaluation of Taking Charge! The results of this evaluation have not yet been released to the public.

Is Workfare Working?

The passing of Bill 36 in 1996 enabled the province to implement involuntary programs that focus on pushing people off the welfare rolls. The previous government pointed to welfare statistics to defend the program's success. As indicated in Table One, total expenditures for social assistance were reduced by 9 percent from 1995 to 1998.

Since 1997, the provincial government has clawed back the National Child Benefit (NCB) supplement from welfare recipients. The NCB is a federal supplement provided to low-income families aimed at reducing child poverty. The provinces were given the option of clawing back this supplement from welfare recipients and "reinvesting" the funds in programming. This is the route the former Government of Manitoba chose to take. Like other low-income families, those on social assistance receive their NCB supplement directly from the federal government. The Province then reduces their social assistance payment by an equivalent amount. This reduction is reflected as reduced provincial expenditures on social assistance. What is significant is that this "savings" in provincial social assistance expenditures comes at the expense of the poorest children in Manitoba. While Table One shows a reduction of Family Services expenditures, it is in part due to a reduction in financial assistance to families who continue to be on the social assistance rolls.

The number of welfare cases involving employable recipients has declined since the inception of Manitoba welfare reform (Table Two). However, there is no empirical evidence to suggest that this reduction is due to welfare reform. Further,

Table 1: Provincial Government Expenditures on Welfare Programs

Year	Family Service Expenditures for Employment and Income Assistance *	Family Service allocation to Making Welfare Work	Education and Training Expenditures on Employment and Development Programs for support for E&IA clients, including Making Welfare Work*	Total expenditures on Welfare programs *
1995-96	374,838	0	7,201.50	382,039.50
1996-97	357,165	3,352.10	7,620.00	368,138.00
1997-98	336,986.**	4,983.00	7,918.40	349,887.4**

* in millions
** $10 million in recovery on National Child Benefit has been deducted from this amount. The government of Manitoba has chosen to deduct this federal supplement paid to low income families from welfare benefits.
Source: Government of Manitoba Annual Reports

there is absolutely no evidence that welfare reform has had any positive impact on poverty rates in Manitoba. The number of Manitobans living in poverty continued to rise in the 1990s (Lezubski, Silver and Black, Chapter Two).

Although Table One shows some decline in welfare expenditures, there has been an increase in food-bank use for individuals who are not on assistance. The number of individuals served by food banks has dropped marginally since 1995, but the number of *working* households assisted has almost doubled in the same period—evidence of the former provincial government's low-wage strategy (Black and Shaw, Chapter Four). The increase in food-bank use by households not on social assistance, along with the increase in the number of people living in poverty, suggests that welfare reform has not contributed to the overall well-being of the poor (Table Three). The decline in the number of welfare caseloads is attributable to a variety of factors that will be discussed further.

For those who have found work, workfare creates a revolving-door phenomenon with no permanent gains in full-time employment. The majority of jobs accessed through welfare reform are unskilled jobs, and few become permanent. "A cost conscious employer who can train people in a few days has no incentive to keep them on the payroll when demand is slack … ." (Jenks, 1997, p. 3). Those who do manage to find full-time employment are most often struggling to make ends meet on minimum or near-minimum wages, as unskilled workers have a

Table 2: Average Monthly Social Assistance Caseload by Category

Category	1995/96	1996/97	1997/98
Children	183	163	133
Single Parents	12,384	12,013	11,256
Aged	398	372	351
Disabled	11,536	11,748	12,115
Crisis Facility Cases	101	111	98
General Assistance	1,556	1,295	1,114
Special Cases	24	28	36
Total	26,182	25,730	25,103

Source: Family Services Annual Reports
** excludes Municipal cases

Table 3: Welfare Statistics vs Food Bank Use

Year	Welfare Cases (for March of each year)	Winnipeg Harvest households served (for March of each year)		
	Provincial and City Combined	Households on Assistance (provincial and city combined)	Harvest households served (not on assistance)	Total individuals served by Winnipeg Harvest
1995	78,325	11,360	2,640	33,000
1996	73,715	12,800	3,200	35,000
1997	68,315	12,576	3,424	35,000
1998	62,805	12,639	3,861	35,150
1999	unknown	11,312	4,582	32,300

Source: Winnipeg Harvest
*Harvest number represent food banks in Winnipeg alone.
In rural Manitoba, food banks have increased from 15 to over 25 from 1995 - 1999

much lower chance of moving out of low-paying jobs (Statistics Canada, 1998). Nor is there a way of knowing how many hours are being worked by those shown as being employed in workfare programs. The Province of Manitoba does not keep statistics on the number of hours worked for those they have determined are "employed," making it impossible to determine how many former social assistance recipients are working only part-time.

Manitoba's largest welfare reform program, Taking Charge!, is a $26.2-million, five-year pilot project targeted at single parents on welfare. At the time of its inception, the government suggested that four thousand single-parent clients would be assisted by March of 1999. This would mean a cost of $65,500 per client with no guarantee that individuals would find full-time work and not require further assistance. The 1998/1999 Taking Charge! Annual Report indicates that the program has had 3,784 registrants. There are currently 3,098 individuals participating in projects and 1453 clients are employed. Whether those 1453 are employed full-time and are self-sufficient is not stated in the Report.

Cutting Where it Hurts

Many initiatives that have in the past had great success in providing training and education for welfare recipients who *voluntarily* chose to participate, have been cut by the government throughout the 1990s. For example:
- Student social allowances were eliminated in 1993. This program allowed individuals to continue to receive social assistance while pursuing their education.
- University access programs were introduced in the 1980s to provide educational opportunities and support for students who would be at high risk of failing in the absence of financial, personal and academic supports. These programs continue to operate but on a shoestring budget after having been cut back throughout the 1990s.
- New Careers South also provided training opportunities to high risk individuals. This program was eliminated entirely.

Other programs including preventive parenting and training programs, childcare, anti-poverty initiatives, support for people with disabilities, foster parents, women's shelters, friendship centres and other initiatives that are especially important in the lives of the poorest Manitobans lost substantial funding, or in some cases were wiped out entirely, as a result of cutbacks. Superficially similar programs have been implemented under the banner of welfare reform. The fundamental difference, however, is the shift in philosophy that has made participation mandatory.

What are the Problems with Workfare?

Opposition to workfare is based on a variety of concerns. The coercive, controlling nature of the program and the absence of choice is paternalistic, humiliating and stigmatizing to an already targeted population. Merely making the program mandatory feeds into the notion that people are unemployed by their own choice.

Workfare does not attempt to address poverty. In fact, it takes the focus away from the issue of poverty by creating the illusion that low-income individuals themselves are responsible for their difficult economic circumstances. As shown in Chapter Two of this volume, poverty in Winnipeg has continued to grow since the inception of welfare reform.

Workfare creates a source of low-wage and free labour by providing subsidies to the private sector and forcing recipients to volunteer in exchange for assistance. Workfare employees do not qualify for the same benefits and protections that other employees enjoy. Free labour is disguised as volunteer labour to avoid contravening labour legislation. The move toward coercing welfare recipients who are not working or training, to "volunteer" their time to community organizations is a concern. This provides free labour to the same community organizations which have suffered as a result of government cutbacks.

There is a very dark irony operating in this latest policy development. The former provincial government cut support to agencies which provide support to the poorest in society. That same government then implemented policy which forces the poor to work for free for those agencies that are no longer able to provide them with support.

Under workfare, poverty advocates become policy enforcers, ensuring that recipients are reporting for duty. This creates a serious ethical dilemma for service providers. In Ontario, where workfare is more advanced, many churches and community groups have refused to take on this policing and supervisory role.[2]

In Manitoba, employers are paid up to $3 per hour toward the wages of a "Work First" participant with no obligations beyond the contractual period. Because subsidized employers need not commit to workers, it is doubtful that this form of intervention results in long-term employment. Many employers fail to hire workers permanently once the subsidized period ends. Most who do keep workfare workers on had a position that needed to be filled with or without workfare. The end result is simply the displacement of a non-workfare worker. A job is not created and the primary beneficiary of the subsidy program is the employer. Economist Robert Solow describes the concept in terms of a game of musical chairs.

> ... the labor market is like a game, or several games, of musical chairs. When the music stops, the players scramble for the available chairs. Since there are fewer chairs than players, the losers are left standing. They are, you might say, the unemployed. If the game were repeated, the losers

might be different people, but the number of losers is determined entirely by the number of players and the number of chairs. Adding more players, which is what forcing welfare beneficiaries into the labor market would do, can only increase unemployment. Some former welfare recipients will find jobs. Perhaps many will, because among other reasons, they are hungry, but only by displacing formerly employed members of the assiduously working poor (Solow, 1998, p. 3).

As competition is added at the level of the least skilled workers, "the costs of adjusting to the influx of former welfare recipients spreads to the working poor, the working just-less-poor, and so on, in the form of lower wages and heightened job insecurity" (Solow, 1998, p. 5).

The mandatory nature of workfare results in individuals being attached to workplaces and training experiences that are often outside of their interests and aptitude. This can be frustrating for employer/trainers and for participants. The stigmatization that accompanies welfare recipients often results in employers not feeling that recipients are worth hiring without the subsidy. They are often not kept on or their hours are reduced to a point where they are forced to leave. Studies of employers' hiring habits have confirmed this. While employers are willing to hire welfare recipients with a subsidy attached, they tend not to continue to employ them. Non-welfare recipients are often chosen over workfare workers for positions that are permanent (Harrison, Bennett, et al, 1998).

Social services workers can cite endless examples of single parents receiving a reduction in hours at their work placements once the subsidized period has ended.[3] Unable to survive on casual hours, they often quit. Unable to collect Employment Insurance or find full-time work, they return to Employment and Income Assistance for help. Unfortunately they find that returning for assistance is not a simple process. Employment and Income Assistance workers question the decision to leave paid employment, regardless of how inadequate it may have been, to seek government assistance. Government officials have stated that even marginal attachment to the workforce is considered a success of welfare reform. Those who choose to leave are subjected to a lengthy investigation before assistance is provided. Of course, the numbers of individuals waiting in limbo while being investigated are not reflected in welfare statistics. There have been reports of people who have waited months before they could get welfare to accept them back on the rolls.

The policy of providing employers with subsidies has further implications. Displacement of non-subsidized workers is clearly a problem. Skill development is *not* a focus of job placements. Without development of skills, workfare participants will remain vulnerable in the market place with little hope of moving on to better jobs.

There have also been concerns expressed about who is actually getting the jobs. One individual interviewed (who wished to remain anonymous) has been actively involved in welfare reform since 1995 and expressed the opinion that there is an ongoing concern with racism. Of all welfare reform participants, it appears that Aboriginal people have had the most difficulty finding work placements. This observation is consistent with U.S. data which show minority groups being least likely to benefit (Holzer, 1997, p. 1).

Table 4: Social Assistance Related Training Support Programs

1997/1998 Fiscal Year	New Careers North	Community Partnerships	Labour Market Training	Employment Connections	Youth Now	Taking Charge
Participants	1387	148	517	310	937	669	1,143
Employed	41	102	164	109	370	330	434
% employed	2.9%	68.0%	31.7%	35.1%	39.4%	49.3%	3.7%
drop out rate	Not known	Not known	Not known	Not known	Not known	Not known	Not known
off assistance	Not known	Not known	Not known	Not known	Not known	Not known	Not known

Source: Manitoba Education And Training Annual Report
N/A Information not available
Total Contribution by Education and Training = $3,986.8 million

98/99 Annual Report	TAKING CHARGE!
Participants Oct 95-Mar 99	3,784
Employed	1,453
% employed	38
Drop out rate	N/A
off assistance	N/A

There are also concerns for those individuals who take the "training" route of welfare reform. Training available to people on welfare is limited to short-term programs that most often result in low-wage employment, if any employment at all. Testimonials such as the following are common.

> My worker showed me a variety of courses that I could choose from. I told her I wanted to go to university but as a single parent I didn't think I could afford the high cost, even with a student loan. I would also need to get upgrading first. The worker said that university wasn't one of my choices. She encouraged me to take a secretarial course. I did. I hated it. I didn't want to be a secretary, I wanted to go to university. I finished but I couldn't find work. There are a lot of us being trained in this field and not enough jobs for us all. I finally got fed up. I am off assistance now and in university. I am accumulating a lot of debt and I don't know if I will ever be able to pay it all back. I had to move back in with my dad because I couldn't make ends meet. Yeah, I am off of assistance but not because of their help. I am far from self sufficient and I am definitely still poor.[4]

One common problem with workfare policy at a time of high unemployment is that it results in recipients moving in and out of the few jobs available. This creates a revolving door through the system. Workfare does not create a long-term solution to poverty and unemployment. Although unemployment in Manitoba is relatively low, the majority of jobs created in the 1990s have been low-skill, low-wage jobs that feed the welfare cycle.

Workfare also violates the U.N. Charter on Social and Cultural rights, which stipulates that workers must be free to choose their work (United Nations Committee on Economic, Social and Cultural Rights, 1998, p. 8).

Although information regarding the costs and outcomes of employment and training programs for welfare recipients is difficult to find, Table Four provides a snapshot of programs including the total number of participants and those employed at the end of March, 1998. The Province of Manitoba defines success as any earnings from employment. This suggests that "employment" in Table Four is similarly defined.

Whether or not individuals continue to be supported by income assistance is not clear. The number of individuals who have dropped out of the programs in Table Four is also not known. The difficulty in obtaining this and related information is of concern. Several requests for information were made to officials in both Family Services and Education and Training. In some cases information was denied or said to be unavailable. The complicated nature of the administrative structure that involves two major departments has also created barriers for researchers. An additional piece of information that was unavailable is the amount of welfare reform dollars that goes directly into the pockets of employers in the form of subsidies. One researcher was told that this information would be next to impossible to access while another was told that it was all in the Annual Report—although it was not.[5]

The Experience in North America

The Manitoba workfare model is not new. It is based on an approach that has been used in other provinces and countries. Evaluations of programs allow us to conclude that the only accomplishment of workfare is that it shuffles people around while keeping them at the bottom. The evidence suggests that the availability of jobs is the single most important factor in determining the number of families on welfare (National Council of Welfare, 1997). The implementation of workfare has had no measurable impact on caseloads. It is the relationship between unemployment rates and caseloads that was found to be direct and consistent over time (University of Wisconsin, 1997, Evaluation of WEJT and CWEP Programs, p. 2).

Workfare programs have been in existence in other Canadian provinces since the mid-1990s. Most Canadian programs are modeled after those in the U.S., which have been around since the late 1980s.

Evaluations of workfare programs in the U.S. highlight a number of concerns. Measuring effectiveness by simply looking at reductions in caseloads is a seriously flawed method of evaluation. Reductions can be attributed to many factors other than workfare. Participants who successfully find work are often those who have higher skills and education and would likely have found work on their own. With private sector involvement in workfare and financial reimbursement based on successful job placement or attendance, there is a tendency to screen out all but the most motivated, well-educated applicants (Hardina, 1997, p. 137).

A comprehensive cost-effectiveness study of mandatory work and job training programs in the U.S. looked at program effectiveness and cost efficiency in eight U.S. states. The study found that "differences between experimental and control groups in terms of both increased earnings and welfare savings were not statistically significant" (Hardina, 1997). The study also found little difference between experimental and control groups in terms of job loss and return to government assistance. Burtless (1995) concluded that these programs could not be judged effective. Programs did not result in "substantial improvement in most recipients' standard of living," and further, "there is no empirical evidence job training, job search, or workfare programs are actually effective in putting people in jobs that will help them leave the welfare system" (Hardina, 1997, p. 144). The evidence is that most people on welfare already do work. They care for their families, work part-time or when work is available, and volunteer in their communities. They do this of their own free will. They do not have to be forced to do so.

The cost of coercion does not come cheap. Many U.S. jurisdictions have abandoned their Workfare programs because they have found the administrative cost to be too high. Florida spent $1 for every 16 cents saved. Georgia spent $1 for every 20 cents saved (O'Keefe, 1995, p. 17).

As in the U.S., Workfare in Canada is expensive and fraught with problems. New Brunswick's much hailed NB Works will cost $59,000 per person if participants complete the program. Manitoba's Taking Charge! program costs $65,500 per person. NB Works had a 60 percent dropout rate. No jobs were created through NB Works, except for the jobs of those hired to deliver, manage and evaluate the program (Mullaly, 1997, p. 57). There has been no change in poverty rates or unemployment levels in New Brunswick.

In Ontario, qualitative research has found that welfare recipients who found permanent work said they did so on their own. They did not cite Ontario Works as helping them in getting off welfare (Report of the Project Team for Monitoring Ontario Works, 1999, p. 29). The Quebec scheme was killed after seven years due to high costs and failure to improve the long-term employment of recipients.

Evaluation of programs in other jurisdictions provide the following lessons that Manitoba could learn from.
1. Good evaluation of programming allows us to understand what works, and what does not.
2. Outcomes are modest but better in jurisdictions where jobs are available. High unemployment equals low success rates.
3. People leave welfare naturally. There is little difference found between participants and non-participants in control group studies.
4. Programs which emphasize long-term skill development and education have a more sustained impact on earnings, access to good jobs and long term employment (Workfare Watch, 1997, p. 18).

Evaluating Programs

There has been a variety of methods used to evaluate workfare programs. It is essential to understand the methods used in order to understand why supporters of workfare claim success, while critics maintain that workfare is a failure.

The most common method of evaluation is to look at the number of welfare cases and to attribute the reduction to the success of welfare reform. This has been the primary method used by the Province of Manitoba. It is extremely problematic.

Without a longitudinal study that follows individuals who have left the welfare system, there is no way of knowing if they remain off the system and are meeting government objectives of self-sustenance. Only through a longitudinal study would we fully understand the implications of workfare in terms of getting and keeping people off the system, and more importantly, whether or not they have been elevated out of poverty.

Comprehensive evaluation must include a control group. This is necessary in order to establish employment patterns of non-participants to determine if work attachment is attributable to workfare policies. Many recipients will enter the workforce as appropriate jobs become available. They may also return to assistance at some point. The rise and decline of welfare caseloads is first and foremost a function of the ups and downs of the economy.

There is no evidence that subsidized employers have contributed to the long-term employment of participants. There is no expectation that employers continue to employ recipients once the subsidy expires. There are sufficient data indicating that employers participate only to take advantage of the cheap labour pool made available through these programs (Shragge, 1997, p. 73).

There is no empirical evidence that workfare programs are effective in putting people in jobs that will help them leave the welfare system permanently (Hardina, 1997). Most programs train for low-wage positions. Training provided through the public purse is often in areas that were previously the responsibility of employers. This suggests that the government has taken on the unnecessary expense of training welfare recipients for jobs that previously required no training. It is employers who are the primary beneficiaries of this policy.

Looking at numbers alone does not measure the well-being of participants. Do welfare recipients past and present feel they are better off, financially and emotionally, as a result of their experience with workfare? Social indicators are required to measure the social impact of workfare. In Manitoba, as in other jurisdictions, there has been no empirical evidence to suggest that welfare reform has been successful. Changes in wages, employment, housing, domestic violence, child maltreatment and foster care placement are among the many indicators that would need to be considered in a proper evaluation. There is a growing acknowledgment that "the development of social indicators is crucial to furthering awareness among Canadians about the impact of political and economic activities" (CCSD, 1998, p. 1).

There is evidence suggesting that mandatory programs are unnecessary and inefficient. A voluntary employment program in Ontario during the early 1990s had significant success at a much lower cost (Reid, 1997). Voluntary programs will attract people who are interested and motivated. The abundance of such individuals would suggest that there is no need for mandatory programs and that they are not a good use of valuable resources.

Manitoba's Employment and Income Assistance Act specifies self-sufficiency as a goal of welfare reform. The decision to consider even marginal attachment to the workforce as success is a far cry from that goal. Marginal attachment to the workforce does not move people permanently off welfare and out of poverty and such a measure cannot be deemed a success by any stretch of the imagination. A single parent with one child needs to work over 80 hours per week at the minimum wage to live above the poverty line.

For all of these reasons, we must conclude that in Manitoba, as in other jurisdictions, there is no empirical evidence to suggest that workfare has been or will be successful.

Poverty, Unemployment and Community Values: the Connection

Workfare is based on the assumption that people on welfare are lazy and dishonest. Proponents of workfare assume that people on welfare do not value work; that they do not already work. But the evidence suggests that there is no difference between welfare recipients and non-welfare recipients in terms of their attitudes toward work (Hardina, 1997, p. 133). This suggests that the decision to implement workfare policies is not about helping people live better lives. It is about decreasing public expenditures on income assistance. It is about providing a source of low-wage labour and distracting the public from the fundamental issues that contribute to welfare dependency in the first place, such as high unemployment, lack of financial incentives, inadequate social supports such as childcare and educational support, and maintaining a low-wage market place which is in part sustained by low-income assistance and involuntary labour.

Recommendations

Before attempting to solve the "welfare problem," policy-makers need to take an honest look at what the problem is. The problem isn't the *people* on welfare. The problem is high unemployment/underemployment, low wages and inadequate redistribution of wealth. This reality needs to be at the forefront of any discussion that attempts to propose welfare reform measures. The focus must move beyond a simple examination of the welfare rolls to a serious discussion about structural solutions. There is no dispute that the existence of large numbers of people on the welfare rolls is a serious matter that requires resolution. Consensus does not extend to how governments can best intervene. It is at this point that ideological differences shine through.

Critics of workfare suggest that progressive, effective welfare reform requires a comprehensive approach to social policy. Progressive solutions would take into account the following:

- The first priority needs to be the creation of jobs that pay a living wage. Welfare recipients, like the rest of society, need to be able to be free to choose jobs they feel are appropriate for them. Workfare does *not* create jobs.
- The Government of Manitoba should drop the policy of penalizing poor families on welfare by clawing back part of the National Child Benefit from welfare cheques.
- The Government of Manitoba should concentrate program efforts on supportive programming that allows people to explore their interests and pursue education and training as appropriate. This does not mean that there cannot be help along the way. That help however should be supportive and encouraging, not coercive and controlling.
- The Government of Manitoba should increase spending in the area of childcare. The lack of affordable registered childcare spaces continues to be a problem which keeps people out of the workforce.
- Welfare rates should be increased sufficiently to enable those on social assistance to meet the basic necessities of life.
- The Government of Manitoba should lobby the federal government to reinstate a national program for income security with clear national standards and adequate cash transfers to the provinces.
- The government should stop contributing to the negative public perception of welfare recipients. The efforts of the government to paint a picture of welfare recipients as lazy and dishonest has been extremely damaging to these families. Contrary to popular belief, it is not the lack of attachment to the workforce that destroys self esteem, as much as it is the day-to-day experience of being told that by virtue of your economic status, you are less of a citizen than your neighbour. As stated by one representa-

tive in the United Nations Committee on Economic, Social and Cultural Rights report (1998) in reference to welfare policy in Canada:

> It is "unbecoming" a democratic society. It is one thing to beat the budget deficit, but not at the expense of bringing about a very harmful, a very inhumane social and economic revolution that is taking place now.

The U.N. Report (1998), strongly urged Canadian governments to abandon workfare programmes. The committee reminded Canada that: "provincial workfare programs violate the international covenant on economic, social and cultural rights."

The government needs to broaden the search for solutions and look at less punitive models that have had success. An excellent example is a four-year community-based program in Ontario. "Going to Work: Waterloo Region Opportunities Planning (OP)" used a participatory approach to include community agencies and social assistance recipients in the design of a program to address unemployment and poverty (Reid, 1997). Opportunities Planning was a voluntary program that allowed clients to identify their personal barriers and assist them in overcoming those barriers. By the end of three years, 1100 people had found permanent jobs or created their own work through self-employment. After one year, 85 percent remained employed. The target population of OP were those least likely to succeed in finding work on their own. The community-based approach ensured that the program was staffed by individuals who themselves had been on social assistance. Cost analyses found that the program had produced $2.2 million in welfare savings on an investment of $1.3 million in the program's first two years. By the end of the program in 1996, "it had generated more than $7.5 million in welfare savings and increased economic activity, equivalent to a return of $2.16 for every government dollar invested in the program" (Reid, 1997). This example is evidence of the value of community-based solutions to poverty.

There has also been some positive work done in Manitoba. Opportunities for Employment has had some success with their job placement model. However, once again, this may be helpful in finding jobs for a select few. It will not resolve the larger problem of poverty and most certainly does not require a mandatory approach. What is needed is a comprehensive approach which addresses poverty at its roots and which employs community-based solutions.

Conclusion

The concern about poverty is not limited to the U.N. and a few anti-poverty activists. In response to the U.S. Government's assertion that the American welfare reform model, which Canada and Manitoba have modeled, has been a success, Senator Paul Wellstone (1998) states:

> The welfare rolls may have been cut in half, but not poverty. I don't quite understand how the White House, or any Democrat or Republican, can proclaim this policy a success when we have done so little to actually reduce poverty in our country, especially the shameful poverty of women and children. Rather than all this boosterism, let's have an honest policy evaluation to find out what is really happening to poor families ... .

The former Government of Manitoba followed other provinces in the implementation of welfare policy without regard to the literature that consistently demonstrates the adverse consequences of this direction. Workfare is a huge step backward in social policy.

It should be stopped.

Notes

[1] "For the period 1992/93 to 1997/98, after adjusting for inflation, the Conservative provincial government had cut expenditures by the following amounts: education, $111.9 million; health, $121.7 million; social assistance, $143.9 million; and total government spending less debt charges, $519.8 million. By 1997 the government boasted that 'the Manitoba government is now smaller than at any time since the mid-1970s'" (Black and Silver, 1999, p. 13)

[2] The United Church of Canada council voted to encourage all its mission units and pastoral charges to refuse to participate in mandatory work programs for social assistance recipients at the 36th general council meeting in Camrose, Alberta, 1997.

[3] Focus groups with Social Assistant clients and anti-poverty advocates (who wish to remain anonymous) in preparation of the Alternative Provincial Budget revealed that this is a common experience.

[4] Interview with a University of Manitoba student who wished to remain anonymous

[5] Researchers were connected with a variety of government employees who failed to provide information requested.

References

Black, Errol, and Jim Silver. *A Flawed Economic Experiment: The New Political Economy of Manitoba* (Winnipeg: Canadian Centre for Policy Alternatives-Manitoba, 1999).

Bobier, Paul. "Workfare Lacks Safeguards, Ontario Works Needs More Funding and Better Standards." CCSD, *Perception*, vol. 22 no. 1, (June) 1998.

Broad, Dave, and Wayne Antony (dds.). *Citizens or Consumers? Social Policy in a Market Society* (Halifax: Fernwood, 1999).

Burtless, G. "Employment Prospects for Welfare Recipients," in D. Nightingale and R. Haveman (eds.), *The Work Alternative* (Washington, D.C.: Urban Institute Press, 1995).

Canadian Council on Social Development. *Symposium on Measuring Well-Being and Social Indicators, Executive Summary of the Final Report* (Ottawa: CCSD, 1998).

———. *Welfare-To-Work Programs in Canada: An Overview* (Ottawa: CCSD, 1998a).

———. *Welfare-To-Work Programs in Canada: A Discussion Paper* (Ottawa: CCSD, 1998b).

———. *Welfare-To-Work Programs: A National Inventory* (Ottawa: CCSD, 1998c).

Gorlick, C., and G. Brethour. *Welfare-To-Work Program Summaries* (Ottawa: CCSD, 1999).

Guest, D. *The Emergence of Social Security in Canada* (Vancouver: UBC Press, 1997).

Gueron, J. and E. Pauly. *From Welfare to Work* (New York: Sage Foundation, 1991).

Hardina, D . "Workfare in the U.S.: Empirically Tested Programs or Ideological Quagmire?" in Shragge, 1997.

Harrison, Bennett, and Marcus Weiss. *Workforce Development Networks, Community Based Organizations and Regional Alliances* (Thousand Oaks: Sage, 1998).

Holzer, H.J. " Welfare Reform and the Labor Market," in *IPPSR Perspectives*, Summer 1997, http://www.ippsr.msu.edu/policy/persp/s97/holzer.html.

Jenks, C., "The Hidden Paradox of Welfare Reform," *The American Prospect*, no. 32, (May-June) 1997 (http://epn.org/prospect/32/32jenkfs.html).

Manitoba. *Taking Charge! Annual Report, 1999*.

—————. *Education and Training Annual Report*, 1997-1998.

—————. *Family Services Annual Report*, 1997-1998.

Manpower Demonstration Research Corporation. *National Evaluation of Welfare-to-Work Strategies: Implementation, Participation Patterns, Costs, and Two-Year Impacts of the Portland (Oregon) Welfare-to-Work Program: Executive Summary*, 1997. Retrieved July 1999, from: http://aspe.os.dhhs.gov/hsp/isp/Portland/xsportld.htm.

Mullaly, Robert. "The Politics of Workfare: NB Works," in Shragge, 1997.

National Council of Welfare. *Another Look at Welfare Reform* (Ottawa: Minister of Public Works and Government Services, 1997).

—————. *Social Security Background #4, Working For Welfare* (Ottawa: Minister of Public Works and Government Services, 1994).

—————. *The 1995 Budget and Block Funding* (Ottawa: Minister of Public Works and Government Services, 1995).

—————. *Poverty Profile 1996* (Ottawa: Minister of Public Works and Government Services, 1998).

O'Keefe, Brian. " Workfare Workfarce," *Our Times*, October/November, 1995, pp. 16-18.

Pulkingham, J. and G. Ternowetsky. (eds.). *Remaking Canadian Social Policy* (Halifax: Fernwood, 1997).

Reid, B. *From Welfare to Work, A Community Success Story in Creating Employment Opportunities* (Waterloo: Community Opportunities Development Association, 1997).

Report of the Project Team for Monitoring Ontario Works. *Plain Speaking: Hope and Reality, Participants' Experience of Ontario Works*, 1999.

Rifkin, J. *The End of Work: The Decline of the Global Labor Force and the Dawn of the Post-Market Era* (New York: G.p. Putnam's Sons, 1995).

Shragge, E. (ed.). *Workfare: Ideology for a New Under-Class* (Toronto: Garamond Press, 1997).

Solow, R. *Work and Welfare* (Princeton: Princeton University Press, 1998).

United Nations Committee on Economic, Social and Cultural Rights. *Consideration of Reports Submitted by States Parties under articles 16 and 17 of the Covenant, Concluding Observations of the Committee on Economic, Social and Cultural Rights*, 1998.

University of Wisconsin-Milwaukee, Employment and Training Institute. *Wisconsin Welfare Employment Experiments: An* Evaluation *of the WEJT and CWEP Programs*, 1997. Retrieved July 1999 from: http://www.uwm.edu/Dept/ETI/pages/surveys/each/wlss93.htm.

University of Wisconsin-Milwaukee, Employment and Training Institute. *Evaluation of the Impact of Wisconsin's Learnfare Experiment on the School Attendance of Teenagers Receiving Aid to Families with Dependent Children*, 1997. Retrieved July 1999 from: http://www.uwm.edu/Dept/ETI/pages/surveys/each/learn292.htm.

Yalnizyan, A. *The Growing Gap* (Toronto: Centre for Social Justice, 1998).

Wellstone, p. "Wellstone Challenges White House Assertion of Welfare Reform 'Success Story,'" News Release. retrieved August, 1999 from: http://www.senate.gov/~wellstone/welfare.htm.

Chapter 4
The Case for a Strong Minimum Wage Policy
By Errol Black and Lisa Shaw

Over the period 1988-1999, Manitoba Conservative governments engineered a significant decline in the province's minimum wage. This decline was imposed despite evidence showing a marked deterioration in the economic welfare of low-wage earners and indeed contributed to that deterioration. Nor was any justification for such a decline ever publicly advanced.

The decline in the minimum wage was partially corrected in 1999 (an election year), when the Conservative government raised the minimum wage from $5.40 to $6.00 per hour effective April 1—an increase of 11.1 percent.

In this chapter we make the case for a strong minimum wage policy for Manitoba. We begin by reviewing the experience with Manitoba's minimum wage since 1988, and by describing the mechanics and politics of changes to the province's minimum wage level.

The core of the chapter is then set out in two parts. First, we describe and critically evaluate the currently popular arguments and the related empirical evidence in support of keeping the minimum wage low or eliminating it altogether. Second, we describe and critically evaluate the arguments and related empirical evidence in support of what we call a "strong minimum wage policy"—one which would raise Manitoba's minimum wage immediately and then index it so that it would not decline in real terms in future.

We conclude by explaining why we believe a strong minimum wage policy is preferable, both for Manitoba's many low-income earners and for the Manitoba economy as a whole.

A Decade of Decline

As shown in Table One, Manitoba's 1988 minimum wage of $4.70 was the highest in Canada. It was 44.8 percent of industrial aggregate hourly earnings for hourly paid employees ($10.49) and 48.4 percent of average hourly earnings in service producing industries ($9.72). A minimum wage earner working full-time (2,080 hours a year) in Manitoba in 1988 could expect to earn $9,776. For a single person, this was 84.5 percent of the Statistics Canada low income cut off; for a family of four, it was 41.6 percent of the low income cut off.

After 1988, the minimum wage in Manitoba was allowed to decline relative to other provinces, relative to average weekly earnings for the economy as a whole, and relative to the Low Income Cut Offs. As shown in Table One, the erosion was especially severe from 1988 to 1998. Some of the lost ground was made up with

Acknowledgements

We would like to thank Wayne Antony, Jim Silver and Susan White for their contributions to earlier drafts of this chapter. Research for this chapter was funded in part by a grant from the Brandon University Research Committee.

the increase to $6.00 in 1999, but conditions for minimum wage workers in Manitoba were still less favourable than in 1988.

As a percentage of industrial aggregate hourly earnings ($13.94) and hourly earnings in service producing industries ($13.29), the minimum wage had declined from 44.8 percent to 43.2 percent and from 48.4 percent to 45.4 percent, respectively, from 1988 to 1999. The decline in annual earnings for minimum wage earners in relation to Low Income Cut Offs was even more pronounced. For a minimum wage worker working full-time in Manitoba in 1999, annual gross earnings were $12,480, which represents a decline since 1988 from 84.5 percent to 75.3 percent of the low income cut off for a single person ($16,565), and from 41.6 percent to 38.0 percent of the low income cut off for a family of four ($32,863).

In addition to this relative decline, minimum wage earners experienced a major cut in their *real wages* from 1988 to 1999. The purchasing power of the minimum wage (the real value of the minimum wage after correction for inflation) was 5 percent less in 1999 than in 1988 (even after the increase from $5.40 to $6.00 on April 1, 1999). This is a reflection of the fact that the increase in the consumer price index of 34.3 percent exceeded the 27.7 percent increase in the minimum wage.

The extent of the erosion in the minimum wage, both relative to other earnings and in real terms, is evident in Table Two, which shows what the minimum wage would have to have been in 1999 simply to maintain the 1988 *status quo*.

The evidence is indisputable: there has been a significant erosion of the minimum wage in Manitoba since 1988. Moreover, if the minimum wage strategy followed by previous Conservative governments—by which the minimum wage was

Table 1: The Manitoba Minimum Wage (1988, 1998, and 1999)

Indicator	1988	1998	1999
Minimum wage	$4.70	$5.40	$6.00
Rank among provinces	1	8*	4**
Minimum wage as a % of average hourly earnings			
Industrial aggegrate ***	44.8%	40.0%	43.2%
Service producing industries ***	48.4%	42.5%	45.4%
Annual earnings at minimum wage (2,080 hours) as a % of low income cutoffs ****			
One person	84.5%	67.8%	75.3%
Four person family	41.6%	34.2%	38.0%

NOTES:
* Tied with Prince Edward Island
** Tied with Saskatchewan
*** Average of first 10 months of 1999
**** Low income cutoffs are for Winnipeg

SOURCES:
Statistics Canada. Annual Estimates of Employment, Earnings and Hours, (10-3000 XKB) 1986-1998.
Statistics Canada, CANSIM L792373, L795353
National Council of Welfare. Estimates for Canada's low income cutoffs

increased only every four years prior to an election—is perpetuated by the current NDP government, there will be further erosion of the minimum wage in the immediate future.

To understand why the decline in Manitoba's minimum wage is important, it is necessary to consider the economic functions served by the minimum wage—specifically, how a healthy minimum wage contributes to a healthy economy.

A Minimum Wage History

The first minimum wage in Manitoba was established in 1921 to end the exploitation of women workers by putting a floor under their wages. It is notable that minimum wage policy has always been and continues to be a policy which disproportionately affects women. The legislation was extended to boys under eighteen years of age in 1931 and to all male employees in 1934. Early minimum wage laws defined different rates for men and women, adults and youth, and urban and rural workers.

As late as 1952, the province had five hourly rates: adult male, $0.60; adult female urban, $0.55; adult female rural, $0.52; youth male and female urban, $0.48; and youth female rural, $0.45. This graded minimum wage system was gradually phased out and on April 1, 1988 a single minimum wage rate was established for all Manitoba workers.

The Rationale For a Minimum Wage

The rationale for early minimum wages and their subsequent extension and reform was that there should be a floor under wages. If people are performing work

Table 2: Minimum Wage Required in 1999 to Maintain 1988 Levels

Relative to:	Actual	Required	Difference
Average hourly earnings			
Industrial aggegrate	$6.00	$6.24	-$0.24
Food & beverage	Monthly data not availble for 1999		
Service producing industries	$6.00	$6.43	-$0.43
Low Income Cutoffs			
One person	$6.00	$6.73	-$0.73
Four persons	$6.00	$6.57	-$0.57
Consumer Price Index	$6.00	$6.31	-$0.31

SOURCES:
Statistics Canada. Annual Estimates of Employment, Earnings and Hours, (10-3000 XKB) 1986-1998.
Statistics Canada, CANSIM L792373, L795353
National Council of Welfare, Estimates for Canada's low income cutoffs

that is of value to an employer and to society, then the pay they earn for doing that work ought to be sufficient to enable them to live and participate in the community with dignity. The idea that people who work deserve a living wage that increases in relation to both the cost of living and the general wage level remains at the core of the case for a minimum wage. That the minimum wage no longer achieves this purpose is shown by the high proportion of those in poverty who are among the working poor (Silver, Chapter One).

The Minimum Wage Board

In Manitoba, a review of the minimum wage is initiated by a provincial government request to the Minimum Wage Board (MWB). The MWB consists of a chairperson, appointed by the government, and an equal number of employer and employee representatives. The province may at any time ask the MWB to evaluate the adequacy of the existing minimum wage and to submit recommendations for revision.

The last such review was conducted by the Board in 1998, when the minimum wage was $5.40. As a result of that review, the Board recommended that the minimum wage be increased to $6.00. The Manitoba government approved an increase to $6.00 effective April 1, 1999.

It is important to recognize that *any decision to change the minimum wage is a political decision*. As part of the review process, the Board invites submissions from all interested parties and conducts public hearings. Invariably, there are two opposing sides on the issue.

Employer organizations such as the Canadian Federation of Independent Business and individual employers in low-wage industries typically oppose increases in the minimum wage. Their opposition is based on their view that any increase to the minimum wage levels will erode the profit levels of business organizations.

Individual employers insist that increases will raise labour costs and either force them into bankruptcy or compel them to hire fewer workers or even lay off some workers. Business organizations also point to the dangers of a ripple effect that would push up all wages, erode the competitive position of Manitoba firms, increase unemployment and add to inflationary pressures.

Support for a rising minimum wage typically comes from labour organizations and organizations and individuals concerned about the plight of low-wage workers. These people stress the need for a living wage, one that is above Low Income Cut Offs. Some organizations, such as the Manitoba Federation of Labour (MFL), propose that the minimum wage be set at "60 percent of average weekly earnings, based on a 40-hour week [and automatically] adjusted every January 1st to a level equal to 60 percent of the previous June's average weekly wage" (MFL, 1994, p. 1).

As well, the MFL has consistently called for an extension of minimum wage coverage to all workers, including in particular agricultural workers, domestic workers working twenty-four hours a week or less for the same employer, and so-called "independent contractors" (workers doing work on a contract basis for firms).

The proponents of higher minimum wages cite a number of favourable effects: increased expenditures throughout the economy, which provide an economic stimulus and benefit small business; reduced government transfers to low-income individuals and increased tax revenues; and significant improvements in the living conditions of minimum wage workers and their families.

After completion of the hearings and assessment of the relevant evidence, the MWB submits its recommendations to the provincial government. The government then decides on the increase in light of its evaluation of the consequences of its decision. Such an evaluation is typically affected by a government's base of electoral support and its ideological disposition. Conservative governments in Manitoba from 1988 to 1999 showed an inclination to accept the position of business interests, as shown earlier, to hold down minimum wage levels.

Given the importance of the minimum wage issue in Manitoba, especially to the immediate beneficiaries of improvements in the minimum wage, but also to the economy as a whole, it is imperative that the arguments on both sides of the debate be carefully evaluated.

Arguments for Keeping the Minimum Wage Low

Historically, the central argument against establishing a minimum wage and, once established, increasing it is that a rising minimum wage kills jobs, thus hurting the very people it is intended to benefit. Recently, a number of right-wing economists and think-tanks have capitalized on the current ascendancy of neoliberal doctrines by pushing for a deregulation of the seller's (worker's) side of the labour market. Some go so far as to advocate the abolition of the minimum wage altogether, either by legislative action or through simply keeping the minimum wage where it is in perpetuity.

Proponents of this strategy argue that it will increase employment, both directly—when the cost of labour is lower, more workers are likely to be hired—and indirectly: lower labour costs will enhance the competitive position of affected employers in external markets and the increased sales will generate more hiring.

The belief that minimum wages and increases in minimum wages reduce employment is based on an economic model which assumes a direct relationship between the wage rate and the rate of unemployment. In short, it is assumed that, as minimum wages go up, employment is reduced and therefore unemployment and the rate of unemployment go up. (For a brief discussion of the theory behind this model, and some of the criticisms of the theory, see the Appendix, "The Debate on the Minimum Wage and the Labour Market.")

The idea that minimum wages should be abolished altogether is promoted by some neoliberal governments and economic think tanks. In 1997, for example, Alberta's Minister of Labour, Murray Smith, said his government was considering the possibility of abolishing the minimum wage altogether (Johnsrude, 1997). The Fraser Institute endorsed the idea, arguing that a minimum wage is no longer necessary because "[t]he strong demand for labour keeps wages up" (UFCW, January 1998, p. 17).

For the Fraser Institute and others like them, the legislative abolition of minimum wages is but one element in a broader campaign to deregulate the worker's side of the labour market.

The bulk of recent empirical research does not support the theory that higher minimum wages will increase unemployment. A comprehensive study of the impact of minimum wage changes in the U.S. by David Card and Alan Krueger (1995), for example, found that the employment effect associated with a minimum wage rise is invariably modest and may even result in more jobs being created than lost.

Moreover, in response to challenges to their 1995 study, Card and Krueger (1998) conducted additional extensive research which confirmed their original conclusions.

A recent Canadian study conducted by Michael Goldberg and David Green (1999, p. ii) reached similar conclusions: "Our analysis clearly disputes the claim that minimum wages are a major "killer of jobs." Frequently, increases in the minimum wage have been followed by increases in employment, demonstrating that other trends and movements in the economy influence employment levels to a much greater extent than do minimum wages."

As well, a comprehensive study of the relationship between the unemployment rate and the wage rate in labour markets in twelve countries revealed that wages and unemployment rates are inversely related: in areas where wages are higher, unemployment tends to be lower, while in areas where wages are lower, unemployment tends to be higher (Blanchflower and Oswald, 1994, p. 360). The study concludes that this relationship cannot be reconciled with the model of the labour market used by economists who counsel *against* the introduction of, or increases in, the minimum wage.

Proponents of eliminating the minimum wage by stealth would adopt a policy of benign neglect. They would simply leave the minimum wage unchanged. This would result in gradual reductions in the minimum wage in real terms (as a result of inflation) and relative to other wages. The argument is that, if the minimum wage is maintained at the current nominal level, the number of workers receiving the minimum wage will eventually approach zero as the general wage level rises.

Such a policy is justified, they argue, on the grounds that the number of people working at the minimum wage is small and therefore presumably not worth the bother. As well, there is implicit in this position a suggestion that, since the majority of minimum wage workers are primarily youth and women, they don't require much money, anyway.

This argument is spurious. The number of individuals actually earning the minimum wage is indeed relatively small. For example, it was estimated that in 1997, 3.9 percent of Manitoba's employed workers (16,900 individuals) were paid the minimum wage of $5.40 (Statistics Canada, 1998). However, when all the workers employed by firms that set and adjust wage rates in relation to the minimum—what are called "near-minimum wage earners"—were taken into account, it was estimated that an additional 6.9 percent of employed workers (30,300 individuals) would benefit from an increase in the minimum wage to $6.00.

Statistics Canada (1999) data provide a basis for evaluating the potential impact of further increases in the minimum wage beyond $6.00. In 1998, 43,100 Manitoba workers (9.5 percent of all workers) were being paid $6.00 or less an hour. An additional 33,600 workers (7.4 percent of all workers) were being paid $6.01 to $7.00 an hour. In sum, an increase in the minimum wage to $7.00 an hour would directly affect 76,700 workers. This is 16.9 percent of all Manitoba workers—approximately one in every six.

There would as well be some impact on workers above $7.00 as a result of a probable spillover effect due to employers adjusting wages in internal labour markets in response to an increase in the minimum wage. The main impact would be for workers earning 10-15 percent above the minimum wage. A minimum wage of $7.00 could potentially have a positive effect on the 30,600 workers (approximately 7 percent of all workers) earning $7.01 to $8.00 an hour.

Table 3: Low Wage Workers in Manitoba By Hourly Wage and Selected Characteristics, 1998

Characteristics	$6.00 or less	$6.01 - 6.50	$6.51 - 7.00	$7.00 or less	$7.01 - 8.00
Number	43,100	13,900	19,700	76,700	30,600
Percent					
Women	61.7%	62.6%	55.8%	60.4%	57.5
20 years of age +	56.8%	75.5%	80.7%	66.4%	89.5%
Married	29.2%	37.4%	40.6%	33.6%	44.8%
Head of family	28.3%	38.8%	39.1%	33.0%	45.8%
Full-time job	48.0%	57.6%	69.0%	55.1%	72.2%
Non-student	66.8%	81.3%	85.3%	74.2%	87.2%

SOURCE:
Statistics Canada, 1999, Work Activity Survey (See Appendix 2)

Further, the very idea that individuals in this wage range do not merit an increase in wages because many are young or women is seriously flawed. As is shown in Table Three, 60 percent of workers earning $6.00 to $7.00 are women.

In short, the minimum wage is an issue that disproportionately affects women and thus is directly related to the "feminization of poverty." As women are disproportionately among the ranks of the poor (Silver, Chapter One), their lower incomes have a direct impact on the problem of child poverty, which reached a rate of 21.5 percent in 1997—the second highest in the country (Silver, Chapter One, Table Seven). Therefore, the poverty of women and children is directly related to low minimum wage levels.

Further analysis of those earning the minimum wage reinforces this observation. Currently, 66.4 percent—almost two of every three—workers earning $6.00 to $7.00 are twenty years of age and older. In addition, 33.0 percent of workers earning $7.00 or less are heads of families, 55.1 percent are in full-time jobs, and 74.2 percent are non-students.

Significant proportions of low-wage earners are adults, heads of households and work full-time. As well, the bulk of workers earning $7.00 or less are non-students. They are not teenagers working part-time for pocket-money, as is implied by the advocates of the benign neglect strategy. Moreover, even in the case of those low-wage workers who are teenagers, students and part-time workers, it is likely that a significant proportion of them are driven to work at minimum or near-minimum wage jobs by the need to augment household income or continue their educational programs or to pay for basic needs.

In summary, the arguments of those who oppose increases in the minimum wage, or suggest its abolition, are ill-founded. There is reason to suspect that their arguments may be based less on sound economic analysis than on a self-serving desire to keep wages low for the benefit of profits. Their justification—that they are concerned about the negative employment effects of a higher minimum wage— is not consistent with the empirical evidence, which suggests that higher wages are associated with lower rates of unemployment and of poverty, and that lowering the minimum wage increases the proportions of those with incomes below the Low Income Cut Offs.

Holding down the level of the minimum wage or recommending its abolition altogether is part of the broader strategy described in Chapter One and elsewhere in this volume—a strategy which includes such measures as cuts to social assistance, the introduction of compulsory workfare, the dramatic reduction of Employment Insurance assistance, and the promotion of more "flexible" work arrangements. In their totality, these measures comprise an unacknowledged but real "seamless web"—a cheap labour strategy—in which a minimum wage which is kept low or even eliminated plays a crucial part.

Holding down minimum wage levels is undesirable in a society which seeks to reduce poverty and to improve the standard of living of individuals who may be trapped at the bottom of the income distribution. If we wish to build in Manitoba a society in which there is a rough equality of opportunity—and we believe most Manitobans, and indeed most Canadians, consider this a desirable objective—then we should be supporting a strong minimum wage strategy.

Arguments for Raising the Minimum Wage

Proponents of raising the minimum wage and of linking its level to particular economic indicators so that its value is not eroded make two types of arguments: first, not doing so contributes to rising poverty and growing inequalities in the distributions of wages and incomes; and second, doing so has beneficial effects for the economy as a whole, including contributing to growth in economic productivity and increasing both aggregate expenditures on goods and services and aggregate employment.

The Minimum Wage and Poverty

Improvements in the minimum wage its proponents argue, are essential to any strategy to alleviate poverty and reduce income inequalities. Statistics show that the proportion of both families and unattached individuals with incomes below the Low Income Cut Offs has been relatively constant in Canada since 1991 (Silver, Chapter One, Table One).

In general, the incidence of low incomes among families and unattached individuals rises during periods of slow growth and rising unemployment, and declines during periods of robust growth and declining unemployment. However, this has not happened in the recent recovery from the early 1990s recession.

What is particularly disturbing in looking at the incidence of low incomes among different types of households is the high incidence of low incomes for families with a single income earner (Table Four).

This is true for two-parent families with children and one earner, for whom the incidence of low income is almost twice that of all families, and it is particulary true for female lone-parent families with one earner, of whom close to one-half are low income. Low wages are not the whole story here—the growth of part-time and self-employment, for example, are also important—but they are a contributing factor (Silver, Chapter One).

Statistics on annual earnings in Manitoba show that in 1995, 16.2 percent of persons working full-year and full-time had earnings of less than $15,000. A higher proportion of women (22.7 percent) than men (12.2 percent) had annual earnings of less than $15,000. The comparable statistics for "other" workers ("persons who worked 29 hours or less per week for 49 to 52 weeks or worked less than 49 weeks") are even more dramatic: 70 percent of male workers and 80 percent of female workers in this category had annual earnings of less than $15,000 (Statistics Canada

Table 4: Incidence of Low Income, Selected Family Groups, Canada 1997

Type of Economic Family	Incidence of Low Income
Economic families, two persons or more	14.0%
Two-parent families with children	
One earner	25.6%
Male lone parent families	23.5%
Female lone parent families	
No earner	95.7%
One earner	42.6%
Unattached individuals	39.6%
Elderly	45.0%
Male	33.3%
Female	49.1%
Non elderly	37.5%
Male	35.1%
Female	40.9%

SOURCE:
Statistics Canada, Income Distributions by Size in Canada (13-207-XPB), 1997.

1995, 13-217-XPB). Without doubt, a significant proportion of these workers were in jobs at or just above the minimum wage.

Studies of the impact of increases in the minimum wage on the distribution of income indicate that the effects are positive—reducing the incidence of low incomes and therefore of poverty and reducing the degree of inequality in the distribution of income. A summary of the results of such studies in the United States argues that "… our empirical results suggest that the most recent round of increases in the federal minimum wage had a narrowing effect on the distributions of wages and family earnings, and that it may have led to a modest reduction in the rate of poverty among workers" (Card and Krueger, 1995, p. 308).

These same authors report that the results of recent studies in Canada indicate that decreases in employment (especially as it relates to teenagers) are insignificant (Card and Krueger, 1995, p. 282).

These views are echoed by Richard Freeman (1994) and David M. Gordon (1996), who argue that the explanation for these favourable effects is that predicted negative employment effects are invariably modest, and are more than offset by the total gains in incomes of minimum wage workers and of other low-wage workers who benefit from spillover effects (for example, the assistant manager in a low-wage retail outlet or service establishment whose salary is adjusted upwards parallel with the minimum wage).

Minimum Wages, Productivity and Employment Levels

Increases in the minimum wage will increase both productivity and aggregate levels of employment in two ways. First, low wages, especially if they persist over extended periods of time, undermine morale. It can be expected that workers stuck at low wages, especially those working in dead-end jobs with no opportunity to acquire additional skills and no prospect for advancement, will become disillusioned with their jobs and may reduce their work effort, thus reducing productivity and raising costs. Turnover is also likely to increase as disgruntled workers leave or are discharged for inadequate performance.

Second, low wages allow inefficient firms to survive and raise the tolerance for inefficiency in other firms. When minimum wages are kept low, firms are able to defer adoption of productivity-enhancing innovations which would improve their capacity to compete in their particular markets.

Increases in the minimum wage mitigate these effects. The beneficiaries of wage increases are likely to feel more positively about their jobs and to put more effort into their work; voluntary quits will decline; and employers will be able to economize on both supervisory (monitoring) costs and turnover costs. As well, marginal employers and relatively inefficient employers will have an added incentive to innovate in order to remain competitive.

At the same time, a rising minimum wage increases total economic activity and employment because the total income of low-wage workers as a group increases. Since individuals and families in this group are likely to spend the bulk of their incomes on necessities and goods and services produced in the local economy, rather than on imported goods and services, the gains in income will translate into increased expenditures on domestic goods and services and increased aggregate employment.

Available information tends to support this argument. For example, in the Prairie region in 1992, households with incomes less than $15,000 spent 91.6 percent of their incomes on goods and services, compared to 71.0 percent for all households and 61.0 percent for households with incomes of $80,000 and over (Statistics Canada, 1994, 62-555). Households with incomes less than $15,000 spent 50.3 percent percent on food and shelter alone, compared to 39.3 percent for all households and 34.9 percent for households with incomes of $80,000 or more.

In addition, as incomes rise at the lower end of the household income distribution, the rate of current consumption remains high (at 87.6 percent for households with incomes in the range $15,000-19,999) and increasing proportions of income are spent on transportation, personal care, household furnishings and equipment, and recreation.

It seems likely, then, that the incremental earnings resulting from increases in the minimum wage would be especially important for families dependent on the earnings of minimum wage workers. This is particularly the case for families where the earnings of low-wage women workers account for either the sole employment income of the family or a significant proportion of total family income.

Summary

Supporters of the minimum wage and of a strong minimum wage strategy argue that the problems allegedly associated with a minimum wage and increases in the minimum wage are exaggerated. This view is supported by the results of recent empirical studies in both the United States and Canada. These studies show that the job loss associated with increases in the minimum wage is minimal, and that cuts to the minimum wage contribute to an increased incidence of poverty, and increased inequalities in the distribution of incomes.

There is little direct evidence that minimum wage increases have positive effects on productivity and the overall economy. This is probably because the number of workers affected by minimum wages is small relative to the total number of workers, and the increment in wages received by low-wage workers as a result of an increase in the minimum wage is small relative to the total wage bill. However, there is much evidence demonstrating that economic growth is adversely affected when real wage increases in the economy as a whole fall relative to productivity. What is true of the whole is likely to be true of the parts—including low-wage workers (Mazur, 1995).

Conclusions

This paper has examined the arguments and the evidence both against and for a strong minimum wage policy in Manitoba. The evidence in support of lowering the minimum wage, or eliminating it altogether, is weak. It is true that increases to the minimum wage may result in some direct job loss in some situations, but the evidence suggests that direct job loss is invariably modest, and is more than offset by several positive effects of higher minimum wages.

The most important of the positive effects of a strong minimum wage policy is *an unequivocal improvement in the economic conditions of low-wage earners and their families*. This suggests that a strong minimum wage policy would be one important element in a broader strategy aimed at reducing both income inequalities and the incidence of poverty. Other positive effects of a strong minimum wage policy include: an increase in aggregate levels of economic activity and of employment, since almost all of any increase in the minimum wage is likely to be spent locally, and a spur to business innovation and efficiency and improved productivity, since higher minimum wages reduce the costs associated with worker dissatisfaction and high levels of turnover and increase the incentive to introduce productivity-enhancing innovations.

Thus, the net effect of a strong minimum wage policy is likely to be improved economic circumstances for those at the lower end of the income scale—we have noted the extent to which these persons are disproportionately women—and increased levels of economic activity and thus of job creation.

Recommendations

It is our view that, given the analysis and evidence presented in this chapter, the case for a strong minimum wage policy is compelling. A strong minimum wage policy would require an immediate increase in Manitoba's minimum wage and, in order to prevent its future erosion in real terms, an indexing of the minimum wage to inflation and/or average industrial aggregate hourly earnings.

Thus, we make four specific policy proposals:
1. *Raise the Minimum Wage to $7.00 Immediately.*
The minimum wage should be raised immediately to $7.00 an hour. An adjustment of this magnitude would more than correct for the erosion in the minimum wage that has occurred since 1988. The impact in relation to the variables identified in Table Two is reflected in Table Five.

Table 5: The Impact of a $7.00 an Hour Minimum Wage in 1999

Minimum Wage Relative to:	$6.00	$7.00
Average hourly earnings		
Industrial aggegrate	43.2	50.2
Service producing industries	45.4	52.7
Annual Earnings at Minimum Wage (2,080 hours) Relative to:		
Low income cutoff single person*	75.3	87.9
Low income cutoff four persons *	38.0	44.3

NOTES:
* Low income cutoffs are for Winnipeg

SOURCES:
Statistics Canada. Annual Estimates of Employment, Earnings and Hours, (10-3000 XKB) 1986-1998.
Statistics Canada, CANSIM L792373, L795353
National Council of Welfare. Estimates for Canada's low income cutoffs

An increase to $7.00 would bring the minimum wage to 50 percent of the industrial aggregate average hourly wage and to almost 90 percent of the low income cut off for a single person. These gains would result in significant increases in the earnings of low income individuals and families, and a significant reduction in labour market and income inequalities.

As well, an increase to $7.00 would improve the real income of minimum wage earners. An increase to $7.00 represents an increase over the $4.70 1988 minimum wage of 48.9 percent, which exceeds the 34.3 percent increase in the Consumer Price Index over the same period. In real terms, therefore, minimum wage workers getting $7.00 an hour in 1999 would be about 11 percent ahead of where they were in 1988.

2. *Index the Minimum Wage*
Beginning twelve months after the initial increase to $7.00, and thereafter every twelve months, the minimum wage should be automatically adjusted by the increase in the Consumer Price Index in the preceding twelve months. Such adjustments will ensure that the purchasing power of the minimum wage is preserved. Automatic adjustments in line with the CPI will establish a floor under the real value of the minimum wage.

3. *Expand Coverage of the Minimum Wage*
The MWB should be directed to review workers who are currently excluded from coverage under the Minimum Wage Act—agricultural labourers, domestic labourers working twenty-four hours or less for the same employer, and independent contractors—with a view to having them covered under the Act. This would seem particularly necessary at the present time given the proliferation of industrial hog farming in Manitoba.

4. *Conduct Annual Reviews of the Minimum Wage Formula*
The MWB should hold annual hearings for the purpose of evaluating the adequacy of the formula for adjusting the minimum wage in ensuring workers in Manitoba receive a living wage.

Appendix: The Debate on the Minimum Wage and the Labour Market

The model of the labour market used by critics of a strong minimum wage policy assumes competitive markets and the absence of market power. In this context, employers and workers are wage takers (i.e., they accept the wage rate as something over which they have no control and adapt their behaviour accordingly) and wage rates are determined by the cumulative demand of employers for workers (which reflects productivity), on the one hand, and the availability of workers with the requisite qualifications, on the other hand.

Equality of these two variables results in a market-determined equilibrium wage rate; employers are able to hire all the workers they want at this wage rate, and all workers who are prepared to work at this wage rate are employed. Any other wage rate—higher or lower than the market-determined rate—will, other things remaining constant, result in adjustments in the employment and availability of workers until an equilibrium is achieved.

In this model, establishment of a minimum wage rate (a wage floor) above the market-determined wage rate will have two effects. First, employers will lay off workers as a means of bringing labour productivity into line with the higher wage rate, and workers who were not prepared to work at the previous market-determined wage rate will enter the labour market in search of jobs. The result is involuntary unemployment, which will tend to persist because market forces have been negated by the minimum wage—hence the claim that minimum wages and increases in minimum wages hurt the very people they are intended to benefit (Gunderson and Riddell, 1993, p. 208).

This argument has been challenged from a number of perspectives. First, many economists have rejected the notion that labour markets are competitive and that firms are passive when it comes to the establishment of wage rates. In fact, there are sound theoretical reasons and solid empirical data which suggest that employers not only set wage rates but also have monopoly power *vis-a-vis* workers, even in markets which appear on the surface to be relatively competitive: for example, the hotel and restaurant industries (Card and Krueger, 1995, p. 369-86). Moreover, changes in economic institutions, especially in labour markets, have accentuated the power of employers in the wage determination process (Rubery, 1997).

Second, the issue of whether low-wage workers as a whole benefit or lose from a strong minimum wage policy depends on the strength of the predicted negative employment effect. If the percentage reduction in employment (measured in either person-hours or person-years) exceeds the percentage increase in the minimum wage, then total wages received by minimum wage earners will be reduced and as a class they are worse off.

If, on the other hand, the percentage reduction in employment is less than the percentage increase in the minimum wage, then total wages of minimum wage earners increase and they are collectively better off.

The bulk of the empirical research done in recent years concludes that the alleged negative employment effect is minimal and therefore that increases in the minimum wage benefit low-wage workers (Marshall and Briggs Jr., 1989, pp. 511-20).

References

Blanchflower, David G and Andrew J. Oswald. *The Wage Curve* (Cambridge, Mass: The MIT Press, 1994).

Card, David and Alan B. Krueger. *Myth And Measurement: The New Economics of the Minimum Wage* (Princeton: Princeton University Press, 1995).

———. "A Re-analysis of the Effect of the New Jersey Minimum Wage Increase on the Fast Food Industry with Representative Payroll Data." Princeton University, *Working Paper #393*, 1998.

Freeman, Richard, B. "Minimum Wages—Again!" *International Journal of Manpower*, Special Issue (Spring), 1994.

Goldberg, Michael, and David Green. *Raising the Floor: The Social and Economic Benefits of Minimum Wages in Canada* (Vancouver: Canadian Centre for Policy Alternatives, B. C., 1999).

Gordon, David M. *Fat and Mean: The Corporate Squeeze of Working Americans and the Myth of Managerial "Downsizing"* (New York: The Free Press, 1996).

Gunderson, Morley, and W. Craig Riddell. *Labour Market Economics: Theory, Evidence, and Policy in Canada (3rd. ed.)* (Toronto: McGraw-Hill Ryerson, 1993).

Johnsrude, Larry. "Dumping minimum wage to be studied" *Edmonton Journal*, November 20, 1997.

Manitoba Federation of Labour. *Brief to the Manitoba Minimum Wage Review Board*, 1994.

Manitoba Labour. *Briefing Notes to Manitoba Minimum Wage Board*, February 6, 1995.

Marshall, Ray and Vernon M. Briggs, Jr. *Labor Economics: Theory, Institutions, and Public Policy (6th. edition).* (Irwin: Homewood, Il, 1989).

Mazur, Jay. "The Minimum Wage Revisited," *Challenge*, July-August 1995.

National Council of Welfare. *Poverty Profile 1996* (Ottawa: National Council of Welfare, 1998).

———. *Poverty Profile 1997* (Ottawa: National Council of Welfare, 1999).

Rubery, Jill. "Wages and the Labour Market," *British Journal of Industrial Relations*, 35:3 September, 1997.

Samyn, Paul. "Child poverty stats grim." *Winnipeg Free Press*, May 12, 1998.

Social Planning Council of Winnipeg & Winnipeg Harvest. *Acceptable Living Level.* (Winnipeg: Social Planning Council of Winnipeg, 1997).

Statistics Canada. *Historical Labour Force Statistics 1997* (13-201-XPB) Ottawa, 1998.

———. *Labour Force Update: An Overview of the 1997 Labour Market* (71-005-XPB), Ottawa, Winter, 1998.

———. *Annual Estimates of Employment, Earnings and Hours, 1984-1996* (10-3000XKB) Ottawa, 1997a.

———. *Income Distributions by Size in Canada, 1996* (13-207-XPB) Ottawa, 1997b.

———. *Earnings of Men and Women 1995* (13-217-XPB) Ottawa, 1997.

———. *Canadian Economic Observer: Statistical Summary* (11-010-XPB) Ottawa, 1997d and previous years.

———. *Family Expenditure Survey, 1992* (62-555) Ottawa, 1994.

United Food and Commercial Workers, Local No. 832, "Another Dumb Tory Idea," *Union*. Winnipeg, January 1998.

Chapter 5
Aboriginal Economic Development In Winnipeg
by John Loxley

Background

Although it is difficult to tell with complete accuracy because of the limitations of the various censuses, it appears that there were remarkably few Aboriginal people living in Winnipeg from 1901 to 1951. In 1901 there appear to have been less than a dozen Indians and only about 700 Métis in the City of 42,340. In 1921 there were 69 Indians counted and by 1951 still only 210 in a city population of 354,000. The Métis were invisible.

In the early 1950s there were already concerns, however, about the living conditions of Aboriginal people in Winnipeg. The Provincial Council of Women noted the sub-standard living conditions of Aboriginal women and that more than half of all the inmates of Portage La Prairie Gaol for women were Métis. But the Welfare Council of Greater Winnipeg, which held the first of fifteen Manitoba Indian and Métis Annual Conferences in 1954, concluded that "it was seriously handicapped in any attempt to help these people, because very little was known about them" (Welfare Council of Greater Winnipeg, 1954, p. 1).

That began to change in 1958 with the first definitive study of the Aboriginal population in Manitoba since the nineteenth century. The Status Indian population of Winnipeg was estimated at 1,200 or 5.4 percent of the total of 22,077 Status Indians living in Manitoba (Lagasse, 1959, pp. 31-37). Winnipeg's Métis population was estimated at 3,500, or 14.8 percent of the total Métis of 23,579 in Manitoba (ibid, pp. 58-75). The Métis figures were likely understated, perhaps by as much as 80 percent, since they did not include people of Métis ancestry who had "integrated to the point of not being recognized by their neighbours as Métis" (ibid, p. 77). But if taken at face value, Aboriginal people appear to have represented just over 1 percent of the City's population.

Sample surveys revealed that about a third of Indians interviewed had lived in Winnipeg for less than a year, 58 percent for less than three. The figures for the Métis were 13 and 20 percent respectively. As many as 45 percent of the Métis had lived in Winnipeg for more than 10 years, compared with only 16 percent for the Indians.

> ## Acknowledgements
>
> Earlier versions of a portion of this chapter appeared in the author's *Aboriginal People in the Winnipeg Economy*, February 1994, amended in 1996. In preparing that paper, which was commissioned by the Royal Commission on Aboriginal Peoples, he was assisted by Bernie Wood, Louise Champagne, E.J. Fontaine and Charles Scribe. The author wishes to thank Anna Rothney for her excellent research assistance in preparing this paper.

The single most important reason for coming to the City, for both groups, was to find a job, and 83 percent of all men and 55 percent of all women who said they had come for work were actually employed at the time of interview (ibid, p60). Just over 55 percent of all Aboriginal people were employed. A third of all Indians employed and 59 percent of all Métis had been in their job for at least a year, and 11 percent of Indians and 17 percent of Métis had been in their job in excess of ten years. At the time of interview, only 13 percent of the Indians questioned and 23 percent of the Métis were receiving social assistance, but about a third had received it over the previous two years. Then, as now, social assistance rates were considered grossly insufficient.

The survey found that the educational performance of Aboriginal children was relatively poor. It identified a number of factors felt to be responsible: perceived cultural superiority on the part of the dominant society from which teachers were drawn; paternalist views of appropriate education for Aboriginal people; poor teachers and facilities; and prominence of religious schools with objectives other than education. A further factor was low attendance rates, felt to be explained by a low value placed on education, given the quality and pessimism about where it might lead in terms of worthwhile employment, discrimination by teachers and other pupils, poor diet, clothing and housing, lack of school supplies and the mobility of the heads of households (ibid, p. 117).

This report was remarkably enlightened for its time. It recommended that a community development program be established by the Province to "help people of Indian ancestry solve their own problems" (ibid, p. 5). It argued that efforts should be made to take industry and jobs to rural and remote communities and that systematic training programs be set up for Aboriginal people. It recommended far-reaching reform of the educational system and of social assistance. It argued for low-cost housing and the enforcement of housing standards. It pressed for services to assist people in settling into city life and to help them develop relations of mutual respect with those they were most likely to come into contact with and face discrimination from—employers, landlords, school administrators, police, etc. It is perhaps no coincidence that the first Indian Métis Friendship Centre in Canada was set up in Winnipeg in 1959 to provide social services to migrants (Fulham, 1981, p. iii).

While the Manitoba Indian Brotherhood (MIB) had been established in 1946 (Daugherty, 1982, although it traced its origins back to 1871, see MIB, 1971), it had focussed almost entirely on the needs of its reserve-based members. Finding an effective means of representing Status Indians in Winnipeg remains problematical to this day. A variety of organizations not affiliated to the MIB or its successor, the Assembly of Manitoba Chiefs, have sought to represent Status Indians and others in the City. In the late 1960s the Winnipeg Indian Council was very active (Damas and Smith, 1975, p. 11), to be replaced by the Winnipeg Council of Treaty and Status Indians and the Urban Indian Association, which amalgamated to form the Aboriginal Council of Winnipeg in 1990 (Aboriginal Council, 1993). The creation of the Manitoba Indian Women's Association (MIWA) in 1969 was another indication that Aboriginal people were beginning to replace well-meaning non-Aboriginal support groups in addressing pressing economic and social concerns, but it complained of being hampered by lack of funding (MIWA, 1973). The Manitoba Métis Federation was set up at this time too (1968), but the importance of having a representative structure in Winnipeg *was* recognized, and the city became one of six regions each of which had a seat on the board (Sawchuk, 1978, p. 48). The prime concern of the Métis was, from the beginning, that of solving the acute housing problems faced by the community in Winnipeg, a problem which grew increasingly as population grew.

Most of the growth in the Aboriginal population in Winnipeg occurred after 1958, and that growth has been rapid. From 1958 to 1979, the number of Status Indians resident in Winnipeg rose almost fivefold to about 6,900, while the number of Métis and non-Status Indians had risen more than three-fold to 12,900 (Clatworthy, 1983a, p. 14). The total Aboriginal population in Winnipeg had grown, therefore, at over 7 percent per annum, to approximately 20,000 or 3.6 percent of the total population by 1979. (These numbers must be taken to be rough orders of magnitude only, given definitional problems and differences between the two periods). Economically and socially, the community remained relatively deprived (Social Planning Council of Winnipeg, 1982: Stevens, 1982).

Our knowledge of the living conditions of Aboriginal people in Winnipeg in the early 1980s is substantial, due mainly to a number of excellent reports by Stewart Clatworthy (1981a,b,c; 1983a,b). He found that migration into the City was proceeding rapidly, though more slowly than previously thought. The main reason for migration among males was economic and among women, social. Aboriginal families were much younger than average and the proportion of single-parent families much higher. Unemployment among Aboriginal people was found to be more than five times that of others, and employment more irregular. Aboriginal household incomes were found to be only half those of the average urban household, and most Aboriginal families were found to be dependent on transfers, mostly social assistance payments. Aboriginal families were four times more likely than others to suffer a combination of shelter poverty, poor housing and overcrowding, and were highly mobile within the City.

Aboriginal Demographics in Winnipeg in the 1990s

The 1991 Census indicates that there were 44,970 Aboriginal people in Winnipeg: 6.9 percent of the total population of the City and 39 percent of the total Aboriginal population of Manitoba. By 1996 their number had risen to 52,500 or to about 8 per cent of Winnipeg's total population. There were 2,660 more Aboriginal females in the City than males, an excess of 11 percent. This imbalance was greatest in the over-fifteen category where there were almost 2,800 or 18 percent more women than men. This imbalance reflects different motivations for migration between men and women. The latter leave rural communities for the city not only for better economic and social opportunities, but also to avoid social problems (Clatworthy, 1981b) including, presumably, violence.

The age composition of the Aboriginal population is quite different from Winnipeg as a whole. There is a much higher proportion of children in the Aboriginal population, with over 35 percent being fourteen or under compared with only 20 percent for the City as a whole, and 13.5 percent being under four compared with only 7 percent in the broader population. Second, a significantly higher proportion of Aboriginal people are in the young working age category, fifteen to twenty-four, than is the case in the city as a whole; 18.4 percent versus 15.1 percent respectively. And third, there is a significantly lower proportion of people over fifty-five in the Aboriginal community, 5.9 percent versus 20.7 percent in the City at large. These demographic characteristics suggest that policy might need to look carefully at the educational needs of the community and the special problems Aboriginal youth might face in entering the job market. They also suggest that childcare needs are likely to be particularly salient in the Aboriginal community.

A comparison of the 1996 Census figures with those of 1991 suggests that the Aboriginal population of Winnipeg has grown at a rate of 3.15 percent per annum, well in excess of the growth rate of the total population of the City, which was only 0.25 percent per annum. The Aboriginal population of Winnipeg also grew at a faster rate than that of Manitoba as a whole, suggesting that migration into the City has continued apace.

The 1996 Census found that 13 percent of Aboriginal people had moved into Winnipeg within the previous five years. Perhaps even more important for social policy purposes, 45 percent of Aboriginal people had changed residence within Winnipeg during that time. This is consistent with a small survey of 144 inner city residents (84 percent Aboriginal) conducted for this study in 1993 (Loxley, 1996). This found a very high rate of mobility within Winnipeg, but suggested a much lower, though still high, rate of migration. Thus, 54 percent of Aboriginal people had lived at their current address for less than one year, while 10 percent had moved to Winnipeg in the past year. While 29 percent had moved into the city in the past five years, 58 percent of Aboriginal respondents had lived in Winnipeg for over 10 years. This suggests that population growth from migration is well in excess of natural growth and that this will have serious implications for the employment, housing and service needs of Aboriginal people. It also suggests that the Aboriginal population is very transient within Winnipeg. This might have implications for the type of economic development strategies that are feasible for the community, perhaps making it difficult for neighbourhood-focussed strategies, unless they are accompanied by efforts to stabilize the population.

Employment and Incomes

The 1991 Aboriginal Peoples Survey (APS)[1] reports that the labour force participation rate of Aboriginal people in Winnipeg was 53.9 percent and the unemployment rate was 27.3 percent (Statistics Canada, 1993). By 1996, the participation rate had risen to 62 percent and the unemployment rate had fallen to 21 percent. While this suggests some progress has been made, these numbers are significantly worse than for those of Winnipegers as a whole, which were 67 percent and 8 percent, and go a long way in explaining urban Aboriginal poverty. They suggest that 59 percent of all Aboriginal adults in the City were without work in 1996.

Why are so few urban Aboriginal people in formal employment? This question has been examined for Manitoba by a number of writers (Clatworthy, 1981a,b, c; Falconer, 1985; Hull, 1984, 1991) and their explanations are remarkably similar to those advanced in other parts of Canada (Wien, 1986). Low participation rates and high unemployment rates are a result of Aboriginal people having much lower levels of education than the average in Winnipeg. Three quarters of the Aboriginal population had less than grade eleven education, the minimum level at which education has a significant impact on participation and employment rates. Aboriginal people also lack suitable training and have, in the past, not been captured by government training programs. Difficulties of gaining work experience are self-reinforcing, as employers usually demand experience. Many employers are prejudiced against hiring Aboriginal people, as stereotyping and racism are widespread. Aboriginal people often do not have access to information about available job opportunities and are not plugged into networks where such information is readily available.

The high frequency of single mothers presents special problems. Childcare facilities are hopelessly deficient and not just for Aboriginal children. The low-skill, low-entry jobs for which the majority of mothers might qualify pay wages so low that there is no incentive to leave social assistance, however inadequate it might be. Social assistance is at least reasonably predictable and allows the mother to spend time with her children; it therefore reduces some risks faced by single mothers. After some time living in poverty, however, it becomes increasingly difficult to break into the labour market because entrenched lifestyles are very difficult to change. And employers tend to look unfavourably at absence from the "formal" labour force.

Aboriginal culture is not, generally, seen as an obstacle to labour force participation. With time for adjustment and a supporting work environment, preferably one in which other Aboriginal people are present, Aboriginal people can and do fit quite readily into new work environments. But time and support are often not made available. Finally, Aboriginal people often find themselves competing for the same kind of limited job opportunities.

Reflecting the lower participation rates and higher unemployment rates which are the outcome of these circumstances, only 56 percent of Aboriginal adults reported employment income in 1996 compared with 67 percent in the population as a whole, while 8.9 percent reported incomes of zero, compared with 5.4 percent in the population as a whole. Of those who earned incomes, 23 percent reported incomes of less than $5,000 per annum, compared with 14 percent in the City as a whole. Only 28 percent of Aboriginal adults reported total income in excess of $20,000, compared with 46 percent in the total population. A much lower proportion of Aboriginal women earned over $20,000, 22 percent, than did non-Aboriginal females (35.8 percent) or Aboriginal males (35 percent).

A major reason for the lower average levels of employment income among Aboriginal people is their concentration in relatively low paying unskilled or semi-skilled jobs. The 1996 Census indicated that, of the 16,640 Aboriginal people in Winnipeg over the age of fourteen who had worked in 1996, 58 percent occupied clerical, non-supervisory sales and service or unskilled manual jobs, compared with 45 percent of the population generally. Many of these positions are not unionized (Hull, 1991). While about 36 percent of Aboriginal employees occupied skilled, supervisory, professional or managerial positions, the rate was 51 percent for the population generally. Furthermore, there was a higher proportion of females among the Aboriginal people employed (48.8 percent) than in the workforce generally (47.4 percent), and apart from being disproportionately represented in clerical and service jobs, there is an acknowledged tendency for females to receive less than males even in the same job. Three other possibilities are that Aboriginal people have less experience and have higher turnover rates and occupy more part-time positions than the average, but we have no evidence to confirm or reject these hypotheses. What we do know from earlier studies is that many Aboriginal people "hold jobs only on a periodic basis" (Falconer, 1985, p. 75), that there is no evidence of "significant upward occupational mobility" (Clatworthy, 1983a, p. 42), and that length of time in the city did not improve the chances of success in the labour market (Clatworthy, 1983b). Each of these propositions needs to be reinvestigated, however, in the light of the rapid growth of the Aboriginal labour force in recent years and, more importantly, in light of what appears to be a significant increase in Aboriginal employment since 1986, as will be shown later.

Just under a third (31 percent) of all Aboriginal adults reported reliance on social assistance payments in 1990, compared with 6.3 percent in Winnipeg as a whole (Social Planning Council, 1992), and two-thirds of these reported that such reliance lasted in excess of six months of the year. These rates of dependence on government transfers are extremely low compared with those found by Clatworthy (1981a) a decade earlier, which were in the 70-78 percent range. Clatworthy's figures included all types of transfers, but welfare dependence alone was more than double that reported in the APS. In our own survey of inner city households in 1993, 67 percent of Aboriginal respondents reported that welfare was their main source of household income, compared with 44 percent for the non-Aboriginal community. Unemployment Insurance was the main source for a further 7 percent.

The net result is that the incidence of poverty among the Aboriginal population of Winnipeg is very much higher than the average, as shown earlier in this volume in Lezubski, Silver and Black.

The Aboriginal community is not, however, accepting of its poverty. Only 13 percent of Aboriginal families report a monthly reliance on food banks, suggesting a discriminating use of these facilities. More importantly, the APS reports that well over a half of those without jobs in 1990/91 and more than double the number formally unemployed reported looking for work, while 18 percent of adults reported being involved in other activities for which they were paid money. Among those looking for work but not finding it, the most frequently cited reasons were that there were few or no jobs available (33 percent) or that their education or experience did not fit the jobs available (27 percent). An additional reason given (18 percent) was that there was not enough information about jobs which were available.

These findings by the APS are echoed in our own survey of 144 residents in the inner city. This found that 72 percent of Aboriginal respondents want full-time work and 53 percent would take part-time work. Only 7 percent had a steady job (only 4 percent of Aboriginal women) but 42 percent expected to obtain one. Indeed, the survey found that a higher proportion of Aboriginal people wanted work than non-Aboriginal people (66 percent). A greater proportion of non-Aboriginal residents of the inner city, however, already had employment (38 percent). This demonstrates that even within the poorest neighbourhoods in the city, Aboriginal people fare much worse than others in terms of employment and that this has little to do with Aboriginal aspirations.

The reasons advanced in the survey for difficulty in finding work echoed those in the APS with one important difference: lack of childcare was given much more weight by respondents to our survey, with 26 percent seeing this as a major obstacle to their finding employment, compared with only 4.7 percent in the APS. This may reflect the preponderance of women in our survey (75 percent). Over 60 percent of both female and male respondents reported that they did not have any special problems holding jobs or looking for work.

Not only do Aboriginal residents aspire to paid employment and actively seek it out, they also engage in a wide range of economic activities best described as self-employment and direct production. Under the heading of self-employment, some 17 percent of people surveyed in the inner city make arts or crafts in the home for sale or engage in auto or electrical repair, while 35 percent provide services for sale, such as home childcare, cleaning, carpentry, etc. It is also apparent from the survey that Aboriginal people spend much more of their labour time producing goods for direct consumption (i.e., for consumption by them or their families) than they do working in either the formal or market-based informal economy, i.e., working for wages or in self-employment. The biggest absorber of time was childcare and supervision, followed by cooking, sewing/knitting, house cleaning, dish washing, laundry and shopping.

The Aboriginal community is not homogeneous. Some 10 percent of the male population and 3 percent of the female population earn over $40,000 per annum; some 1300 now own their own business, while in the inner city survey, 24 percent report that they have a business idea they are working on. In 1996 there were over 4,100 Aboriginal people in the City occupying supervisory, semi-professional, professional, and managerial positions, and 51 percent of these were women.

A balanced view of the Aboriginal community must recognize, therefore, not just the prevalence of poverty, but also a desire to secure paid employment, both part-time and full-time, an active participation by many in informal sector activities, an unusually heavy workload in terms of household labour, contingent upon family size and a diversified community in which many Aboriginal people are employed in reasonably well-paying jobs and in business or, at least, have aspirations to enter business.

Institutional Structure and Capacity for Economic Development

The three principal Aboriginal political organizations in Winnipeg are the Assembly of Manitoba Chiefs (AMC), the Manitoba Métis Federation (MMF) and the Aboriginal Council of Winnipeg (ACW). The first two are province-wide bodies headquartered in Winnipeg. The ACW was established in 1990, a product of the amalgamation of the Winnipeg Council of Treaty and Status Indians, which represented Status Indians, and the Urban Indian Association, which represented Status Indians, non-Status Indians and Métis.

Of these organizations, only the MMF has developed an institutional capacity for economic planning and development, backed up with financial resources. The Federation established the Manitoba Métis Community Investments Inc. (MMCII) in 1984 to undertake economic development initiatives essentially in rural Métis communities. In January 1991, the MMF establised the Louis Riel Capital Corporation. It is capitalized at $7.6 million, has an annual operating budget of $270,000, and employs three staff, two of whom are Métis. To date it has advanced $1.5 million in a range of economic sectors, from agriculture to retail. While none of the loans has so far been advanced in Winnipeg, there are no constraints on its ability to lend there except the viability of borrowers. The MMCII has also established the Métis Construction Company and an office/warehouse complex in Winnipeg. In 1998, the MMF–Winnipeg Region established the Winnipeg Metis Development Corporation to help Winnipeg Metis establish small businesses, initially by providing micro-lending.

The MMF, therefore, has a pool of capital, some economic and financial expertise and some office, storage and construction capacity. While these resources are minimal and quite inadequate for a frontal assault on Métis and non-Status economic problems, they constitute a base from which to start. The other political organs have no such base.

The Assembly of Manitoba Chiefs has no capital corporation and only a tenuous attachment to a single position for an Economic Advisor. It suffered the elimination by the Filmon government of its core funding from the Province, while the federal government first cut back and later abolished its Regional Opportunities Program (ROP), from which the Economic Advisor was financed.

The Chiefs have proposed the creation of a First Nations Economic Development Advisory Council, consisting of representatives of tribal councils, unaffiliated reserves, urban Indian organizations and women's groups. Assisted by a small technical secretariat, the Council would operate at arms length from the AMC and would be responsible for developing and advising on economic development policy. In this way the Chiefs, as politicians, would retain some distance from the technical aspects of development, while the Advisory Council would service the broad needs of the community for economic development and not merely be a creature of the Federal government.

The refusal of the federal government to make resources available to the AMC for this purpose suggests the government is not really interested in developing the capacity of the First Nations' community to shape their own economic development agenda. Rather, the government has a narrow preoccupation with involving First Nations' organizations in its economic programs, but on its terms, and in a purely advisory capacity. The Chiefs are concerned about being co-opted into structures which duplicate their own and over which they have little control and about being seen by their constituencies as being party to decisions which may often be unpopular. The end result is a stalemate. The situation remains one in which the Status Indians have no central economic development institutions and no source of capital over which they have control.

Once they leave the reserve, Status Indians find themselves in an ambiguous position. Since the Federal government does not accept the principle of portability of Treaty rights and since bands have no incentive to transfer funds to urban areas to provide services to migrants, their own funding being hopelessly inadequate, urban Indians find themselves in a nether land. They have no obvious representation and by and large, the AMC has not, until recently, directed its attention to their predicament because it does not have the resources to do so. Yet there are some urban Status Indians who believe that the tribal council approach is not the way to further their interests and these have tended to throw their support behind the Aboriginal Council of Winnipeg (ACW).

The Aboriginal Council has the backing of numerous Aboriginal institutions in Winnipeg and of some very prominent urban Aboriginal activists, Status, non-Status and Métis alike. Its position is that Aboriginal people should have the right to self-determination regardless of place of residence. In those urban neighbourhoods where Aboriginal people are a majority, they might exercise a degree of territorial jurisdiction. Otherwise, since urban Aboriginal people have no land base, they will have to exercise jurisdiction through the development of self-determining institutions. The ACW believes that "status blind" institutions would best serve the interests of urban Aboriginal people, delivering services regardless of legal distinctions between Aboriginal people (Aboriginal Council, 1992). At the same time the ACW is careful to point out that it does not believe in a '"melting pot" approach to urbanisation. Rather, it respects the diversity of the different groups and believes in the portability of Treaty rights.

The Aboriginal Council also suffers from a lack of resources, receiving only $45,000 in core funding from the Province. It has no in-house economic development capacity, but it does have a huge volunteer base and close ties with numerous inner city Aboriginal organizations, and it draws on these to lever resources from government agencies for specific development projects.

A number of non-urban tribal councils have their headquarters physically located in Winnipeg (though legally based on reserves for tax reasons). The largest and most significant of these is the Southeast Resource Development Council, Inc., which represents nine bands in south-eastern Manitoba. This Council owns two extremely profitable buildings, a parking lot and a junior hockey team in the city. It also provides significant educational supports in Winnipeg for students coming into the city. It has an economic development capacity through its Economic Development Division, which employs seven staff, four of whom are Aboriginal, but this focuses entirely on community development on the reserves. Southeast has, however, discussed plans to set up a fast food outlet in the centre of the city and has, in the past, discussed establishing a travel agency and a cheque-cashing facility. The Council has a number of economic ventures designed to service its reserve members, such as a building supply store, an electrical contractor and an airline, but all of these are based outside of Winnipeg.

Aboriginal women have felt the need for their own political organizations for some years and, with the emphasis they have been putting in recent years on male violence, their organizations have become very prominent. In Winnipeg, the main women's bodies are the Aboriginal Women's Unity Coalition, the Original Women's Network and the Indigenous Women's Collective. None of these has the resources to develop its own economic decision-making capability, but the first two work closely with the Aboriginal Council and all contain women with considerable experience in building development projects from the ground up. What is clear is that any efforts to strengthen the institutional capacity for Aboriginal organizations to formulate economic policies and plans and to implement them must also involve making resources available to women's organizations so that their particular experiences and insights can be given full expression, and so that their particular problems and needs can be addressed.

Strategies of Economic Development Proposed by the Aboriginal Community

One of the most influential statements on economic development for urban Aboriginal people in Manitoba, dating back to the early 1970s, comes from Stan Fulham (1981). Fulham proposed the creation of a Native Economic Development and Employment Council (NEDECO) appointed by representatives of Aboriginal organizations and senior levels of government. The Council would establish a Native Development Corporation (NDC) which would operate a number of subsidiary companies, offering them financial and administrative services. The NDC would set up a Native Industrial Centre, a business complex to house companies. The Council would negotiate contracts with government, crown corporations and private business for Corporation subsidiaries to supply goods and services employing Aboriginal people. It would concentrate on labour intensive activities, would work with government to set up appropriate training schemes, and would maintain an inventory of Aboriginal people—their skills and employment experience—so as to maximize their employment opportunities, within the Corporation and elsewhere.

The Native Industrial Centre would house a credit union for staff and businesses, and several other personal service enterprises, such as a cafe/restaurant, barbershop, hairdresser, and shoe-repair shop. By sharing premises, both subsidiaries and other businesses would economize on costs (subsidized where justified), and would have ready access to managerial expertise and a source of finance. Fulham also advocates the "setting aside" of government purchasing of supplies and services to benefit specifically Aboriginal businesses. While relying heavily on government resources for purchasing and for training and while drawing on community input for the Council and the Corporation, Fulham saw the aim of his proposal as being, primarily, "to establish and promote a private business sector for Native people" (p. 74).

Fulham poses this strategy in opposition to affirmative action, which he views as a "negative approach" (p. 75) and, in this respect, his views are quite at odds with those currently held by Aboriginal groups in the city. Also at odds with contemporary thinking in the Aboriginal community is the degree of state supervision of the, quite cumbersome, institutional structure which Fulham envisages.

Some of Fulham's thinking embraces ideas put forward initially in 1969 by the Indian and Métis Friendship Centre for the Native community in Winnipeg. The proposal was fleshed out in some detail between 1972 and 1975 as Neeginan—a Cree expression which can be translated as "Our Place" (Damas and Smith, 1975, p. 10). This envisaged the creation of an ethnic quarter in Winnipeg for Aboriginal people, to serve as a transitional milieu for those moving into the City. It would have its own housing, social service and economic facilities and would be run by Aboriginal people. It was seen as a more enlightened alternative to a proposal being put forward at that time by Kahn-Tineta-Horn of an urban reserve to be located ten miles outside of Winnipeg (Damas and Smith, 1975, p. 6). A 1975 report went into considerable architectural detail for the community services centre which would be the focal point of the community, housing social service agencies, shops, schools, residential accommodation and Aboriginal political organizations. The report also examined alternative locations in the inner city.

The Neeginan proposal was quite thoroughly developed and had considerable support both inside and outside the community. For many years, however, governments were not prepared to fund it and, after much frustration, its proponents simply lost steam (Krotz, 1980, p. 60).

Though formulated over twenty years ago, Fulham's views and related proposals such as Neeginan have a remarkable currency and continue to surface. Thus, the centrepiece of *An Economic Strategy for The Manitoba Métis Federation*, prepared by Thunderbird Consulting (1992) and endorsed by the MMF, is the proposal for government "setting aside" markets for Métis businesses. The incubator proposal (or "franchise" as Fulham would have it) also surfaced again in recent years, albeit in modified form, in the proposal to establish the Aboriginal Centre of Winnipeg in what used to be the Canadian Pacific Railway Station, which is located in the heart of the core area.

The idea behind the Aboriginal Centre was that it would bring under one roof a variety of Aboriginal organizations providing services to the community. Existing organizations would be encouraged to move their offices there. It would house an Aboriginal Institute which would deliver existing and new employment and training-related services. Attempts would also be made to bring in public sector agencies providing services to Aboriginal people. A restaurant and childcare facility would be set up to cater for those working or being trained in the building. Finally, there was provision for light industrial activities, such as catering, printing and publishing, etc., and for conferences in the huge, 146,000-square feet building.

Considerable progress has been made in realizing this plan, which contains many elements of the Neeginan proposal, especially the community service centre component, without the emphasis on building a separate neighbourhood as such. The building was purchased in December 1992, initially by means of the CPR taking back a mortgage, and later by means of loans from the Assiniboine Credit Union. Since March 1993, several Aboriginal organizations have moved in. As a National Historic Site, the Centre qualifies for special funding for restoration and maintenance from the federal government, but provincial, civic and other forms of federal funding were pursued too, while a charitable organization was established to accept public donations, needed to lever government grants.

By 1999, the Centre had twenty-five tenants and was fully occupied. Aboriginal firms which have established there include a security company, a woodworking enterprise, a printer, an auto body shop, a restaurant (which is in part a training initiative) and an art gallery. Many other tenants provide important services to the community, such as counselling, employment advice and training, and health and wellness. The Aboriginal Council of Winnipeg is also located there as are a number of non-Aboriginal entities which provide services to the community, such as the post office, legal aid and human resources organizations of government, and the Aboriginal Business Development Centre, a federally funded organization which offers counselling to small businesses in an "Aboriginal friendly" environment.

This represents a considerable accomplishment for the Aboriginal community of Winnipeg. The Aboriginal Centre will undoubtedly become a focal point for the community and represents the realization of an idea long in the making, having been envisaged by the Urban Indian Association which the Aboriginal Council replaced.

The Centre is not, however, without some potential dangers. First of all, due to its large size, it may expose Aboriginal tenants to a degree of risk they might not otherwise carry. Thus, failure to obtain the break-even occupancy level might put pressure on tenants to raise rents and/or associated fees. Occupancy problems were in evidence until 1999 when, after successfully creating a high school campus in the Centre, the space was fully rented out. Annual rents now bring in over $700,000 a year.

Second, the project is likely to remain highly dependent on state funding for rental income. This is not, of course, unusual for Aboriginal institutions, but the centrality of that funding to the ongoing commercial viability of the Centre is, perhaps, somewhat unique. Diversifying the tenants helps reduce risk in this regard, as does diversifying the types and sources of state funding. In late 1999, there were twenty-five tenants drawing funding from the federal, provincial and City governments, as well as Aboriginal educational authorities, so one could argue that this risk has been recognized and addressed to some degree.

Third, the *geographic* concentration of Aboriginal organizations in one building limits the extent to which they can be incorporated into holistic, community development based on "balanced growth" within neighbourhoods. It could be argued that this is a necessary, structural, weakness of the incubator approach.

Fourth, the incubator concept has been only partially successful with regard to commercial businesses. The ones listed earlier are important initiatives but are not highly integrated, sharing little but a common roof. Some of the services which might have accomplished this and which were originally in the plan have not materialized—for example, the credit union—perhaps because of scale problems.

Finally, the large concentration of Aboriginal institutions, each with a different mandate and agenda, will call for a high degree of diplomacy in the handling of problems and disagreements among tenants and between tenants and the Centre. Initially, there were grounds for optimism that the key institutions behind this proposal, the Aboriginal Centre and Ma Mawi Wi Chi Itata Centre, an Aboriginal child and family services organization, would be equal to this task, as both are the product of broad alliances within the community. Unfortunately, the board of Ma Mawi pulled the organization out of the Centre in the mid-1990s, ostensibly on the grounds that the building was unsafe because of the presence of asbestos-lined pipes.

Since local regulatory agencies had declared the building safe, one has to question what the real motivation for the move was, but the net result at the time was a huge hole in the operating revenue of the Centre of some $100,000 per annum (*Inner City Voice*, January, 1994), and the resignation of the Executive Director of Mama Wi, who was also the Chairperson of the Board of the Centre. This most unfortunate development cast a large question mark on the viability of the Centre until alternative tenants were found. As a result, the Centre experienced financial problems for most of the decade. Only in 1999 was full occupancy accomplished and a net profit on operations earned. This helped reduce an accumulated loss on operations of some $350,000 to that date (although it has net assets of over $5.5 million, on account of the building), and the Centre entered the twenty-first century with its financial prospects looking better than ever. The importance of diplomacy and a process for managing disagreements cannot, however, be overstressed.

The biggest success of the Aboriginal Centre may prove to be that of resurrecting the Neeginan concept and pushing it through to implementation. The serious problems of the inner city became apparent in the late 1990s with extensive Aboriginal gang activity, a rapidly deteriorating housing stock and an outbreak of arson. In 1999 the Pan Am Games were held in Winnipeg and the politicians decided that Main Street needed a face-lift. Proceeding with the Neeginan concept was felt to be a way of meeting several objectives at once: clearing up derelict hotels on Main Street; replacing them with an impressive structure celebrating Aboriginal strength and culture; placating the Aboriginal leadership and offering financial support (over $6 million) to the community's own solutions to the economic and social problems it faces. Neeginan seemed to offer all of this.

Construction of the Thunder Bird House, Neeginan's home, was completed in early 2000. This strikingly impressive building was designed by Douglas Cardinal who sees it as "a place of rebirth and vitality; a place of healing and sharing" (Cardinal, undated). It will have several components: a place for Aboriginal art and culture; a youth complex; and a "commercial complex/business incubator." The incubator component is exactly the same as that envisaged for the Aboriginal Centre and Douglas Cardinal describes it thus: "In this village, we will provide stores which will offer an assortment of goods and merchandise such as: food, clothing, gardening equipment, leather goods, and other necessities. We will have banks, bookstores, video stores, pool halls, movie theatres, arcades, and restaurants" (ibid). It remains to be seen, however, whether or not Neeginan will have more success in this regard than the Aboriginal Centre, which is located just across the street.

Perhaps the most clearly articulated approach to community economic development for the Aboriginal population of the inner city of Winnipeg is that put forward by members of the Neechi Foods Co-op Ltd. (a community store) in their *Its Up To All Of Us* guide (Winnipeg Native Family Economic Development, February 1993). They lay down ten community development principles by which to assess proposed or actual community initiatives. The first three of these essentially advocate a "convergence" approach to economic strategy: they provide for the use of local goods and services, the production of goods and services in the local economy, and the reinvestment of profits locally. The point here is to emphasize the potential of the inner city market to sustain economic livelihoods. This means that income *earned* in the inner city should, as far as possible, be spent there, and preferably on goods and services which are actually *produced* there. This contrasts with the current situation in which substantial inner city income leaks away in expenditures elsewhere in the city on goods and services which are not produced in the inner city. Neechi encourages Aboriginal residents and non-Aboriginal residents and others earning incomes in the core to use their purchasing power to the benefit of the local community. The idea is to spend in such a way that leakages from the inner city economy are minimized and economic linkages within it strengthened. This would reduce dependence on outside markets and build greater community self-reliance.

The fourth principle is to create long-term employment for inner city residents, so as to reduce dependence on welfare and food banks, enable people to live more socially productive lives, and build personal and community esteem. In the process, of course, more income would be available for spending in the community. Related to this, the fifth principle calls for the training of local residents in skills appropriate for community development.

The sixth principle or guideline is the encouragement of local decision-making through local, cooperative, forms of ownership and control and grassroots participation. The aim would be to strengthen community self-determination as people work together to meet community needs (see Hunter, Chapter Six).

Principles seven and eight recognize the importance of community development promoting public health and a safe and attractive physical environment. The ninth principle stresses the centrality of achieving greater neighbourhood stability by providing more dependable housing, encouraging long-term residency and creating a base for long-term community economic development.

Finally, the whole approach is premised on the safeguarding and enhancement of human dignity. While there is a personal dimension to this, in the form of promoting self-respect, much of the emphasis is social, recognising the need to generate community spirit, and to encourage equality between the sexes and respect for seniors and children. The Neechi criteria also call for the promotion of social dignity regardless of physical or mental differences, national or ethnic background and colour or creed. Above all, community development should promote Aboriginal pride.

This is an exhaustive and demanding set of criteria by which to evaluate community development proposals. Underlying it is a definite vision of both the *process* and the *goal* of community economic development.

The Neechi approach to economic development is not merely an intellectual one. It is rooted in and shaped by practical experience. Its origin can be traced back to the Northern Plan exercise in the mid-1970s (Loxley, 1981 and 1986). The ten principles evolved during two training programs conducted in the early 1980s for Métis and Indian economic development and finance officers. Sponsored by the MMF and the All-Chief's Budget Committee of the AMC, but run independently, these programs have produced over fifty well-trained Aboriginal staff, most of whom are now employed by Aboriginal organizations in the Province (see Métis Economic Development, 1986). Out of these courses, which combined rigorous classroom work with practical on-the-job experience, came a series of community planning meetings in the summer of 1985, run by the trainees. Four projects were identified in these meetings as being high on the list of priority needs in the community in Winnipeg—a food store, a housing co-op, a commercial daycare and a crafts shop—and the trainees proceeded to appraise each, working in conjunction with project working groups. All but the last of these has now been implemented and, in the early years, they were loosely 'federated' under the umbrella of the Winnipeg Native Family Economic Development (WNFED), a mutual support group.

Neechi Foods Co-op is an Aboriginal workers' co-op operating a grocery store and Aboriginal specialty shop in the inner city. The objectives of the co-op are to offer Aboriginal people a better selection of food at better prices, to promote community health (which it does in a number of ways, for example, by not selling cigarettes and by subsidising sales of fruit to children), to promote Aboriginal pride and employment, to keep money circulating in the community, to foster sharing, co-operation and local control and to create capital for new projects. The store employs four full-time and five part-time employees, all Aboriginal, and annual sales are now in the region of $500,000.

The housing operation affiliated with WNFED is the Payuk Inter-Tribal Co-op, which has a forty-two unit apartment block and five duplex units. One of its aims is to provide a safe and supportive environment for Aboriginal women and children (alcohol is prohibited in the building). Rents are tied to ability to pay. The Nee Gawn Ah Kai Day Care is located in the Payuk building, has space for thirty children and employs six people. The Ma Mawi Wi Chi Itata Centre, Canada's first major urban Aboriginal child and family support service which now employs fifty-five, largely Aboriginal, staff was also associated with WNFED. This organization was the outcome of efforts by the Winnipeg Coalition on Native Child Welfare, which also worked closely with the Economic Development Training Program, underlining the holistic, integrated approach to economic and social reform subscribed to by an influential section of the community.

The Neechi approach has clearly influenced the thinking of the Aboriginal Council in its formulation of an economic development strategy for Aboriginal people in the City. It argues for "a community economic development planning process geared towards developing a convergent, self-reliant local economy based upon community economic development principles: maximising income retention, strengthening and promoting economic linkages, and maximising community employment." (Aboriginal Council, 1992). It argues for the development of linkages between the urban Aboriginal community and reserves and rural Métis communities, but it would also like to see Treaty administration centres established in Winnipeg to meet the needs of off-reserve Indians. The Council puts a major emphasis on the Aboriginalisation of the staff and control of the social service delivery system catering to Aboriginal clientele. They see Aboriginalisation as an important component of community economic development and extend it to education (with calls for an Aboriginal school board and control over all aspects of urban Aboriginal education), health, services to women, seniors, youths, and ex-inmates; in short, to all sections of Aboriginal society. This "decolonisation" would be based on the principle of participation by all sections of Aboriginal society and would be accomplished, ideally, in cooperation with the other political organizations. This strategy has, therefore, some unique features, but at root, as a convergence strategy, it is essentially that which is proposed by Neechi.

The Neechi/WNFED approach to economic development shares some things in common with the Fulham approach. They both recognize the importance of Aboriginal organizations in the process; they both stress the importance of developing linkages and mutually supporting economic initiatives, both within Winnipeg and between the City community and Aboriginal communities outside; they both recognize the importance of having support services available to Aboriginal businesses, and especially of appropriate training; both argue the importance of providing decent long-term housing; and both admit the social desirability of non-Aboriginal support for Aboriginal ventures even when more lucrative investment outlets or cheaper purchases could be had elsewhere.

There are, however, crucial differences between these two approaches which need to be highlighted. First of all, the Neechi approach is much more clearly grounded in grassroots community activism than is the Fulham model and its variants, and envisages a much less significant role for Aboriginal political organizations in the economic development process. Second, the Neechi model attaches a much greater importance to community ownership and control than does Fulham, who is more wedded to the promotion of private Aboriginal business. In this respect Neechi appear to have strong community support for their views. In the survey of 144 inner city households mentioned earlier, 69 percent of households responded that community ownership of business would be best for the neighbourhood, and only 7 percent said private ownership. Third, the Neechi approach is a much more holistic one, in which economic development is seen as one aspect, albeit a very important one, of healthy communities, in which economic opportunity, health and educational development and social and environmental stability go hand in hand. It is not that Fulham et. al. would necessarily disagree with this, but they do not articulate their philosophy in such a comprehensive, holistic fashion. Fourth, and related, Neechi would attach less importance to the physical aggregation of economic enterprises under one roof, preferring more spatial balance and securing supportive services and economies of scale in other ways. Finally, the Neechi model promotes restoring economic balance and community self-reliance through economic restructuring which in some ways challenges the logic of the market economy. Fulham's approach, on the other hand, accepts the dominant market on its own terms and seeks to break into it with government assistance.

In their most recent variant, the Neechi principles now include support for other community economic development initiatives. These principles have been adopted by the Community Development Business Association (CDBA) and its more than twenty-five members.

The Assembly of Manitoba Chiefs has taken an eclectic approach to economic development in Winnipeg. It is supportive of both the "incubator" concept and of community-based initiatives of the kind advocated by Neechi. It also argues for aggressive employment equity initiatives in the public sector and for the opening up of employment opportunities in the private sector. The AMC has been particularly insistent on greater accessibility to mainstream employment opportunities and has developed a close working relationship with some large-scale private employers, such as the banks. Over the years, the AMC and its forerunners have also advocated a much greater Aboriginal presence in those governmental institutions dealing directly with Aboriginal people. This emphasis has paid off in one or two federal departments in Winnipeg having fairly high rates of Aboriginal employees. The AMC would argue, however, that there is a long way yet to go in the federal civil service as a whole, and has, in fact, taken up the matter of the general lack of progress with the Canadian Human Rights Commission.

The Chiefs of Manitoba have argued also for the creation of funding vehicles to promote Indian economic development in the City of Winnipeg, as well as in the reserve communities. As early as 1969, the Manitoba Indian Brotherhood argued for the creation of a Manitoba Indian Development Inc. which would serve as a development bank to give financial and other supports to First Nation economic ventures. This idea surfaced in somewhat amended form in the mid-1980s as the Manitoba Indian Development Association, MIDAS (All-Chiefs' Budget Committee, 1984). Eventually, however, the chiefs decided to pursue the capital corporation approach with the tribal council, or associations of tribal councils, as the focal point. The result of this has been the institutional development outlined earlier and a situation in which, while new capital corporations are empowered to lend money in Winnipeg, there is no institution set up *specifically* to cater for First Nations' people in the City. This is being recognized as a problem now, as there is insufficient funding to cater for the needs of reserve communities which is where the existing capital corporations must first focus their attention. Thus, consideration is being given to how best to rectify this problem. Had the Winnipeg Tribal Council emerged as a viable entity with strong grass-roots support, then this could have been a vehicle for launching a new financial institution for First Nations' people in Winnipeg, but this does not appear to be the case, and an alternative approach will likely be needed.

In November 1998, the AMC, MMF and ACW participated in a Round Table on Aboriginal People in Winnipeg's Urban Community (Human Resources Canada, 1998). They agreed on the need for an economic development strategy which would create 2,000 jobs every year. They proposed the adoption of a common vision which would promote community level ownership of economic ventures. The need to break away from dependence on welfare and government services was acknowledged as was the necessity to move from non-profit to for-profit activities. While much was made of building "partnership" among the three groups, the AMC argued its case for the portability of Treaty rights into the urban setting while the MMF advanced its claim to be the legal representative of all the Métis in the province and asked for funds so that they could be properly enumerated. The superficial cooperation hides, therefore, some deep political divisions, and these became apparent when Neeginan was announced. The AMC and MMF were critical of the project on the grounds that they had not been part of the decision-making process (*Winnipeg Free Press*, June 22, 1998).

Thus, a variety of approaches to economic development in Winnipeg are to be found within the Aboriginal community. The supporters of these different viewpoints co-exist quite amicably and even with some degree of cooperation, although some struggles have been waged within organizations over the preferred approach. There is so little happening in the field of Aboriginal economic development at this time, relative to the problems of Aboriginal need, that there is ample room for eclecticism and disagreement over strategy.

The Core Area Initiative

The most significant policy intervention in the City of Winnipeg in the recent past was the Winnipeg Core Area Initiative (WCAI). All three levels of government shared equally in providing funding to improve the "economic, social and physical conditions" of the core, where a large proportion of Winnipeg's Aboriginal people reside. The first phase of the Initiative was 1981-86, and the total direct funding involved was $96 million; the second was 1986-91, and the cost was $100 million. Since many projects "leveraged" funds from elsewhere, the impact of the Initiative was much greater than these figures indicate and it dominated urban policy during its lifetime.

In the first agreement, $4.4 million went to administration, evaluation and information (Sector 3); $11 million to industrial development and small business assistance and $35.4 million to large scale physical redevelopment of the city (Sector 2); $12.9 million to housing, $14.7 million to employment and affirmative action and $16.5 million to various community initiatives (Sector 1). In the second agreement, $4 million went to administration (Sector 3), $8.4 million to industrial and entrepreneurial support and $49 million to large scale redevelopment (now transposed as Sector 1); $10.5 million to housing, $12 million to employment and training and $16.2 million to neighbourhood and community development (now transposed as Sector 2). It was the Sector 2 category of program funding in WCAI 2 and Sector 1 in WCAI 1 that had most relevance for Aboriginal people.

The evaluation of the Employment and Affirmative Action component of the first agreement documents quite carefully its impact on the Aboriginal community (Clatworthy, 1987). Over 500 residents of the core were trained and placed in both public and private employment. Over 200 of these were Aboriginal, of which 25 percent were single parents and 26 percent were youths. The unemployment rate of graduates fell from 83 percent before training to 12.5 percent after; their total incomes rose, on average, by two-thirds and earned income tripled, while dependence on government transfers had declined by 80 percent in cash terms (ibid, p. 41). Although no new jobs were created by this program, inner city residents, including Aboriginal people, gained opportunities to work which they would otherwise not have had. The cost of training each graduate was, however, almost $31,000.

Two other parts of this component trained nurses and social workers, again with great success. Of the ninety-three people trained, over a half were Aboriginal. By March 1987, forty-one people had been placed in employment and about one-half were Aboriginal.

While the evaluation found that this component had, by and large, met its objectives, it also found that there was a failure to integrate the training component of the WCAI with its other job creation components (p. 21). This would help explain why the Economic Stimulus programs (Sector 2) and the Industrial Development Program failed to hire Aboriginal people (Epstein Associates, 1987, pp. 48 and 51)

Although WCAI did not reduce the overall unemployment rate in the Core, it has been argued that "conditions would have been significantly worse in the absence of the CAI" (Working Margins, 1991 p. 36). For Aboriginal people in the Core there was, in fact, a large rise in the unemployment rate between 1981 and 1986 from 27.7 percent to 31.5 percent, due to a huge (67 percent) increase in the Aboriginal labour force in the core between 1981-1986 (for which the CAI was, of course, partially responsible). At one level, the initiative was successful; yet given the demographic trends it was not equal to the task of stabilizing, leave alone reducing, the Aboriginal unemployment rate.

Data on employment creation appears to be a little more comprehensive for the second agreement. A total of 1,968 jobs not directly connected to CAI construction projects were created by all components of the agreement. Of these, 298 or one-third, were Aboriginal. Most of the jobs, 72 percent, were in the private sector: 28 percent of the total were in manufacturing, 15 percent in finance and 10 percent in construction. Two-thirds of the jobs paid under $20,000 per annum which, according to the evaluation, suggests that most were in entry-level or lower-level positions (Working Margins, 1991 p. 20), but 60 percent of the jobs paid more than $15,000 a year, or much more than the average Aboriginal worker would earn in Winnipeg.

A total of 2,241 individuals benefitted from training programs. Aboriginal people represented 43 percent of all trainees, and about a half the number of Aboriginal people unemployed in 1986 received training during the five-year period (Working Margins, 1991, pp. 26-27). Some 250 Aboriginal trainees were placed into employment. In contrast to the first agreement, training and affirmative action were not only aimed at the private sector, NGOs and other sections of government, but were firmly integrated into Core Area Initiative projects themselves. The average cost for graduates placed in employment, at $14,394, seems to be under half that of the first agreement.

A major problem with CAI placements, however, appears to be a high turnover rate, especially in manufacturing and construction. A survey of employers, in all sectors including the public, found that only 41 percent of those placed were still working with their original employers (Working Margins, 1991 p. 23).

In contrast to Sector 2, it appears that Sector 1 and related initiatives, accounting for 57 percent of all funding, provided little if any benefit to the Aboriginal population of the core. Most of this money went into financing high profile real estate and property development transactions such as the Forks project, North Portage Place and the Exchange District improvement.

The overall assessment of the impact of WCAI 2 on employment creation would be similar, but less favourable in relative terms, to that of WCAI 1. About the same number of jobs were created, but the Aboriginal labour force continued to grow significantly in the 1986-91 period. The Initiative itself also raised labour supply by more than it did demand.

Apart from training and job creation, the WCAI was important to Aboriginal people for the funds it provided for improvements of housing and community infrastructure. A total of $12.9 million was earmarked for housing under the first agreement and $10.5 million under the second. The first upgraded over 6,000 houses and helped build in the region of 500 new houses. Most assistance was to individual home owners, but $2 million was put into non-profit housing (Epstein Associates, 1987). The second added 327 units to the housing stock and renovated just over 1,000 houses or 5 percent of the core's total housing stock. Many more houses were inspected and their owners forced to undertake repairs. It was not possible, however, to assess the effect of these on "stabilizing the area's population base and neighbourhood" (Winnipeg Core Area Initiative, 1992, p. 94).

Under the heading of Neighbourhood and Community Development, WCAI 2 provided over 300 grants totalling more than $14 million to community facilities and services. These were taken advantage of by most agencies operating in the core area. Some projects were specifically aimed at the Aboriginal community, and Aboriginal organizations received $1.8 million for a whole variety of projects. The largest of these were the $216,000 received by Ma Mawi Wi Chi Itata Centre's New Directions Project to promote self-identity and self-esteem among Aboriginal youth; $161,000 for the Manitoba Association for Native Languages; $236,000 for the Native Women's Transition Centre for a new facility and programming; and $98,000 for background studies related to the Aboriginal Centre.

Very little funding under the Neighbourhood and Community Development component was aimed at community economic development "per se." Indeed, of the $14 million assigned to this envelope, only $667,000 was earmarked for economic development projects in the community; $341,000 was actually invested in community ventures, of which there were only three in total. Most of this, $201,000, went to Neechi Foods, $107,000 went into a greenhouse project for the mentally handicapped and $33,000 into a cooperative laundromat. This failure to more aggressively promote community economic development was recognized by the community as the most glaring weakness in the WCAI.

We have a very clear idea of what the community, including the Aboriginal community, of the core area actually felt about the WCAI because in 1990 a Community Inquiry into Inner City Revitalisation was held, prompted by the impending expiry of the WCAI 2 and the anticipation of future government initiatives in the city. What the Inquiry found was that inner city residents and groups recognized the value and accomplishments of the tripartite initiative, had benefitted greatly from it and wished it to continue, but with certain improvements in direction and focus (Community Inquiry Board, 1990, p4).

The Inquiry found that residents wanted a much greater role in planning and decision-taking, a much greater emphasis on promoting ownership, self-help and self-determination and a much greater focus of capital expenditures on housing, infrastructure and community facilities (as opposed to the grandiose town planning gestures). Concern was expressed that many innovative programs and services would disappear along with the WCAI and that no provision had been made for their long-term funding. This was related to the critique of the WCAI for its lack of emphasis on community economic development. Without such development, the core area would not be able to build the financial base of the community and make it less dependent on state funding in the longer run. The Inquiry called for a closer link between education and economic development and a greater commitment to affirmative action hiring by companies benefitting from government finance .

The Inquiry called for the drawing up of an economic development strategy for the inner city by the Aboriginal community in conjunction with the WCAI and governments. It also supported the idea that priority should be given to Aboriginal business development and diversification generally, and to the establishment of the Aboriginal Centre specifically. There was support for easily accessible loans for small and micro businesses and for earmarking a portion of available funds for community groups to undertake development initiatives. There should be greater community control over Aboriginal education and training and more emphasis put on training Aboriginal women.

The Inquiry revealed that improving both the quality of housing and Aboriginal access to the ownership of housing are considered crucial to stabilizing the core. A variety of financing schemes were proposed including sweat equity, rent-to-own, deferred mortgage loans and the redirection of social assistance funds for rents. There was strong support for cooperative and non-profit housing and for using housing to encourage community-based economic development through worker cooperatives for building and renovation.

What emerges from the Inquiry report and what is clearly evident in recent community initiatives is a very clear recognition of the problems facing inner city residents and a strong desire to rectify them. This is not a community given over to fatalism or one trapped, irrevocably, into some "culture of poverty." On the contrary, it is a community with an impressive depth of leadership which has shown resolve and creativity in building institutions to serve the needs of Aboriginal people. It is a community full of ideas and energy but one also starved of resources and one which meets severe institutional obstacles when it attempts to give concrete substance to its creative ideas.

Unfortunately, the three levels of government were unmoved by the Inquiry recommendations and the WCAI was replaced by a city-wide Winnipeg Development Agreement. While this has given important financial support to a number of specific initiatives, such as the Aboriginal Centre, Neeginan, SEED Winnipeg and Just Housing, these account for only a small proportion of the $75 million to be spent between 1995 and 2000. Of the $60 million committed to the end of March 1999, only about $12.5 million or 21 percent was directed to Aboriginal projects and of this amount, fully $7.1 million was accounted for by Neeginan ($4.6 million) and the Aboriginal Centre ($2.5 million) (Winnipeg Development Agreement, 1999).

Acknowledging that "what we've been doing simply isn't working well enough," Lloyd Axworthy, Winnipeg's senior Liberal MP and cabinet minister, announced a $30 million Urban Aboriginal Strategy in July 1999 (*The Sun*, Winnipeg, July 14, 1999). This provides $4 million for economic development, $15 million for employment and training initiatives and $9 million for Aboriginal youth centres and housing improvement. Details are hard to come by so it is hard to know how much of this is new money. Also, the strategy does not appear to have been developed with the participation of the community, leave alone other levels of government.

Other Developments

In addition to the initiatives discussed above there have been numerous efforts to increase Aboriginal participation in the Winnipeg economy through business development, training, affirmative action and employment equity. Many of these were outlined and assessed in Loxley (1996). The training scene, in particular, has evolved rapidly since the mid-1990s with significant Aboriginal "ownership" (both figuratively and literally) and staffing of the schemes themselves. Elements of the

SEED Winnipeg

SEED Winnipeg is a development loan scheme for micro and community businesses, overseen by a volunteer board. It facilitates three loan programs: a micro loan scheme, a lending circle scheme and a community project loan scheme. In its micro lending it advances start-up capital in the form of loans of up to $10,000 to economically disadvantaged people, who are usually unemployed or on welfare. Special consideration is given to Aboriginal people, members of visible minority communities, people with disabilities, ex-offenders or inner city residents. Borrowers typically cannot meet the requirements of mainstream institutions for collateral and require training in business planning and management. All would-be applicants must first attend a three-hour orientation session. The credit circle program consists of groups of ten or so borrowers who take it in turns to borrow, support each other and act as a pressure group for loan repayment. Community projects are larger, collective ones requiring more development work and larger sums of finance. SEED provides experienced mentors to assist borrowers. It has little capital funding of its own, and draws mainly on funds from an inner city credit union which has earmarked funds specifically for this purpose and which works with SEED in evaluating applications. Operating funds are provided by The Community Education Development Association (CEDA), the Mennonite Central Committee (MCC), various charitable organizations and, as SEED has developed a track record, from government. Mentors are drawn from the Mennonite Economic Development Associates (MEDA). These various organizations, the Aboriginal community and the Provincial Government are all represented on either the board or the advisory committee to the board. While SEED is a relatively small institution, it is important as a model, and it underscores the point made by members of the Aboriginal community that there is, indeed, a scarcity of start-up capital for small businesses. Its average loan size, and credit cost per job, is under $5,000, or only 15 percent that of the Aboriginal Business Development Program. The mentor dimension of SEED is also something which has proven invaluable to clients and could usefully be emulated elsewhere. Finally, SEED has been successful in negotiating the continuation of social assistance payments during the initial period of business activity, thereby reducing pressure on the borrowers until break-even is achieved. More recently, it has assisted CEDA in helping realize the creation of a development corporation in one of the poorer sections of the city. The North End Community Renewal Corporation was created in 1999 and will offer a full range of community economic development services.

SEED also administers the Christmas Lite campaign which started as an adjunct to the Christmas Cheer Board, raising funds for Christmas hampers but buying food from Aboriginal, inner city businesses so as to help create permanent jobs in the community donors are seeking to help.

private sector, including the Winnipeg Chamber of Commerce, have also recognized the need to strengthen the Aboriginal business and employment presence in the city and have committees which encourage purchasing from Aboriginal suppliers. The Royal Bank, among others, has also actively promoted Aboriginal employment and business development.

Social organizations within the inner city have for many years pressed for private and public support of community economic development projects that would benefit Aboriginal people. The most persistent and most successful in this regard has been CEDA, which in 1999 brokered a proposal for a housing trust fund that would see a mix of financial contributions from the three levels of government and the community to buy, repair and sell inner city housing. The Assiniboine Credit Union has also been actively supporting community economic development initiatives in recent years, including SEED, housing and a variety of community business projects.

Finally, many Aboriginal people enter the labour market in Winnipeg without any form of special assistance and a number of Aboriginal businesses are also formed and operated entirely on their own initiative.

What Have These Initiatives Accomplished?

There are indications that Aboriginal employment in the City increased significantly between 1986 and 1996. The 1986 Census data suggests that 7,974 Aboriginal people were employed in that year (calculated from Census data contained in Social Planning Council, 1989). The 1996 Census records 16,640 Aboriginal employees, an apparent growth rate of 7.6 percent per annum over the decade. There may, however, be problems with these numbers in that some of this increase might reflect not new employment, but simply the capturing in the data of people not previously described as Aboriginal in 1986. One should be extremely cautious, therefore, about these findings. Whatever the accuracy of the 1986 base, however, there is other evidence of high growth rates in Aboriginal employment. On the basis of estimates of Aboriginal employment in 1991 in Loxley (1996), it appears that Aboriginal employment grew by about 6.4 percent per annum between 1991 and 1996, a remarkably strong performance.

If these numbers are anywhere near to being accurate, they paint an encouraging picture of Aboriginal employment growth in the city. The total number of people employed in Winnipeg rose by only 1.7 percent between 1986 and 1991 and by 1.3 percent between 1991 and 1996. This means that the proportion of those employed who were Aboriginal people rose from about 2.7 percent in 1986 to about 4.0 percent in 1991 and 5.1 percent in 1996. This increase undoubtedly owes something to the initiatives described above, but how much is impossible to tell.

At the same time, because the Aboriginal labour force itself doubled, the number of unemployed Aboriginal people also rose over this period, from 2,197 to possibly 4,000 in 1991 and to 4,445 in 1996, or at about the same rate as employment grew over the same period, *in spite* of the numerous economic development, employment equity and training initiatives. One can only speculate how bad the situation might have been without such programs. The numbers suggest then, that the growth of the Aboriginal labour force in Winnipeg is so rapid that a whole new *scale* of intervention is required if the unemployment rate and the total number of unemployed in the Aboriginal community are to be reduced. This will mean building on what appears to have been successful in the past and modifying or replacing initiatives which have had less success. It may also suggest that government initiatives are not equal to the task of coping with the rapid growth of the Aboriginal labour force and that the time is ripe for an entirely new *approach* to Aboriginal economic development drawing, as much as possible, on the strategies proposed by Aboriginal people themselves.

Recommendations

A number of proposals to strengthen *institutions* emerge logically from the above. First, the main representative Aboriginal organizations in Winnipeg need resources to build up an economic development planning, policy and advisory capacity. If self-government is to have any meaning, then governments must be prepared to transfer to Aboriginal organizations not just responsibilities but also resources. The strengthening of economic capacity should apply as much to the organizations of Aboriginal women, where they express a desire for it, as to the three main political bodies or their technical arms. The main purpose of these organizations would be to work with the local community to promote and support economic development initiatives and to ensure a coherent approach to economic development.

There is also a pressing need for a pool of capital controlled by and used to the benefit of the Aboriginal community. The MMF has an institution in place, and perhaps all that is needed there is additional funds earmarked specifically for urban Métis. Status and non-Status Indians have no such institutional structure. Theoretically, the mandates of tribal council capital corporations do extend to Winnipeg but, institutionally, this is an unwieldy way of addressing the capital needs of City residents which, if resorted to extensively, might face opposition from the constituent bands. There seems to be a case, therefore, for the creation of at least one new capital corporation with representation from the different communities or, if that cannot be agreed upon, one institution for First Nations people and one which would be status blind, to complement any urban activities of the existing capital corporations. The main point is that there is a lacuna in the City which needs to be filled quickly.

This pool of capital would be available to promote and support all forms of initiative in the community, be it small scale business or community development initiatives. Lack of funding for the latter is particularly acute, and yet the Aboriginal community in Winnipeg has a strong preference for community ventures.

There are no shortages of ideas in the Aboriginal community, at the levels both of strategic approaches to economic development and of specific projects. There is, however, a need for resources to be made available at the neighbourhood level to enable people to develop and realize their ideas.

Education for community economic development is currently conducted essentially on a voluntary basis, with two notable exceptions. The Community Education Development Association (CEDA) has long been active in this area, but it operates on a tight and vulnerable budget. The Crocus Investment Fund, a labour-sponsored venture capital fund has also contributed on a sporadic basis by bringing in practitioners to speak to Winnipeg activists. To involve the Aboriginal community more fully in the development process, additional funding for community development education is essential, as is more explicit encouragement and funding of community development projects. One without the other is unlikely to work for, as Neechi have pointed out, inner city development projects must rely for their long-term viability on a commitment from local residents and those earning their incomes in the inner city to help retain local incomes in the community. The Neechi/WNFED approach also requires the local community to consider the development potential of all activities taking place in the community, from house building to medical services, and even to food banks. Such an approach is quite alien to the way governments and those working and/or living in the inner city tend to think and behave (Rothney, 1992). To transform current patterns would require a good deal of community activism and the availability of resources to work out in detail how alternatives might be developed.

Some of these resources ought to be channelled into training programs for community economic development officers, with strong business and planning skills, specifically for the inner city. There is a model on which to build, namely the All-Chiefs and Métis training programs of the mid 1980s. These officers could be sponsored and later hired by the economic arms of the Aboriginal institutions, revamped according to the first recommendation, and/or they could be attached to CEDA, SEED or directly to neighbourhood organizations. The absence of this capacity in the city is particularly striking.

More attention needs to be given to stabilizing the urban Aboriginal population. This is important not only in building a sense of geographic community, but also for improving the educational accomplishments of Aboriginal children. More quality housing at affordable prices is needed and should be attainable. This may mean diverting the housing component of social assistance into innovative housing schemes, be they privately or cooperatively owned, for the Aboriginal community and others. It may mean giving greater weight to sweat equity in calculating down payments for CMHC loans. It will certainly require a commitment of finacial resources by all three levels of government, along the lines of the housing trust fund proposal put forward by inner city groups. However it is accomplished, it ought to be possible to increase or improve the housing stock in ways which involve little or no net drain on government resources since the indirect returns from improvements in housing should more than offset the direct cost.

Economic development initiatives by the Aboriginal community must be complemented by bolder and more systematic efforts at employment equity and affirmative action (Loxley, 1996). At all three levels of government, employment equity programs are encountering serious problems. The number of Aboriginal recruits is too low, their turnover is too high, they are concentrated in junior and impermanent positions, and they tend to be ghettoized in certain occupations or departments. If significant progress is not made in the immediate future, the Aboriginal community should press for legislative changes to make employment equity targets mandatory and to sanction non-compliance.

Our preference is for Aboriginal capital corporations, with boards which are representative in terms both of gender and age, to ultimately replace funding agencies of the federal and provincial governments to which Aboriginal people apply directly. These should be funded adequately to cover overhead costs and a reasonable level of inevitable bad debts.

Addressing the poverty of single-parent families will require action on a number of different fronts at once. Clatworthy's three-pronged approach still has relevance (Clatworthy, 1981b). This combines longer-term occupational training programs with increased access to stable, relatively high-paying jobs, facilitated by a relaxation of the barriers to participation in the labour force. The principal barrier is, of course, adequate childcare facilities (Loxley, 1993). The state ought also to "recognize the productive work of parenting" (Falconer, 1990, p. 205) and adjust transfer payments so that they provide a decent "wage" to those who choose to stay at home and care for their children. Finally, as the movement to self-government proceeds, it is vital that Aboriginal institutions be fully representative of single-parent women, of women generally and of all age groups, including youth and the elderly, so that the particular economic concerns of these groups will not be overlooked or given insufficient weight and so that the community can draw to the fullest on their talents and experience.

Funding for the Access Program and New Careers ought to be restored. Both levels of government could link some aspects of the programs more explicitly to their own employment equity goals and to the needs of Aboriginal self-government, but the programs have a much wider rationale than this. The Provincial government should also reinstate social assistance payments for youth returning to school to complete their education.

Ultimately, however, it will be the extent to which the Aboriginal community can be mobilized to draw on its inner strengths and abilities which will determine the pace of Aboriginal development in Winnipeg. State resources will have an important role to play but Aboriginal pride and determination to be self-reliant in the long term will be more important. It is for this reason that the holistic approach of Neechi, with its emphasis on using available resources as fully as possible to meet the needs of the community and its recognition that one cannot separate economic development from social and cultural development, appears to offer the most coherent way forward for Aboriginal economic development in the City of Winnipeg.

Note

[1] The APS counted Aboriginal people on the narrower basis of self-identification, rather than ancestry or ethnic origin, on which the 1991 Census was based.

References

Aboriginal Council. *Discussion Paper: Self-Determination for Urban Aboriginal People, (Based upon Assorted Aborginal Experiences from the Urban Area of Winnipeg)*, Presentation to Royal Commission on Aboriginal Peoples, Edmonton, Alberta, June 21-23, 1992.

All-Chiefs' Budget Committee. *Midas Economic Development Institution: A Manitoba Approach to Indian Economic Development Concept and Proposals*, Assembly of Manitoba Chiefs, April 1984.

Black, Errol, and Jim Silver (eds). *Hard Bargains: The Manitoba Labour Movement Confronts the 1990s* (Winnipeg: Manitoba Labour History Series, Winnipeg, 1991).

Cardinal, Douglas. *Neeginan: A Vision of Hope and Healing*, for the North Main Task Force, Winnipeg, undated.

Clatworthy, Stewart J. *Patterns of Native Employment in the Winnipeg Labour Market*. (Winnipeg: Institute of Urban Studies, University of Winnipeg, 1981 a).

———. *Issues Concerning the Role of Native Women in the Winnipeg Labour Market*. (Winnipeg: Institute of Urban Studies, University of Winnipeg, 1981b).

———. *The Effects of Education on Native Behaviour in the Urban Labour Market*. (Winnipeg: Institute of Urban Studies, University of Winnipeg, 1981 c).

———. *Native Housing Conditions in Winnipeg*. (Winnipeg: Institute of Urban Studies, University of Winnipeg, 1983 a).

———. *The Effects of Length of Urban Residency on Native Labour Market Behaviour*. (Winnipeg: Institute of Urban Studies, University of Winnipeg, 1983 b).

———. *Final Evaluation of the Winnipeg Core Area Agreement Employment and Affirmative Action Program* (Winnipeg Core Area Initiative, September 1987).

Community Inquiry Board. *Community Inquiry into Inner City Revitalization: Final Report*, June 25, 1990.

Damas and Smith Limited. *Neeginan: A Report on the Feasibility Study*. Prepared for Neeginan (Manitoba) Incorporated, April, 1975.

Daugherty, Wayne. *A Guide to Native Political Associations in Canada* (Ottawa: Treaties and Historical Research, 1982).

Epstein Associates Inc. *Final Evaluation of the Winnipeg Core Area Agreement Economic Stimulus Programs* (Sector 2 Programs), Submitted to Stewart J. Clatworthy, Evaluation Manager, Winnipeg Core Area Initiative, November 1987.

Falconer, Patrick. Appendices for the Report on: *Urban Native Community Economic Development and NEDP's Element II: Problems, Prospects and Policies*, submitted for consideration, August 30, 1985.

———. "The Overlooked of the Neglected: Native Single Mothers in Major Cities on the Prairies," *The Political Economy of Manitoba*, edited by Jim Silver & Jeremy Hull (Regina: Canadian Plains Research Center, 1990.

Fulham, Richard Scott. *Economic Strategy for Urban Indians*. Urban Indian Assocation of Manitoba, October 1987.

Fulham, Stanley A. *In Search of a Future* (4th ed.) (Winnipeg: KINEW Publishers, January 1981).

Hull, Jeremy. *Native Women and Work: Summary Report of a Winnipeg Survey*. (Winnipeg: Institute of Urban Studies, University of Winnipeg, 1984).

———. "Aboriginal People and the Labour Movement," in Black and Silver, (eds) 1991.

Human Resources Canada. *Report on First Nations, Métis, Inuit and Non-Status Peoples in Winnipeg's Urban Community: Information Generated from the Place Louis Riel Round Table held November 9 and 10, 1998*. (Ottawa, 1998).

Krotz, Larry. *Urban Indians: The Strangers in Canada's Cities* (Edmonton: Hurtig Publishers, 1980).

Lagasse, Jean H. *A Study of the Population of Indian Ancestry Living in Manitoba* (Winnipeg: The Social and Economic Research Office, Dept. of Agriculture and Immigration, 1959). Appendix: *The People of Indian Ancestry in Greater Winnipeg*.

Loxley, John. "The Great Northern Plan," *Studies in Political Economy*, vol.6, 1981.

———. *The Economics of Community Development*, A Report Prepared for the Native Economic Development Program, H.K.L. and Associates, Winnipeg, 1986.

———. *Childcare Arrangements and the Aboriginal Community in Winnipeg*, A Report Prepared for the Royal Commission on Aboriginal Peoples, Winnipeg, November 1993.

———. *Aboriginal People in the Winnipeg Economy*, A Report Prepared for the Royal Commission on Aboriginal Peoples, Winnipeg, February 1994, revised, September, 1996.

Manitoba Indian Brotherhood. *Wahbung: Our Tomorrows*. (Winnipeg, 1971).

Manitoba Indian Women's Association. *Summary Report of Meeting and Organization Chart*, Manitoba Indian Women's Association Annual Meeting at the Balmoral Hotel, Winnipeg, Manitoba, November 20 - 22, 1973.

Métis Economic Development. *Currents of Change* (Winnipeg: Pemmican Publications Inc., 1986).

Rothney, Russell. *Neechi Foods Co-op Ltd.: Lessons in Community Development* (Winnipeg Family Economic Development Inc., July 1992).

Sawchuk, Joe. *The Métis of Manitoba: Reformulation of an Ethnic Identity* (Toronto: Peter Martin Associates Ltd. 1978).

Social Planning Council of Winnipeg. *Winnipeg Census Data Insights & Trends Aboriginals*, An Information Kit, 1989.

———. "Toward a Solution to End Child Poverty in Manitoba," *Child Poverty in Manitoba: An Approach Towards its Elimination*, Winnipeg, 1992.

———. *A Review of Changes in the Demographic, Educational, Economic and Social Conditions of the Registered Indian Population of Manitoba—1971 to 1981* (Winnipeg: May 1982).

Statistics Canada. *Schooling, Work and Related Activities, Income, Expenses and Mobility*. (Ottawa: 1991 Aboriginal Peoples Survey, 1993).

Stevens, Harvey. *A Review of Changes in the Living Conditions of the Registered Indian Population of Manitoba During the 1970s*. (Winnipeg: Social Planning Council of Winnipeg, 1982).

Thunderbird Consulting. *An Economic Strategy for The Manitoba Métis Federation*, Presented to The MMF Economic Development Technical Group, Winnipeg, 1992.

Welfare Council of Greater Winnipeg, *Annual Report*, Winnipeg, 1954.

Wien, Fred. *Rebuilding the Economic Base of Indian Communities: The Micmac in Nova Scotia*. (Montreal: The Institute for Research on Public Policy, 1986).

Winnipeg Core Area Initiative. *Canada-Manitoba-Winnipeg Tripartite Agreement 1986-1991*, Public Information Program of the Winnipeg Core Initiative, 1986.

———. *Status Report*, Programs and Projects to September 30, 1989, 1986-1991 Core Area Agreement, Public Information Program of the Winnipeg Core Area Initiative.

———. *Final Status Report*, Program Activities to September 30, 1987 Under the 1981-1986 Core Area Agreement, Public Information Program of the Winnipeg Core Initiative.

———. *Canada-Manitoba-Winnipeg Tripartite Agreement for Development of the Winnipeg Core Area*, Selected Indicators of Program Objectives Achievement, prepared by the Evaluation Program, August 1992.

———. *Partnerships for Renewal—Canada-Manitoba-Winnipeg Tripartite Agreement 1981-1992*, Public Information Program of the Winnipeg Core Area Initiative, 1992.

Winnipeg Development Agreement. *1999 Update*, Governments of Canada, Winnipeg and Manitoba.

Winnipeg Native Family Economic Development Inc. *It's Up to All of Us: A Guide to Community Economic Development in Winnipeg's Inner city*, February 1993.

Working Margins Consulting. *Evaluation of the Winnipeg Core Area Employment and Affirmative Action Initiative: Detailed Findings Report*, Winnipeg, September 1991.

Chapter 6
In The Face of Poverty:
What a Community School Can Do
By Heather Hunter

William Whyte Community School is located in one of the poorest urban neighbourhoods in Canada. It is an inner city school serving 325 children and youth from nursery to grade eight. The overwhelming poverty in Winnipeg's inner city is a major obstacle to the educational attainment of these children.

Families with children in the William Whyte Community School catchment area experience severe economic deprivation. In 1996, 69 percent of households had incomes below the Statistics Canada Low-Income Cut-Offs, 62 percent of families with children were lone-parent families, the unemployment rate was 25.8 percent, and the proportion of individuals with less than grade nine education was 26 percent. For each of these indicators, William Whyte was among the three worst-ranked elementary schools in Winnipeg School Division No. 1 (Winnipeg School Division No. 1, 1997/98, Part E, Table One, p. E3).

The mobility rate—total student transfers as a percentage of average month-end enrolment—was an astonishing 89.8 percent in 1997/98. Average enrolment that academic year was 243; there were 218 total transfers. William Whyte's mobility rate and total number of transfers was the highest among inner city elementary schools (Winnipeg School Division #1, 1997/98).

The adverse impact of such mobility and such a high incidence of poverty on childrens' ability to learn is dramatic. This has been confirmed repeatedly in the literature on poverty and educational attainment (Coleman, 1969; Kozol, 1991; Cole, 1997).

This research finding is simply obvious when one works daily with children in the inner city. They spend their childhood in substandard housing where heat, light and water may be absent. They often are not adequately clothed. They are often cold. They face scarcity of food. They lack safe recreation opportunities, sports equipment, music lessons, fun clubs like Brownies and Cubs. There is a dearth of community club facilities, community hockey, soccer and baseball leagues. They have to learn, as best they can, to adjust to the cyclical life events of having money and not having money, of having food and of having none left, of having a safe place to live and having it turn unsafe.

Acknowledgments

I wish to acknowledge Jim Silver's significant contribution in re-working and consolidating parts of earlier drafts of my PhD dissertation into this single chapter, in order that the story of the William Whyte Community School could be told. I am also very happy to acknowledge the commitment and dedication of the William Whyte staff and the neighbourhood families, without whose efforts the work done at William Whyte Community School would not have been possible.

Poverty can savage the collective spirit of our community. Students transfer often, in and out, right through the school year. Parental involvement ebbs and flows corresponding to family mobility in the neighbourhood. Changes can be tragic and unpredictable. Two students, nine-year-old girls, on their way to the local swimming pool, are struck and killed by a drunk driver suspected to be on his way to the "low track"—where adolescent girls work as prostitutes. A sniffer burns to his death in a house just down the street from the school. He was set on fire by students, ten- and twelve-year-old boys, who'd had enough of his solvent-related abuse. School and families become destabilized when children are apprehended, older students have charges laid or get taken into custody, parents go missing, children go missing, someone does not come home the night before, or children get hurt, even die in house fires, in the kind of accidents and unanticipated life events which seem to occur too often in this community. These are day-to-day realities which impede educational attainment.

All the evidence is clear: stronger and more stable families and communities are the key to better school performance by children in poverty. What is needed, therefore, is a way to stabilize family and community life and to create economic opportunities for people in the community. That is what we tried to do at the William Whyte Community School from 1992 to 1999.

The Need For a Community Focus

Traditional educational approaches focus on individual learners and on the need to provide them with the various skills and competencies needed to escape poverty. Even when successful, the result of this approach is that change is of the individual, not collective, sort. The underlying problem—the poverty that prevails in the community—remains unchanged, and continues to adversely affect families and communities, and therefore educational attainment, even though some individual students may overcome their conditions of poverty.

Even worse, this focus on the individual student may lead to dealing with inner city school children in a manner referred to by some as the "pedagogy of poverty." The pedagogy of poverty is characterized by teaching practices that have been reduced to emphasizing basic skills. The lack of emphasis on academic learning is attributable, in part, to the fact that the research makes clear that achievement test scores of poor children are affected primarily by their socio-economic class. The evidence suggests that pre-education supports and strong school leadership can to some extent counteract the effects of poverty, but too often the knowledge of the adverse effects of poverty on students' educational attainment leads only to low expectations on the part of teachers and schools, with the result that a self-fulfilling prophecy is set in motion: it is assumed that poor kids will do poorly in school, so school educational standards and expectations are set very low, with the result that children in poor neighbourhoods do poorly in school. This kind of "pedagogy of poverty" is completely inappropriate, because as long as the individual students and their disadvantages are the focal point of an inner city educational strategy, the real problem will continue to go unattended.

This focus on the individual student as the problem, rather than on conditions of poverty as the problem, has a long pedigree. Typical approaches to failure in school have moved over time from the genetic hereditarian explanation, to the notion of cultural deprivation, to the now commonly-held concept of "at risk" students:

Community Change

In the mornings on my drive to work and as I walk through the front doors of the school and even before I set down my brief case on my office chair, I find myself always newly aware of this school and our community. Sometimes it is an awareness which hits me even prior to my arriving at the school's receiving doors. There are always so many physical changes which alter the neighbourhood landscape. Perhaps a house has burnt to the ground during the night, or is boarded up and newly decorated with a "Condemned" notice nailed to plywood covering the front door, or is left empty, unexpectedly vacated by a family who more than filled it the day before. In front yards, on sidewalks and boulevards, can be seen other evidence of changes—broken glass in the street, broken furniture left for trash, a broken door or a bullet hole through a front window. Very young children play in the school yard an hour and a half too early for the breakfast program which starts the school day.

This community awareness of change is fundamental to teaching and learning at our school. We learn of these events from the news on the radio, when it turns itself on in the morning to begin a new day, or as we listen in morning traffic, or from the looks on the faces of fellow staff already at work in the office but without their usual cheery salutations and good-natured griping which characterize the beginning of the school day.

> The popular "at risk" construct, now entrenched in educational circles, views poor and working class children and their families (typically of colour) as being predominantly responsible for school failure, while frequently holding structural inequality blameless (Valencia, 1997, ix).

This "blame the victim" approach applies not only to education, but also to racism and health care:

> In race relations, we have social engineers who think up ways of "strengthening" the Negro family, rather than methods of eradicating racism. In health care, we develop new programs to provide health information (to correct the supposed ignorance of the poor) and to reach out and discover cases of untreated illness and disability (to compensate for their supposed unwillingness to seek treatment). As we might expect, the logical outcome of analyzing social problems in terms of the deficiencies of the victim is the development of programs aimed at correcting those deficiencies. The formula for action becomes extraordinarily simple: change the victim (Ryan, 1976, p. 8).

It is clear that the problem is not the victim; the problem is poverty and its effects on families and communities. If it were possible to promote the development of the community—to overcome the adverse effects of poverty by creating opportunities for families in the community—then overall educational attainment would improve. As Maeroff argues:

Those who want to raise educational standards and improve classroom learning must acknowledge—especially so far as the one in five students who live in poverty are concerned—that the out-of-school lives of these students cannot be ignored.... Families and communities, too, need help if they are to structure relationships that provide children with values and opportunities in harmony with productive learning (Maeroff, 1998, p. 425).

What, then, can a local school in a low-income inner city neighbourhood do to have a positive effect on the community and on families in the community in order to improve the levels of educational attainment? The answer, I believe, is in large part to be found in community economic development, and the role that a community-based school can play in a community economic development strategy.

Community Economic Development

Community economic development (CED) is an effective strategy for combating poverty and building community. It is a response to the fact that the inner city's economy is like a sieve: most of the money that flows into the inner city drains right out, without producing any local benefits. Inner city schools can play a part in blocking this drainage and keeping money in the inner city by hiring and purchasing locally. Doing so is community economic development: using local resources to meet the needs of the community.

In Winnipeg's inner city the most comprehensive articulation of the principles of community economic development has arisen from the work of an inner city Aboriginal workers' cooperative called Neechi Foods Community Store. These principles first appeared in 1993 in the Neechi Foods document titled *It's Up To All Of Us* (Loxley, Chapter Five). They have been endorsed by numerous inner city organizations, including William Whyte Community School, where they serve as a guide for CED initiatives.

As John Loxley pointed out in Chapter Five, the first three of the CED principles in *It's Up To All Of Us* constitute a "convergence" approach—income earned in the inner city should be kept in the inner city. At William Whyte Community School we attempted to do this by purchasing and hiring locally.

William Whyte Community School

William Whyte was rebuilt in 1975, at a time when ideas about open area and community schools—or at least what were then thought of as community schools—were optimistically identified as solutions to the special needs of inner city education. The old school building was a large, three-story, wooden structure—a school house classic of its day. The classrooms featured big windows, worn wooden desks, old-fashioned cloakrooms and actual black boards.

The now not-so-new William Whyte Community School is a modern structure, with somewhat the appearance of a concrete bunker. Indented entrance-ways, initially designed to be invitational with sheltered access into the school, are now blocked by additional fire doors. This means that children have to go through three sets of heavy doors just to get into the school. The few exterior windows

Inner City Communities

I asked four inner-city school principals how things in their schools were different from schools in the wealthier districts in the city. They looked at each other, laughed for a moment, then began talking non-stop, frequently interrupting each other. In their schools the kids often came to school hungry. A great many were poorly dressed. In the winter few had adequate warm clothing. Many suffered severe emotional stress. There were not field trips. They couldn't afford to belong to the community leagues. No movies, no going to see hockey games. There were no computers in their homes. Few books. Some kids even came to school not knowing what a book is. In the summer there was no place to go. By mid-June many of the children became distressed; without the school lunch program, what would they eat?

The list went on and on and on. After about half an hour I asked them how many kids they had in their school, and how many played organized hockey. They answered quickly, one after the other: "240-none," "220-none," "306-one," "198-none," (Hurtig, 1999, p. 25).

have been caged in black mesh metal. A covered courtyard along the south side of the building, meant to be a place for the younger children to get fresh air playtime even on wet days, is also caged in and inaccessible. These changes were ostensibly made to prevent glass breakage and to discourage people from urinating in the doorways during the evening and early morning hours. Still, the overall effect makes the school seem inaccessible, and gives it a physical appearance more like a community jail than a community school.

The schoolyard occupies a full city block. Across the street is an aging brick building, a former Jewish parochial school, circa 1900. A few years back, our school and community council were responsible for developing a plan and securing funds to refurbish this site. It now houses the Andrews Street Family Centre. The rest of the neighbourhood is residential, but since the school yard is the only green space around, the school takes on the feeling of a community centre with lots of children using the swings and play structure after school and in the early evening. Benches in several places are used by the older students and adults to hang around and watch neighbourhood activity.

When I started as Principal of William Whyte in 1992 I was greeted by a frenzy of meetings, with many workers in attendance, and a line-up of children in the school office coming with difficult-to-control behaviours starting even before opening exercises at 9 a.m. Five families had their children apprehended directly from the school with little or no information or follow-up. This was clearly not a school in which it was going to be easy to accomplish our educational mission.

The first steps were to listen to and share ideas about practical improvements with the teaching staff. Some of the most obvious areas of concern became the take-off points to our becoming community-based. Perhaps the most obvious difficulty in 1992 was the overwhelming number of special needs children and high-risk families. Of the 280 children then enrolled at William Whyte Community School, 190 were listed as special needs, open to some kind of Child Guidance Clinic intervention, or for whom other special education programming had been

Anna

I will always remember my encounter with Anna on my first day back at work after being on maternity leave. Anna was eight years old and in grade three and very much at risk, having already found her way onto the street.

She has the brightest eyes, glossy dark hair, and when she is smiling, she's just a little more beautiful than when she's not. At the morning recess, she was sent in with a couple of other girls for being too bossy about who uses the swings. Our enrolment generally builds steadily throughout the school year, so that by March, the playground equipment goes from being not good enough to do the job to being woefully inadequate. After a short mediation session, which is how we deal with conflict at the school, my recalcitrant group was back to the playground. Just before noon, the secretary asked if I had time to see Anna. Strange, I thought. Anna seemed to take ownership and contribute to solutions to the problems she was involved with earlier. She usually wasn't the kind of child who would be on the look out for more difficulties to bring to the office.

I was right. What Anna had to share with me was her individual initiative. She had crayoned a colourful poster of children on swings, lots of swings. It was captioned "Dear Ms. Hunter, I'm glad yur back so I will help you raiz money to buy more swings: My friends will help, to. From Anna ." Yes. I'm glad that I'm back, too.

---

requested. In terms of child protection and family support, Winnipeg Child and Family Services (CFS) were also very involved. In the year prior to my appointment, 450 referrals were made from the school to the CFS neighbourhood office. Given the 200 teaching days in the school year, this referral rate averages more than two calls a day.

This was the climate in which we introduced community-based schooling at William Whyte.

The Practice of Community-Based Schooling

Community-based schooling as it was practiced at William Whyte from 1992 to 1999 was based on the assumption that the local school is an important site for community development initiatives. Community-based schooling starts with the local school, but it extends to the development of the community that the school is intended to serve. This approach considers the local school as, in effect, a form of capital that can be used to support children and families and to strengthen the local community.

At William Whyte Community School, we did this in two ways. The first had to do with the implementation of community economic development strategies intended to strengthen the neighbourhood economic base. The second had more to do with community education and the use of school resources to create for members of the community more opportunities for voice, sense of agency and responsibility for action as the means to promote individual development and collective strengthening of the community.

Community Economic Development: Strategies at the Local School Level

Our community economic development initiatives were intended to keep money in the community by hiring and purchasing locally, and creating jobs and training programs for local people wherever possible.

At our school, food was purchased for the nutrition program from Neechi Foods Community Store. In this way, from its nutrition budget the school supported another community development initiative by contributing in excess of $10,000 to its annual retail sales. This money stayed in the community, creating local jobs and adding to the stability of the community—a pre-condition for educational success in the inner city. The practice of providing nutritious daily snacks to all of the students at the school was supported by an annual grant of $5,000 from an anonymous donor. This money, too, was spent locally.

Another initiative, community-based hiring practices at the school, had the most significant results. Several years back, an ad hoc hiring committee with membership from staff and parents determined that criteria for hiring at the school would be that any one hired: must first care for children; should be a First Nation or Métis person; should be Access-trained (the provincial Access program enables members of disadvantaged groups to take advantage of post-secondary education) with an understanding of the inner city and of community education; and should have facility in a First Nation language. If one or more of these criteria were missing in a candidate, then he or she had to possess very special talents to share with the children and the community.

The result was significant changes in staffing at William Whyte. In 1992/93 there were no Aboriginal teachers and only two teachers with Access education training. By 1998/99 over 60 percent of professional staff were Aboriginal, from the community, and/or Access-trained.

In addition, there were significant changes to the staffing of teacher assistant positions at the school. In 1992/93, there were 6.5 teacher assistant positions. Of these, less than 30 percent were Aboriginal and/or community people. By 1998/99 the number of paraprofessional jobs potentially available for community people had tripled to 19 positions, of which more than 75 percent were filled by Aboriginal and/or community people.

Much of this increase can be attributed to the practice of trading off professional time in order to increase the number of teacher assistant positions in the school. The decisions for this aspect of school staffing were, for the most part, left to the local school. This was made possible by the School Division's support for local school decision-making, and its commitment to equity in school staffing. Yearly planning processes at the school consistently ranked the assignment of a teacher assistant to every classroom in the school as being a top planning priority.

Other employment opportunities were created at the school. The "community school project" generated three positions—community, family and youth workers—with annual salaries of approximately $30,000 each and a program budget of $15,000. The money was raised on a project basis, largely from various government sources but also from the United Way and from local foundations. Grateful though we were for this essential financial support, it is nevertheless the case that in the absence of *sustained* funding, an inordinate amount of time is consumed by the seemingly endless paperwork involved in preparing funding applications and meeting varying reporting and accounting requirements.

The three workers were responsible for an exceptional amount of after-school and summer programming to support community-based schooling at William Whyte and to build linkages with the community. This alone was of enormous benefit in a community starved of recreational facilities. But also, this project injected over $100,000 annually into the local economy. All of these positions were occupied by women who lived in the community—two of them had children attending the school—and who first became involved at William Whyte as volunteers, then got jobs as teacher assistants. They are now in these higher paying positions carrying out, in highly responsible ways, "cutting-edge" community development work.

There is a pattern of parental involvement at the school, by which individuals first volunteer at the school and then move to paid positions either working in the school or in another community organization. For example, Andrews Street Family Centre, which emerged out of the community-based schooling efforts at William Whyte, has hired more than ten parents who had been volunteers at the school. Since its opening, Andrews Street has hired many others from the community. These hiring practices are considered to be one of the strongest ways in which community-based institutions can contribute to stabilizing the economic base in an inner city neighourhood. Between the two, William Whyte Community School and Andrews Street Family Centre added approximately forty jobs to the local William Whyte community in the 1990s—an important contribution to strengthening and stabilizing local families and the community.

Community Education Development at the Local School Level

A second kind of activity strengthened the local community by using the school as the means to create opportunities for individuals in the neighbourhood to be involved in school decision-making. A model of local control of school organization and governance creates opportunities for input from families, staff and students about all aspects of school programming. This effort to democratize school decision-making by opening it to the community and seeking the active involvement of parents is predicated upon the view that creating opportunities for decision-making by members of a community who are normally overwhelmed by the decisions of others, or are immobilized by institutional structures, is an important way to promote individual development and to strengthen community. People who live in poverty will benefit from schools which operate in such a way that they become the actors—the ones who shape and create their world—rather than the acted upon. It is an essential element of community-based schooling.

Twenty years ago, William Whyte Community School was known as a "community" school. But, it was different. I know, because I was there. I taught grades five and six as a beginning teacher. Back then, the school reflected the philosophy of the community school movement. We had a community education worker whose job was to involve parents in the school and to assist teachers to connect with families. As a workplace, it was probably more democratic than most schools are now, thanks to the leadership of the principal at the time. All areas of school life were planned and organized by the staff. The school was hot with new ideas for open area, whole language, thematic and concrete math activities, with a strong commitment to a child-centred, experience-based philosophy of learning, and to the community school movement. Parts of this worked wonderfully; parts just flopped. But this could be said to be the case with most approaches to school administration.

What didn't work well—and this wasn't evident to me until my years of teaching began to be influenced more strongly by the ways we learn from history and from the poor—is that this inner city community school of twenty years ago was a school where the teachers were doing *for* the community. We certainly were not working *with* the community, at least not in the ways where community is the centre and has voice.

At William Whyte from 1992 to 1999, community-based change efforts did not appear, on the surface, to be that much different from conventional school change initiatives, but they were.

Right inside the front entrance to the school was a classroom that had been converted into the community room. It was a large, bright room with a small fridge and stove, sink, drink machine and phone. Tables and chairs for meetings of forty to fifty people were moved to one side to allow for a less formal seating arrangement for parents who used the room on a daily, drop-in basis. The cupboards held supplies from Winnipeg Harvest and other food donations. Generally a plate of crackers or day-old muffins was out for people to help themselves. The coffee was always on, started by whichever parent was first in for the day. In the corner of the room, preschool children played with toys, crayoned at a small table, or just ran around. While this room and the parents and other community people and staff who occupied it appeared as the most tangible evidence of community presence in the school, it represented only part of the changes which took place at the school.

Members of the community council were the most frequent occupants of the community room at the school. Over the years, it served as point of entry for many who would otherwise have been reluctant to spend time at the school. Following the model which has the school functioning as an extension of the family, the community room was like a second living room away from home.

School organization, the instructional program and support to students all reflected a community-based approach. School planning involved staff and parents in annual processes of goal setting, action planning, evaluating outcomes, and reestablishing school purpose. There were opportunities for everyone—not only staff but also parents—to have a voice in important decisions. Community school organization meetings were held in the afternoon of the second Friday of each month so that staff and parents could carry on with this planning. Afternoons of the fourth Friday each month were used for school-directed professional development which included parents if the sessions were relevant for them, such as training sessions on the Internet and e-mail held in the school's computer lab, or if parent input was needed, such as discussions about expectations for students or core educational outcomes.

The school community council met weekly as a morning coffee club, and in the evening once a month. This group of parents concentrated their efforts on addressing larger community issues which affected the school. They took action on issues of community safety, housing, youth recreation, and family services. They also worked to establish more cultural programming and opportunities for learning First Nations languages. For example, an immersion Ojibway language program for parents was introduced with two hour sessions twice a week after school. This was an entirely volunteer effort with elders from the community assisting with language instruction and parents making potluck and childcare arrangements.

All of this is consistent with the philosophy of community-based schooling. The school was organized to function as an extension of the family at the student level. If there were problems for a child at our school, school policy required that the family was to be the first contacted to discuss these concerns. This was the responsibility of the classroom teacher. The assumption was always that the family cared about the child's problem and would be able to help. For each child, the teacher was responsible for the planning and implementation of an individual educational program which would foster development of the whole child. For some children, those who present severe learning challenges, this responsibility for planning is shared with other community services. While the school received resources similar to those of other inner city schools, staff and parents made decisions about the nature of supports for students that represented a radical departure from conventional student support systems. This occasioned some resistance from within the system, but it produced positive results, and we persevered.

Support for teachers who had this larger responsibility for their students was planned and reviewed yearly. Class sizes were kept under twenty and teacher assistants were assigned full time to each classroom. Daily physical education, cultural arts and computer classes were scheduled so that classroom teachers had about three times more planning and preparation time than the 180 minutes per cycle prescribed by Manitoba Education. This allowed them time to respond to their students' needs. A strict protocol for student support at the school required parental consultation and agreement to individual educational plans or other interventions, which made the daily presence of so many parents at the school a very useful thing for staff. The school was not separate from local families and community.

Andrews Street Family Centre

Several years ago, the William Whyte Community Council arranged funding to establish a family centre located across the street from the school. Andrews Street Family Centre assists families, youth and young children to participate in practical activities to improve their own situations. Evolving out of the model at the school, this community development initiative was aimed at gaining local control of social service resources. The Andrews Street Family Centre does not try to help families learn how to "live with" their current situation. Instead, it provides a supportive environment to facilitate growth in self and neighbourhood capacity. Activities at the Centre are guided by the principles of empowerment, sustainability and social action.

The intent of the Andrews Street Family Centre is to provide a focal point within the community where families can become involved in meaningful ways to solve their own problems and meet their own needs. It represents an amalgamation and integration of existing and new programs and supports located within one neighbourhood and operating under a community ownership framework. Programming is not intended to serve primarily as a referral service where individuals or families are directed to professionals for assistance with their needs. Nor is it intended to be a crisis-intervention centre. It is intended to build internal capacity within individuals and families and to support the enhancement of existing family structures and strengths.

Community Council

While the principal doesn't get to vote, she does attend community council. Next to visiting and learning from the children and staff in the classrooms, it's one of the most affirming experiences on the job. I think back to how tired I was, really feeling beat when I left school on a second Monday of the month, the night for our community council meeting. It had been a crazy day. Just ask me if I got one thing done that I had planned to do and I would tell you "NO." Regardless, I needed to get home to be with Stepheny until her daddy could take over to let me get back for the school meeting. Did I feel like going back? Not at all. But I did.

The parents on the community council bring their children to the meeting. The daycare was set up in the nutrition room and it was really nice to see the kids having fun together. We always have dinner at community council meetings and it is a good thing to be able to share a meal with people you care about. The laughter and games are special too. On this night, chicken and rice are on the menu. The raw materials were purchased earlier in the day by Jennifer and Sitara, our family worker and community worker. They elicited the help of a few other parents to cook and serve food for the thirty parents in attendance and for the more than fifty children who have come along with their parents. The meal is served first to the children; then we adults line up to fill our plates. Everything tastes great and the meeting begins. On the agenda are the regular reports and, on this night, there is also a presentation from the Block Parent Association which seems to fall on less than impressed ears. I am not sure but I think I know why.

Nevertheless, the meeting goes on and on to a point where I am beginning to feel my obligations at home will not get done if we don't end soon. As we come to the end of the meeting, I hear Jennifer and Sitara cry out "don't anybody leave yet!" They refer to the "birthday board" they had constructed as parents came in. Even before we could sit down, we had to give them our birthdate. This information got written on a very bright, cheerful looking display board. Now, to end the meeting, we are instructed by these two to go around the group saying one thing we like about someone in the group and then wish them "Happy Birthday." Never mind that it was nobody's birthday in particular on the night of the council meeting. Their push was to get us to celebrate with each other now. So, what I got to say was "I'm Heather, Principal of this school, and I'm very glad that Eleanor is here. She is starting work in our Nursery program as a teaching assistant. Apart from the fact that Eleanor is a mom at our school with her three children attending, she was also my student at Argyle Alternative High School some ten years ago. I have always admired and respected Eleanor's determination and capacities as a student and a mother over the years. Happy Birthday, Eleanor."

Andrews Street Family Centre

I think about a visit I made recently to our Family Centre, remembering that a few years ago, the building that houses the Centre was mostly vacant, unkempt and vandalized. Situated directly across the street from our school, it sat unused and deteriorating like so much of the neighbourhod infrastructure. This Family Centre now employs twenty-seven people from the community and provides many resources previously unavailable in the neighbourhood. And so, it is with a certain feeling of pride and sense of accomplishment that I entered its doors.

It was ten o'clock Monday morning, late February. The place was humming. At the top of the stairs, a small office houses the community patrol. The past president of our parent council heads up this project— another example of peoples' skills blossoming when given opportunities. To the right, another room serves as a community store run as a cooperative. Selected items are priced low to benefit people in the neighbourhood whose main alternative is the corner store economy. The reception area has an assortment of people working and utilizing services offered by the community kitchen, childrens' play area, and a washer and dryer available for community use. I approach the crowded office of the Director. She's on the phone trying to nail down some funding for a project involving some neighbourhood moms attending a weekend camp. The potential for sharing and building community is powerful. My guess is that if she is successful in getting the funds for this camp, the women who participate will return with yet another long list of things to be done to strengthen families and improve the neighbourhood.

Many useful community-based programs are run out of the Andrews Street Family Centre. The place is a bee-hive of activity. The purpose is to create the environment in which the community itself can build the capacity to meet their own needs. Programs run out of Andrews Street include, among many others, a Moms Helping Moms Support Program, the pre-school Oshki-Majahitowiin Program (Aboriginal Head Start Initiative), a parent-child drop-in centre, sharing circles, a community kitchen at which people get together to plan and cook meals, a food-buying club, and the much-used free access to laundry and telephone facilities. These programs involve people in the community working together to meet their own needs.

All of this work has been based on the direct requirements of the neighbourhood, as identified through an initial community survey. The primary focus of efforts to date has been family support and stability, child development, and the development of an overall "model" for local ownership and support in dealing with neighbourhood issues.

The Andrews Street Family Centre is very much a part of community-based schooling. The idea is that lower levels of educational attainment in poor inner city neighbourhoods are best addressed by strengthening community, and families in the community.

Conclusion

Most schools could lay claim to being community schools. Fewer schools could be described as being community-based. In this study, I have considered the fundamental ideas behind community-based schooling and have argued that its purpose is to contribute to the development of an economic response to the problems of poverty and education.

This model of community-based schooling has developed from ideas tested, first hand and in practical ways, at one of the poorest inner city elementary schools in Canada. In my experience, the manner in which the business of living and learning is conducted in our neighbourhood school can go a long way to strengthen the economic base in our community.

Seven years is probably not a long time-frame to test the approach of community-based schooling as a concrete and practical way to respond to the issues of poverty which have confronted educators in Winnipeg's inner city. But it was long enough for me as the Principal of William Whyte Community School to see some constructive gains. Much more remains to be done, of course: what we tried to do at William Whyte Community School was only a beginning. But it was a good beginning. Sometimes I have been accused, albeit in friendly ways, of being overly positive and hopeful when it comes to explaining the successes we had at the school. People may be left with the impression that we found, in our community-based approach, a perfect solution to the issues of poverty and education. Such flawless outcomes are not possible. Nevertheless, for those who live and/ or work daily in the harsh circumstances of Winnipeg's urban core, a positive and constructive outlook is necessary for survival. The community-based initiatives that I have tried to describe here are grounds for a positive and constructive outlook.

References

Albert, Michael. *Thinking Forward: Learning to Conceptualize Economic Vision* (Winnipeg: Arbeiter Ring, 1997).

Apple, Michael W. *Education and Power* (New York: Routledge, 1982).

——. *Ideology and Curriculum* (New York: Routledge, 1990).

Aronowitz, Stanley, and Henry A. Giroux. *Education Still Under Siege* (Toronto: Ontario Institute for Studies in Education, 1993).

Barlow, Maude and Heather-Jane Robertson. *Class Warfare: The Assault on Canada's Schools* (Toronto: Key Porter Books, 1994).

Blakeley, Edward J. *Planning Local Economic Development: Theory and Practice* (Thousand Oaks, CA: Sage Publications, 1994).

Boomer, Garth, et al. (eds.). *Negotiating the Curriculum: Educating for the 21st Century* (London: The Falmer Press, 1992).

Boscardin, Mary Lynn, and Stephen Jacobson. "The Inclusive School: Integrating Diversity and Solidarity through Community-based Management," *Journal of Educational Administration*, Vol. 35, No. 5, 1997.

Bowles, Samuel, and Herbert Gintis. *Schooling in Capitalist America* (New York: Basic Books, 1976).

Brown, Rexford G. *Schools of Thought* (Oxford: Jossey-Bass, 1991).

Chernomas, Robert. *The Social and Economic Causes of Disease* (Winnipeg: Canadian Centre for Policy Alternatives-Manitoba, 1999).

Chambers, Robert. *Rural Development: Putting the Last First* (Essex: Longman Scientific and Technical, 1983).

Christenson, James A. and Jerry W. Robinson Jr. *Community Development in Perspective* (Iowa: Iowa State University Press, 1981).

Cole, Mike, et al. (eds.) . *Promoting Equality in Primary Schools* (London: Cassell, 1997).

Coleman, J.S. *Equal Educational Opportunity* (Cambridge: Harvard University Press, 1969).

Connell, R.W. *Schools and Social Justice* (Toronto: Our Schools/Our Selves Education Foundation, 1993).

Darling-Hammond, Linda. *The Right to Learn*(San Francisco: Jossey-Bass Inc., 1997).

Freire, Paulo (ed.). *Mentoring the Mentor: A Critical Dialogue with Paulo Freire* (New York: Peter Lang Publishing, 1997).

——. *Pedagogy of the City*(New York: Continuum, 1995).

——. *Pedagogy of Hope: Reliving Pedagogy of the Oppressed*(New York: Continuum, 1992).

——. *The Politics of Education*(Massachusetts: Bergin and Garvey, 1985).

——. *Education for Critical Consciousness*(New York: Seabury Press, 1973).

——. *Pedagogy of the Oppressed*(New York: Seabury Press, 1968).

Furman-Brown, Gail. "Editor's Foreword," *Educational Administration Quarterly, Special Issue: School as Community*, Vol. 35, No. 1, 1999.

Greene, Maxine. "What Counts as Philosophy of Education," in Wendy Kohli (ed.), *Critical Conversations in Philosophy of Education* (London: Routledge, 1995).

——. *Releasing the Imagination: Essays on Education, the Arts, and Social Change* (San Francisco: Jossey-Bass Publishers, 1995).

Hammond, Barry, and Ken Gibbons. "Testing in Schools," *Quarterly Review of Economic and Social Trends in Manitoba* (Winnipeg: Canadian Centre for Policy Alternatives-Manitoba,) Vol. 1, No. 2 (Spring) 1999.

Henderson, Anne T. and Nancy Berla (eds.). *A New Generation of Evidence: The Family is Critical to Student Achievement* (Washington: Centre for Law and Education, 1994).

hooks, bell. 1994. *Teaching to Transgress: Education as the Practice of Freedom* (New York: Routledge, 1994).

Hull, Jeremy. *Natives in a Class Society* (Regina: University of Saskatchewan, 1979).

Hurtig, Mel. *Pay the Rent or Feed the Kids: The Tragedy and Disgrace of Poverty in Canada* (Toronto: McClelland & Stewart Inc., 1999).

Illich, Ivan. *Deschooling Society*(New York: Harper and Row, 1970).

——. *After Deschooling, What?* (New York: Harper and Row, 1973).

Kozol, J. *Savage Inequalities: Children in America's Schools* (New York: Harper Perennial, 1991).

Leistyna, Pepi (ed.). *Breaking Free: The Transformative Power of Critical Pedagogy* (Cambridge: Harvard Educational Review, 1996).

Levin, Benjamin. "Poverty and Education," *Education Canada*, 1995.

Loxley, John. "The Great Northern Plan," *Studies in Political Economy*, No. 6 (Autumn) 1981, Pp. 151-182.

Maeroff, Gene I. "Altered Destinies: Making Life Better For Schoolchildren in Need," *Phi Delta Kappan*, Vol. 79, No. 6, February, 1998.

McLaren, Peter. *Revolutionary Multiculturalism: Pedagogies of Dissent for the New Millennium* (Boulder, CO: Westview Press, 1997).

Miron, Louis F. *The Social Construction of Urban Schooling: Situating the Crisis* (Cresskill, NJ: Hampton Press, Inc., 1996).

Nemiroff, Greta Hofmann. *Reconstructing Education: Toward a Pedagogy of Critical Humanism* (Toronto: Ontario Institute for Studies in Education, 1992).

Nozick, Marcia. *No Place Like Home: Building Sustainable Communities*(Ottawa: Canadian Council on Social Development, 1992).

Ryan, William. *Blaming the Victim*(New York: Vintage Books, 1972).

Simon, Roger I. *Teaching Against the Grain: Texts for a Pedagogy of Possibility* (Toronto: Ontario Institute for Studies in Education, 1992).

Tierney, William G. *Building Communities of Difference: Higher Education in the Twenty-First Century* (Toronto: Ontario Institute for Studies in Education, 1993).

Valencia, Richard R. *The Evolution of Deficit Thinking: Educational Thought and Practice* (London: The Falmer Press, 1997).

Wells, Gordon. *Changing Schools from Within: Creating Communities of Inquiry* (Toronto: Ontario Institute for Studies in Education, 1994).

Chapter 7
Solutions that Work:
Fighting Poverty in Winnipeg's Inner City
By Jim Silver

A close examination of Winnipeg's inner city reveals a contradictory reality. The socio-economic circumstances of a large proportion of inner city residents continue to deteriorate, generating a wide range of problems, while at the same time, in the midst of these inner city problems, exciting and innovative community-based initiatives are underway. These community-based initiatives, together with adequate levels of public investment in people, constitute the basis of a long-term solution to the problem of inner city poverty in Winnipeg.

The Problem of Poverty in Winnipeg's Inner City

In Chapter Two, the appalling growth of poverty in Winnipeg was documented in quantitative terms, using customized Census Canada data. These findings are confirmed over and over again by those struggling daily to deal with the consequences of poverty in Winnipeg. What follows are but a few of a great many such examples.

In April 1997, in an unprecedented move, the United Way of Winnipeg released a report that arose out of a series of five meetings with the executive directors of forty-seven United Way member agencies and that expressed their concerns with the seriously worsening circumstances of lower-income Winnipegers. Since the United Way has traditionally been at pains to avoid any hint of political controversy, the mere fact that the report was publicly released is significant. The United Way agencies reported that "while the demand for their services is growing and becoming more complex, the resources to respond to these demands are shrinking and shifting" (United Way, 1997, p. 4). The head of one health-related agency is quoted as saying: "We can now only meet the needs of those who come by their own personal initiative. There are many more out there who need help" (p. 10). In many cases, "basic physical supports such as food, bedding and housing" are no longer being met (p. 9). Among the results are:

> ### Acknowledgments
>
> For their useful comments on earlier drafts of this chapter I am grateful to Jean Altemeyer, Wayne Antony, Errol Black, Paul Chorney, Parvin Ghorayshi, John Hofley, Bob Jones, Margaret Little, John Loxley, Greg Selinger and Tom Simms. I also want to thank the many inner city organizers and administrators, whose names are listed at the end of this chapter, who generously agreed to speak with me about their work in Winnipeg's inner city. They are putting into practice the solutions that work.

… increasing levels of anger and despair among young people, even in six and seven year olds. This hopelessness translates itself many times in involvement in gangs, petty crime and prostitution (United Way, 1997, p. 10).

The roots of the problems are in worsening levels of poverty. "Again and again," the report stressed, "agencies made the link between poverty and increasing needs," and from there to a wide variety of increasingly serious social problems.

Similar conclusions were drawn in a study prepared for Manitoba Health in March 1995. Health care costs are directly affected by poverty: those in the poorest income groups are ten times more likely to be admitted to hospital than those in the highest income groups; indeed, "there is no determinant of health that impacts more on the health of individuals than poverty" (Manitoba Health, 1995, pp. 30 & 58). Numerous studies confirm that poverty is a major contributant to rising health care costs (See, for example, Toronto Food Policy Council, October, 1997; Wilkinson, 1996).

Child and Family Service (CFS) agencies are massively overloaded and are struggling under the weight of the rapidly growing demands being placed on them by the multifaceted results of growing poverty. Between 1985 and 1995/96 the number of children in care in Manitoba grew by 62 percent and reports of physical and sexual abuse of children grew by 242 percent (CUPE, 1996, pp. 1 and 5). An external review of CFS Winnipeg reported in March 1997 that government funding for the agency had grown from $45 million in 1992/93 to $60 million in 1996/97, and that costs are projected to continue to grow very rapidly over the next five years (Prairie Research Associates Inc., 1997, pp. 5 and iii).

So constrained are the resources made available to CFS agencies relative to the explosion in demand for services that a survey of social workers and support staff at CFS Winnipeg and CFS Central, conducted by the Canadian Union of Public Employees in 1996, found that 92 percent of social workers who responded "… did not believe it was possible/realistic to comply with all aspects of the Child and Family Services Act," and "almost 90 percent of all respondents indicated they did not feel that the current Child Welfare System is able to adequately meet the needs of families and children" (CUPE, 1996, Appendix IV, pp. 6 and 9). In 1998 the *Winnipeg Free Press*, describing an internal report prepared by Winnipeg Child and Family Services, listed "… the issues upon which everyone seems to agree":

- "There are more children being taken into custody by Child and Family Services, a result of increasing stress on families;
- There are not enough foster parents to meet the demands of a province that takes more children per capita into care than any other;
- More money is going into the child welfare system but with little positive result;
- Child welfare workers—the front-line staff in the war to protect at-risk children—are horrendously overworked;
- Not enough preventative measures are in place … ."

The result, not surprisingly, "… is a system paralyzed by uncertainty and under threat of being swamped by demand" (Lett, June 3, 1998).

Manitoba also has the highest rate of violent youth crime and of youth incarceration in the country: "Both the Manitoba Youth Centre and Agassiz Youth Centre are occupied beyond their capacity" (Manitoba Health, 1995, p. 67).

The Hughes Report, arising out of the independent review of the riot at Headingley Correctional Institute on April 25 and 26, 1996, concluded that massive public expenditure was needed to solve the problems he found. The inmate population at Headingley has changed dramatically very recently: "... in 1992, there was not a gang problem. By 1993 it was beginning to emerge. By 1994 it was firmly there" (Manitoba, 1996, p. 53). Members of these gangs, especially the Indian Posse and Manitoba Warriors, actively and often violently recruit new members while incarcerated—making counterproductive a strategy that leads to Manitoba having Canada's highest rate of youth incarceration—and, "... once a member, it is ... often close to impossible to withdraw from membership when back out on the street" (Manitoba, 1996, p. 53).

These gangs and the Headingley population generally are largely Aboriginal. A September 1996 survey found that "... the prison population at Headingley was approximately 70 percent Aboriginal" (Manitoba, 1996, p. 96). This proportion has grown dramatically in recent years. The Aboriginal Justice Inquiry(AJI) reported that in 1983, 37 percent of admissions to Headingley were Aboriginal; in 1989, 47 percent of Headingley's population and 55 percent of Manitoba's total jail population were Aboriginal. The Inquiry added that: "On October 1, 1990, 64 percent of the Manitoba Youth Centre's population and 78 percent of Agassiz's population were Aboriginal youths" (Manitoba, 1991, pp. 9-10).

Why is gang activity growing? Hughes, a former Deputy Attorney-General of British Columbia, offers this explanation:

> Gang membership offers an attractive and often glittering alternative to many who are poverty stricken, have few if any skills to market on their own, and are caged within a life without hope ... .They are likely candidates for recruitment, because so many of them have lives full of despair, flowing from the poverty that besets them (Manitoba, 1996, p. 123).

The United Way report said the same: "We are competing with gangs because they are perceived as having more to offer" (United Way, 1997, p. 10). Keith Cooper, then CEO of CFS Winnipeg, added, "We will continue to feel significant impact from poverty and hopelessness resulting in street gangs and violence" (CFS Winnipeg, 1994/95, p. 5). And why are gang members and prison inmates disproportionately of Aboriginal descent? Justices Hamilton and Sinclair, authors of the Aboriginal Justice Inquiry, suggest the following:

> ... we believe that the relatively higher rates of crime amongAboriginal people are a result of despair, dependency, anger, frustration and sense of injustice prevalent in Aboriginal communities, stemming from the cultural and community breakdown that has occurred over the past century (Manitoba, 1991, p. 91).

Aboriginal people in Manitoba are disproportionately poor. The Aboriginal Justice Inquiry said: "In Manitoba, Aboriginal people are the poorest of the poor" (Manitoba, 1991, p. 92). Approximately 50 percent of Manitoba's Aboriginal children and youth live in poverty. The death rate and the rate of suicide among Manitoba's Aboriginal youth are respectively four times and six times the provincial average (Manitoba Health, 1995). Although less than 10 percent of Manitoba's children are Aboriginal, approximately 50 percent of the Children's Hospital beds at any given time are occupied by Aboriginal children and almost 70 percent of the wards of CFS Winnipeg are Aboriginal (Manitoba Children and Youth Secretariat, 1997, p. 23). More than half of Winnipeg's street prostitutes, many of them adolescents, are Aboriginal.

Although levels of educational attainment correlate strongly with employment rates and income levels for Aboriginal people, educational attainment is made particularly difficult by the persistence not only of poverty but also of racism. An internal report prepared for the Manitoba government in 1998 refers to "... subtle yet powerful attitudes of bias and racism toward Aboriginal people ... at all levels of the system," and concludes that "... the 93 percent of Aboriginal youth who do not graduate from high school needs to have the highest priority"(Lindberg Consulting, 1998, p. 12). The educational needs of Aboriginal students do *not* have the highest priority. Indeed, the entire system is under-funded and over-stressed, and the particular needs of Aboriginal children, the products of a century of colonization and marginalization, are not being adequately addressed (Spillett, February 5, 1999).

Racism is deeply rooted and widely pervasive in Winnipeg. "White people don't know how prevalent it is ... and the effects just keep piling up" (Maracle, June 9, 1998). Unless addressed, these problems will get worse. The proportion of Manitoba's children under the age of 14 who are Aboriginal is growing rapidly: it was 9.1 percent in 1991; it is projected to be 17.4 percent, or more than one in six, by 2011 (Manitoba Health, 1995, p. 21).

Yet, as Keith Cooper, out-going Chief Executive Officer of Winnipeg Child and Family Services, said in his final Report: "... there is more and more a rhetoric that refuses to acknowledge the very existence of poverty and marginalization and their impact, let alone ensure resources that might assist the victims" (Winnipeg Child and Family Services, 1996/97, p. 5). When such a mind-set prevails, real solutions to poverty are not likely to be implemented.

Solutions that do not work

The Market-Based Approach

The market-based approach practised by the former provincial government was described by then Premier Filmon in December 1996. He said: "Nobody would ever suggest that there isn't a problem [with poverty]. But if we are going to help the disadvantaged, the first thing we're going to have to do is to have a healthy economy"(*Winnipeg Sun*, December 6, 1996). The implication was that the benefits of a healthy economy would "trickle down" to those who are poor.

The evidence makes clear that this did not happen. The public investments needed to address poverty were cut in the interests of a "healthy economy"; wages were kept low to attract capital from afar (Black and Silver, 1999). A study by the Canadian Council on Social Development found that many poor families, particularly in the Prairies, are fully employed, "... indicating that low wages were a major contributor to their market poverty" (Schellenberg and Ross, 1997, p. 38).

The decline in the minimum wage is evidence of what was a consciously-chosen low-wage strategy (Black and Shaw, Chapter Four).

An important study of the growth of inequality in Canada concludes that economic growth alone will not solve the problems of inequality and poverty, and conversely, attending to problems of inequality and poverty is likely to improve a society's economic capacity.

> The larger the segment of the population that is underhoused, underfed, undereducated, understimulated and underdeveloped in their economic political and recreational opportunities, the smaller the harvest of innovation, leadership or productivity. Conversely, invest in this group and you magnify your society's capacity to grow" (Yalnizyan, 1998, p. 75).

Associated with the growing levels of poverty that are a product of the market-based approach is an increased degree of "poor-bashing," of blaming the victim (Northcott, June 4, 1998; Riley, May 21, 1998; Selinger, June 3, 1998; Wiebe, May 27, 1998). Poor people in Winnipeg's inner city are increasingly labelled by those in positions of authority as "lazy," "incompetent," "untrustworthy" (Helgason, June 5, 1998; MacKinnon, Chapter 3). This response to the growth of poverty is no different than that of Ontario Premier Mike Harris, who justified cuts to pregnant mothers' prenatal benefits by saying that he did not want them using the money for beer, and of Prime Minister Chrétien, who is reported to have told a well-to-do audience that welfare recipients should be working rather than "... sitting at home, drinking beer ..." (Rebick, 1998). The clear implication is that poverty is the fault of the poor.

Such an interpretation has become dominant in North America since the 1980s. The work of the neoconservative American academic Charles Murray is often seen as having been particularly influential in the emergence of this interpretation, and it has since worked its way into Manitoba. Murray argued that welfare programs have removed poor peoples' incentive to work. The problem is lack of incentives; the cause is welfare; the solution is cuts to welfare and the introduction of workfare (Murray, 1984).

> Murray blamed lenient 1960s social policies for rising poverty, which provided a rationale for eliminating the right to welfare in the U.S. Indeed, in the Republican Party's 1994 "Contract With America," welfare reform became the "Personal Responsibility Act" (H.Silver, 1996, p. 123).

The 1994 "Contract With America" was followed in Ontario by the Harris government's 22 percent cut in welfare rates effective October 1, 1995, and the June, 1996 launch of Ontario's workfare program (Ontario Works), which in turn was followed in Manitoba by the former provincial government's sharp cut in welfare rates and introduction of workfare in 1996. These measures are rooted in the belief that welfare recipients are undeserving, that their behaviour and their values make them the authors of their own misfortune, and that therefore they need to be induced, by reduced welfare payments, or *forced*, by workfare, to take paid employment (MacKinnon, Chapter Three).

This appears to be what has been happening in Winnipeg's inner city. Many inner city administrators and organizers report that increased and sometimes unreasonable pressure has lately been put on single mothers on welfare to push them into low-wage jobs which, given the lack of supports, do not make economic sense for their families (Northcott, June 4, 1998; Riley, May 21, 1998; Wiebe, May 27, 1998). At the same time, the monitoring of small amounts of extra income earned by welfare recipients has been tightened, ironically creating a disincentive to work (Helgason, June 5, 1998).

The current welfare system is an insidious contradiction. It is not the solution to poverty in Winnipeg's inner city. In fact, it is part of the problem. It is a dependency model— it locks people into a dependency status, traps them, takes away their right to make their own decisions, demoralizes them, grinds them down, and erodes their dignity and sense of self-worth (Forest, May 20, 1998; Helgason, June 5, 1998; Riley, May 21, 1998; Simbandumwe, June 4, 1998). And yet, destructive though welfare is, current welfare rates are far too low, and must be raised— as a matter of urgent priority (Bruce, June 4, 1998; Northcott, June 4, 1998; Wiebe, May 27, 1998). Many of those on welfare in Winnipeg's inner city are unable to provide adequately for their families on the reduced levels of money they receive from welfare. The result is that poverty and associated problems are reproduced across generations. This is the strongly-held view of community administrators and organizers with years of inner city experience (Hammond, May 21, 1998; Helgason, June 5, 1998; Hill, June 17, 1998; Northcott, June 4, 1998; Wiebe, May 27, 1998). Blaming the poor for the growth of poverty simply distracts attention from real causes.

The same can be said for the rise of the "charity model" as a response to inner city poverty. As public expenditures have been cut, increasing reliance has been placed on charitable donations. There is an immense capacity in the volunteer sector to respond charitably to peoples' immediate needs. But the response, though genuine, is generally simplistic and non-systemic. It does not get at the roots of the problem of poverty. It responds to symptoms, not causes. It cannot provide solutions that work. The growth of food banks is an example. People contribute because it meets their genuine need to act, to help those in need. The corporate sector contributes because, among other reasons, they are strong advocates of the former Conservative government's market-based approach and its associated expenditure cuts. They prefer charity to a coherent strategy of public investment to combat poverty. But charity, like blaming the poor, serves merely to distract attention from the need to find and implement real solutions to poverty.

Blaming the poor for the problem of poverty, reducing welfare rates, resorting to workfare and responding to the problem with charity are not solutions that work. They are, however, responses to poverty that are logically associated with a market-based approach to managing the economy—an approach which has contributed significantly to the growth of poverty in Winnipeg's inner city.

However, the traditional public sector approach—the top-down design and delivery of social service and other programs by government officials to inner city residents—is also a solution that does not work. It is a strategy that turns the intended beneficiaries of such programs into "clients" rather than into active participants in solving their own problems.

Government Delivery of Programs to and for Inner City Residents

Public investment is an essential part of any anti-poverty strategy directed at Winnipeg's inner city. But it cannot come in the form of programs delivered from the top; it must take a form that facilitates and encourages the active participation of those who would be its beneficiaries. This is a conclusion borne out by the failure of recent Winnipeg-based anti-poverty programs. In an analysis of their failure can be found the seeds of an approach which, when combined with adequate public investment in people, can provide the basis of solutions that work.

The evidence suggests that those strategies used to date in Winnipeg's inner city—i.e., those strategies involving the delivery of programs to and for inner city residents—have been largely unsuccessful. The deterioration of the inner city has advanced steadily throughout the entire post-war period, and the poverty and related problems now appear to be more severe than ever. This is the case despite numerous government programs. Consider, for example, the Winnipeg Core Area Initiative (Loxley, Chapter Five).

A conflict around the proposed Sherbrook-McGregor Overpass and the fate of the Logan neighbourhood, together with the important role played by federal Liberal Cabinet Minister Lloyd Axworthy, led to the creation in 1981 of the ambitious Core Area Initiative (CAI), a multi-faceted, tri-partite, five-year program which was extended with additional funding for a further five years, and was extended yet again, but with no additional funding, for a final year. A more recent version of this initiative is the Winnipeg Development Agreement—a five-year, tri-level, $75 million program that began in 1995 and that targets all of Winnipeg, not just the core area.

The two Core Area Initiatives directly pumped $196 million into Winnipeg's downtown and inner city between 1981 and 1992 (Winnipeg CAI, 1992). However, while some aspects of its comprehensive strategy appear to have been successful—housing and job training for example (Clatworthy, 1987; Winnipeg CAI, 1992; Decter and Kowall, 1990)—and although it has been called "without precedence in Canadian urban planning practice," and "… one of the most ambitious urban revitalization efforts in North America" (Kiernan, 1987, p. 23; Winnipeg CAI, 1992, p. 9), the CAI was nevertheless limited in its impact on poverty in the inner city (see Loxley, Chapter Five).

This is so for several reasons. First, the dollar amount contributed was not as large as may at first appear—$20 million per year, which is less than 2 percent of the estimated $1 billion total annual income of core area residents (Winnipeg CAI, 1992, p. 15). Second, a large portion of the CAI's investment went into "bricks and mortar" projects, such as the North Portage Place, and as an Economic Council of Canada study concluded:

> Major physical projects such as North Portage are vulnerable to the criticism that while they relocate economic activities from suburban areas to the downtown, they do little to address poverty and unemployment in the inner city (Decter and Kowall, 1990, p. 46).

The Director of an inner city agency added sarcastically: "Our concern is the way the resources were allocated …. For example, Portage Place must be the most expensive drop-in centre for inner city children in North America" (WFP, July 4, 1991). The overemphasis on such large capital projects and their irrelevance to the socio-economic circumstances of Winnipeg's inner city has been a constant throughout the post-war period (Jim Silver, 1996; Silver and Black, 1998). The same will almost certainly prove to have been the case with the more recent Winnipeg Development Agreement(Santin, December 5, 1999). Writing about Winnipeg's inner city in 1975, when he was Director of the University of Winnipeg's Institute of Urban Studies, Lloyd Axworthy, later the driving force behind the Core Area Initiative, and co-author Pat Christie, said:

> The major efforts at physical renewal, those undertaken by government and the private sector at a cost of many millions of dollars have limited relevance to the real problems of the core. The problems ... poor housing, poverty, alcoholism, lack of jobs, are not helped in any significant way (Axworthy and Christie, 1975, p. 78).

The 1990 Community Inquiry into Inner City Revitalization made another criticism of the CAI, and it is this criticism which contains the seeds for fruitful change. The Inquiry found that the CAI was not sufficiently participatory; it did not involve inner city residents to the extent that was possible and desirable. This theme emerged repeatedly at the 1990 Community Inquiry and was expressed succinctly by the Inquiry Chair, former Director of the University of Winnipeg's Institute of Urban Studies, Professor Tom Carter, who observed after the Inquiry's hearings that:

> It was obvious from the many well-articulated presentations at the Inquiry that there is a substantial level of expertise in inner city communities, and this expertise is begging for the opportunity to play a more active role in planning and program delivery (Carter, 1991, p. 4).

The Manitoba Association of Social Workers was one of many presenters to the Community Inquiry calling for a more active role for the community in planning and program delivery:

> Neighbourhoods must be more directly involved in the planning process and not just serve in an advisory capacity ... .The MASW believes that the overriding goal of a new agreement should be to transfer ownership of the revitalization process and resources to the community itself and allow the residents of the core area to shape their own future (MASW, 1990, pp. 61-62).

The rationale behind the inner city community's call for control of the revitalization process was put most clearly by the Inquiry Coordinator, in her summary of the May 9, 1990 hearings:

> The basic case was put as follows: inner city residents hold the key to sustained revitalization efforts. In principle, they have the most at stake, and their needs and aspirations—not those of outside institutions or investors—should prevail. In practice, a number of organizations and projects have demonstrated that residents can assume effective decision-making and administrative control over local issues and initiatives, given appropriate developmental support. If public sector intervention is to be preventive rather than remedial in nature, resources should be allocated to community and self-help, grassroots projects/groups that foster local ownership and responsibility" (Inner City Inquiry, Summary of May 9, 1990 hearings).

Solutions That Work

Further Evidence in Support of a Community-Based Approach

The merits of a community-based approach to governance have been argued repeatedly in recent years, in a wide variety of contexts. For example, the case is forcefully advanced in an empirical fashion by Robert Putnam, in his analysis of regional governments in Italy since 1970 (Putnam, 1993). What Putnam found is that those regional governments which have performed best on a range of government responsiveness and effectiveness indicators are those with a strong civic tradition—ie., those regions "... blessed with vibrant networks and norms of civic engagement," those regions characterized by "... patterns of civic involvement and social solidarity," those regions where "... a dense network of secondary associations both embodies and contributes to effective social collaboration" (Putnam, 1993, pp. 15, 83 and 90). It follows from Putnam's study that efforts to build and support community and community organizations in inner cities make sense. "By far the most important factor in explaining good government is the degree to which social and political life in a region approximates the ideal of the civic community" (Putnam, 1993, p. 120). Putnam also refers to other empirical work which substantiates this view.

> Summarizing scores of case studies of Third World development, Milton Esman and Norman Uphoff conclude that local associations are a crucial ingredient in successful strategies of rural development: 'A vigorous network of membership organizations is essential to any serious effort to overcome mass poverty under the conditions that are likely to prevail in most developing countries for the predictable future ... we cannot visualize any strategy of rural development combining growth in productivity with broad distribution of benefits in which participatory local organizations are not prominent (Putnam, 1993, p. 90, quoting Esman and Uphoff, 1984, p. 40).

Esman and Uphoff also find, however, that "... local organizations 'implanted' from the outside have a high failure rate," and that the "... most successful local organizations represent indigenous, participatory initiatives in relatively cohesive local communities" (Putnam, 1993, p. 91).

And in Manitoba, a 1998 evaluation of three community-based projects, two in Winnipeg and one in The Pas, which fit the "healthy community concept"—an approach which seeks "... to put control into the hands of residents and their neighbourhoods"—suggests that the impact of these community-building projects is likely consistent with the findings of Putnam, and of Esman and Uphoff. The evaluation concludes that: "Even with less than two years of action, each community shows evidence of progress towards achievement of their intentions ... ." The community-based approach appears to be "... a method of breaking the cycle of hopelessness," leading the evaluators to conclude that: "Over the longer term, stronger communities can provide community-based support to individual residents (particularly youth and others at risk) before crisis situations occur, providing an alternative to costly and dependency-building service interventions" (Social Planning Council of Winnipeg, May 1998, pp. i, ii, iii and 28).

A complement to this community-building approach is community economic development (CED). There is considerable evidence that inner city organizations want a CED approach. In Winnipeg's Aboriginal community, for example, there exists a well-articulated vision of a locally-based, CED strategy based on a "convergence" approach to economic development. The convergence approach is rooted in the notion of local production for local needs and local reinvestment of profits (Loxley, Chapter Five).

Similarly, Marcia Nozick calls for "local production for local needs," and the meeting of local demand with "smaller scale industries and technologies which can be more easily managed by the community" (Nozick, 1992, pp. 14-15). Nozick provides examples of such local economic development: building and housing retrofit strategies to improve housing save energy and create jobs; co-op housing and other programs enabling home ownership to stem the outflow of rent money to absentee landlords; community construction companies that hire and train local residents; locally based financial institutions with local investment mandates; storefront science and technology centres to contribute in a practical fashion to local creativity and inventiveness. For as Nozick argues: "Entrepreneurial inventiveness and creativity are two of the most important human resources we have in creating new wealth for local communities" (Nozick, 1992, p. 57). The challenge is to use those abilities for the benefit of lower-income communities.

How this might be done, at least in part, has been demonstrated recently in very practical terms by the Winnipeg Community Economic Development Resource Group, whose detailed analysis and recommendations for hiring and purchasing practices by agencies and businesses located in the inner city is a model of community economic development planning (Muldrew and Simbandumwe, September, 1997). That this convergence approach can be put into practice has been demonstrated in the 1990s by, among others, the William Whyte Community School (Hunter, Chapter Six).

My hypothesis is as follows: inner city residents want to control the process of inner city revitalization through their own, indigenous organizations; there is considerable empirical evidence that doing so is a necessary condition for social and economic development; and this approach has not yet been tried in Winnipeg on the scale that is needed. With respect to this latter point, as one observer of former inner city initiatives put it, referring to the CAI: "Resources were not available for major citizen involvement, although planners had by now developed routine methods for limited involvement" (Kubiski, 1992, p. 9). It is real involvement that is needed.

It is clear that such a community-based strategy is not a passive welfare approach. Rather it calls for a new, more active role to be played by the state, in promoting and facilitating a local economic development strategy driven by the skills and hard work of the very people intended to be its beneficiaries. A coherent economic strategy that could achieve this end has long been articulated and promoted by community leaders in Winnipeg's inner city.

In what follows, I sketch the beginnings of a community-based strategy that is significantly different both from the market-based strategy of the former Conservative government, and the state-delivered strategies of most social democratic governments. My contention is that this community-based strategy, in conjunction with a strong economic commitment to job creation and the generous public funding of programs that invest in people, would in time begin to make serious progress in the eradication of inner city poverty.

Community-based organizations and their work in Winnipeg's inner city

To test these ideas, interviews were conducted with twenty-five inner city leaders—people who work in the inner city with community-based organizations and who have a close familiarity based on personal experience with the circumstances and the needs of inner city communities and with social and economic development strategies that do and do not work. They were asked three broad questions, and open-ended answers were encouraged. The questions were:
1. What are the main problems in Winnipeg's inner city?
2. What innovative and effective things are being done to counter such problems?
3. In what way(s) could a progressive government contribute to solving such problems?

There emerged a remarkable consistency of responses to the questions, not only as to the nature of the problems—their responses consistently confirmed the observations about the severity of inner city poverty outlined elsewhere in this volume—but also, and more importantly, as to the character of the solutions. There appears to be a set of views about inner city solutions that is widely held by skilled and experienced inner city administrators and organizers, and that is broadly consistent with the findings of empirical studies linking good governance and socio-economic development to the existence and active involvement of community-based organizations.

(i) Many of the Community-Based Institutions Are Already in Place

The foundations of such a community-based strategy are already in place. The strategy is rooted in the further development of a range of institutions, many of which are already operating in Winnipeg's inner city. These include, among many others: Andrews Street Family Centre, Community Education Development Association (CEDA), Native Women's Transition Centre, North End Women's Centre, Northern Star Collection, North End Community Renewal Corporation, West Broadway Alliance, Rossbrook House, West Broadway Development Corporation, William Whyte Community School, Niji Mahkwa School, Aboriginal Ganootamaage Justice Services, SEED Winnipeg, Just Housing, Inner City Housing Coalition, Neechi Foods Community Store, Christmas LITE (Local Investment Through Employment). These and many other similar institutions have emerged in response to the real and immediate needs of inner city residents. They are creative and flexible and are structured and operated and staffed in a fashion that is attuned to and suitable for the circumstances of those who use them.

However, most are currently too small and insufficiently resourced to make a serious dent in the problems at which they are aimed. This has long been the case in Winnipeg's inner city. More than twenty years ago Lloyd Axworthy and Pat Christie, after describing the limits of conventional approaches to inner city problems, referred with optimism to "… a number of new kinds of services [that] have emerged that are more activist and innovative than many of the traditional agencies," and which had emerged out of "… the work of community organizations." However:

> The difficulty with all these programs is that they are small, generally poorly funded, or in a pilot project stage. Therefore, they make only a small dent in the overall mass of need. What they do provide, however, are clues about the future direction that social service programs might take to change from a remedial passive role to more of a self-help, social entrepreneurship function (Axworthy and Christie, 1975, p. 48).

Little has changed since those words were written. Innovative inner city agencies continue to emerge, but most are so small and underfunded as to be little more than "demonstration projects."

(ii) The Problem of Underfunding

The underfunding of such agencies is a debilitating problem. Far too much staff-time is consumed in the seemingly endless search for more project-based funding—the Community Inquiry identified a primary concern with "the extent to which community energy is being diverted from program development and service delivery in order to patch together budgets from diverse, short-term funding sources" (Community Inquiry: Summary of Public Meeting, April 5, 1990, Rossbrook House)—and the numbers of those who wish to take advantage of such services far out-strip the capacity of these institutions to respond. As one experienced inner city organizer puts it: "Right now there's a lot of good projects, but their funding is always in question. We need to move from demonstration projects to programs that have continuity ..." (WFP, Nov. 29, 1998). Axworthy and Christie's observation, made almost a quarter-century ago and noted above, remains true today.

(iii) The Problem of Top-Down Bureaucratic Approaches

While more funding is needed, it is essential that it not take the form of the state delivering programs to and for inner city people in a top-down bureaucratic fashion. The needs of inner city residents are best served if programs are delivered by locally based, grassroots organizations that are staffed primarily by people who are drawn from and intimately knowledgeable about and committed to the inner city. It is those who are actually doing the work in the community who know what works, what does not work, and what is needed. They are the "experts." Government should be coming to them and asking what is needed, rather than designing rigid programs from a distance into which the community must fit (Knol and Goodman, January 26, 1999; Spillett, February 5, 1999). Programs designed by "someone on the sixteenth floor" (Simms, May 25, 1998)—what others working in the inner city have called "made in Charleswood"(a wealthy Winnipeg suburb) solutions (Hammond, May 21, 1998), or "template approaches" (Helgason, June 5, 1998)—delivered by "consultants" who are soon gone (Tetlock, January 21, 1999), by people who "fly into the community and fly out," serve to create only a "superficial relationship with the community" (Hill, June 17, 1998). They do not involve inner city people in solving their own problems.

    As observed earlier, many millions of dollars have at various times been poured into the inner city, but so long as they are top-down, outside-in approaches or short-term solutions they provide few real and lasting benefits. In their recent evaluation of community-based projects, the Social Planning Council of Winnipeg observed that existing inner city services "... predominantly take the form of service interventions to deal with immediate or crisis situations," and "... little long term 'success' can be identified when the focus is upon problems, or deficits."

> Generally, these formalized services are viewed as being external to the community and deal with the individual or family, not through building collective capacity of neighbourhood residents to deal with their own issues. In many instances, further dependencies are created through the need for such periodic interventions (Social Planning Council, May 1998, p. 6).

This has long been the case. Twenty-five years ago Axworthy and Christie observed that:

> Generally, the social service agencies in the core area provide only remedial or rehabilitative assistance rather than measures for developmental self-help. The paternalistic approach of social agencies has resulted in the creation of a whole series of dependencies from welfare to housing to employment. Consequently, the vast amount of resources going into the core area is minimal in its impact, and conditions in the area are not improving (Axworthy and Christie, 1975, p. 108).

Despite its numerous strengths, this was to a very considerable extent the case with Winnipeg's Core Area Initiative (CAI). Over and over again, as already shown, those inner city organizations and individuals making presentations to the March 1990 Community Inquiry Into Inner City Revitalization complained about the top-down decision-making process that characterized the CAI. What is needed is solutions that are made in the inner city by inner city residents.

(iv) A New Role for Government

The role of the state, of governments, is neither to design nor to deliver solutions. Rather, the role of governments, in consultation with inner city organizations, is to define and enforce a set of criteria and standards, and evaluation and accountability mechanisms, by which such organizations are to operate. And it is to fund, so as to make financially stable, those organizations which continue to meet such criteria and standards and which appropriately account for the expenditure of such funds. The state, in this model, does not design and deliver programs to and for the inner city, but enables and co-monitors—with inner city citizens—the design and delivery of programs by inner city organizations and residents. This is because, as Lucille Bruce puts it: "Most successful programs are those created within the community because the people understand the issues and [because they] hire community people."

(v) The Importance of Local Hiring, and the Need for a Staged Process

Although the hiring of community people to work in community-based organizations is a central part of the strategy being advanced here, this is not as straightforward an approach as might first be thought. A "staged" approach to moving into paid employment is needed. Many inner city people need entry-level jobs with built-in personal and work supports—indeed, such supports may in many cases be needed as part of a pre-entry-level work preparation program—in order to develop confidence and self-esteem as well as specific skills. It is the opportunity to work which builds confidence and self-esteem, but people lacking those attributes need to be brought into the paid labour force in a staged, step-by-step fashion, with adequate and appropriate supports in place. The provision of such supports is a labour-intensive process—it requires that would-be labour market entrants be the beneficiaries not only of accessible and appropriate training and educational opportunities and childcare facilities, but also of personalized attention. Such supports are best provided by community-based organizations staffed by people drawn from and personally knowledgeable about the inner city community and its people. In short, the job of providing the necessary institutional and personal and work supports to would-be labour market entrants requires a set of skills best attained by having lived in and become intimately knowledgeable about inner city communities.

Hiring locally thus sets in motion a virtuous cycle. At the Andrews Street Family Centre, for example, the initial premise was that the Centre would be professionally staffed, but professional staff were intended to work themselves out of a job on a fixed schedule. Local people would be hired and mentored to take the place of the professionals (Hill, June 17, 1998). Community people come to use the facilities at Andrews Street, as often as not to use the most basic things, like washing machines and telephones. Frequently they come just to talk with someone, with another adult. They may begin to build a relationship with others, and with staff, out of which emerges a clearer sense of their circumstances and their needs, which may result in their volunteering at the Centre. The philosophical foundation of Andrews Street includes a committment to identifying and building on peoples' strengths, not their weaknesses. Volunteer opportunities are plentiful: in the food-buying club, the clothing exchange, the community kitchen, the children's and teens' programs, the moms-helping-moms program and others. Those who demonstrate ability may be hired. Andrews Street has started a catering cooperative which provides casual and part-time employment to as many as ten people, has trained and hired people for home renovations and repairs, and also employs local staff in the moms-helping-moms program, among others (Knol and Goodman, January 26, 1999; Social Planning Council, May 1998). These opportunities give local residents not only much-needed income, but also equally-needed confidence and self-esteem.

Those working at Andrews Street can see, because they are immersed in the community, what else is needed. For example, they would like to open a "centre for practical learning," which would provide community-based education in literacy and computers and a variety of other needed skills. Such a centre would provide an intermediary step in the staged process, between volunteer work with one or more of the many Andrews Street programs and either paid employment or more advanced education at the Winnipeg Education Centre(WEC). (WEC is the university-level, community-based institution offering degree programs to inner city residents in education and social work). It is essential, say Dilly Knol and Janice Goodman, that such training be local, that it be physically located in the community and that it be run by people from the community. This community-based approach of creating sequenced opportunities through which people move at their own pace and in familiar, supportive and culturally appropriate surroundings is the philosophical foundation that makes this approach successful. It is an example of using local resources to meet local needs.

A similar process is set in motion when community-based schools hire locally to fill teacher aide positions (Hunter, Chapter Six; Selinger, June 3, 1998). This is a strategy begun in the late 1970s and re-introduced in the early 1990s, especially at William Whyte Community School. In the 1970s funds were available which:

> ... allowed schools to hire local residents as teacher-community aides and community workers to organize local residents so that the residents could articulate their needs. These programs met with some initial successes, but the overall effect of the effort has been limited by the short life-span of the programs (Johnston, 1979, pp. 187-188).

Nevertheless, the earlier effort appears to have been effective in developing local leadership (Johnston, 1979, p. 188; Selinger, June 3, 1998; Tetlock, January 21, 1999) and the same appears to be the case today (Hunter, Chapter Six).

At the North End Womens' Centre women pay a dollar for membership in a clothing exchange, which gives them access to clothing free of charge. Out of local womens' involvement in this initiative there emerged a sewing club to make things from tattered clothes. This enables staff to see who has what skills, who attends regularly, who would benefit from particular forms of training or education. Out of the successful experience of the sewing club, the North End Womens' Centre has started a small business, the Northern Star Collection, where traditional Aboriginal star blankets and winter parkas are made. The Northern Star Collection employed ten people in January 1999, including a general manager with experience in Winnipeg's garment industry. Plans are to expand to no more than twenty-five employees, and the expectation is that within two years the operation can be self-sustaining. The intention is to stay relatively small because to get too large would defeat the purpose. As Chris Tetlock, Director of the North End Womens' Centre, and Leroy White, Northern Star Collection's General Manager, point out, the inner city women now working at Northern Star have reached that point by way of a staged process. They have come through the North End Womens' Centre Sewing Club where they have acquired not only sewing skills but also, gradually, the self-confidence that they need to be productive employees. Moreover, Tetlock and White maintain, going directly into one of Winnipeg's large mechanized and impersonal garment factories would prove too alienating and would simply not work for most of these women. Therefore what is needed is both the more intimate and personal and staged approach that is typical of effective inner city organizations and the kind of practical business skills, tailored to the cultural circumstances of small inner city organizations, being used at the Northern Star Collection.

Yet another example is the Native Womens' Transition Centre, which is locally staffed by women who know from their experience about the needs of those who use the facility. The women admitted to the Native Womens' Transition Centre have multiple needs: they are frequently the victims of violence, often have low levels of formal education, rarely have experience in the paid labour force, have in some cases been forced to work the streets to feed their families, are in many cases the victims of racism, and are usually severely lacking in self-esteem and confidence. According to Lucille Bruce, it generally takes at least three months for women who come to the Native Womens' Transition Centre simply to begin to feel comfortable with and trusting of the staff. Healing, and the development of self-esteem, are long-term projects. Yet this past year two such women were successful in reaching the final stage in their applications to become students at the Winnipeg Education Centre.

The issue here is that community-based organizations staffed with community-based people are best suited to be able to identify and respond to the needs of the community, and to find the ways to move such people in a staged fashion into more productive roles in the community.

(vi) Specialized Education: The Winnipeg Education Centre

At the upper end of a staged approach to bringing inner city residents into the paid labour force is the Winnipeg Education Centre. WEC plays a crucial role in re-building the inner city from within. Many of the most skilled and dynamic administrators/organizers with inner city institutions are graduates of WEC, and in many cases they have entered WEC after the kind of staged and supportive introduction to the paid labour force described above. WEC offers university-level programs in social work and education, but it does so in a manner specifically designed to meet the needs of inner city residents. It is located in its own building, physically separate from either of Winnipeg's two university campuses, and it uses an Access model of education—ie., programs are tailored to meet the needs of, and supports are provided for, students. The physical separateness of the off-campus WEC site contributes to overcoming the alienation that inner city students might otherwise feel at either of the regular campuses, both of which have student bodies which are large and mostly culturally mainstream and middle class. The supportive environment and specially-tailored programs enable talented inner city students to compensate for the lack of preparedness for formal education that many bring with them to WEC.

The result is a much larger number of inner city students than would otherwise be the case who have university-level education. What is more, and what constitutes the enormous social and economic value of WEC, an exceptionally large proportion of WEC graduates return to the inner city to work—as teachers, school principals, social workers, administrators. The result is that a growing number of leadership positions are filled by people who possess not only formal educational qualifications, but also the crucially important job qualification of personal familiarity with the particular circumstances and needs of inner city residents. WEC therefore plays a major role in creating culturally-appropriate role models and of overcoming the numerous problems associated with bringing in and relying upon "experts" from outside the community.

The WEC model is such an important part of the solution to inner city poverty that it deserves to be expanded. The program ought to be expanded beyond education and social work to include a community economic development stream. There is emerging in the inner city a number of institutions committed to community economic development, such as Winnipeg Native Family Economic Development, SEED Winnipeg, the North End Community Renewal Corporation, the West Broadway Alliance. Such institutions—small and underfunded to date—aim to promote economic development in a fashion consistent with the socio-economic needs and circumstances of the inner city. Appropriately skilled people are needed to do this complex work, and in the long run it is best that these people come from the inner city. However, the post-secondary business training currently being offered at the University of Manitoba Faculty of Management, for example, is largely inappropriate, both for the educational needs of inner city students and for the socio-economic development needs of inner city communities. The Faculty of Management trains people for work in the corporate world; most graduates occupy positions in large, well-established corporations; they will have imbibed and will work in the context of a highly competitive and individualistic neoliberal ideology. The socio-economic needs and circumstances of the inner city are different, and thus both the institutions and the academic preparation for meeting those needs and working in those institutions ought to be different. WEC could be expanded to fulfil this need. The result would be community economic development workers who brought to their work not only formal and appropriate educational skills in areas such as finance and management, but also the equally important job qualification of personal and intimate knowledge of and committment to the inner city.

(vii) The Need For an Inner City Development Fund or Funds

While an expanded WEC would be funded by the same means as it is now—as part of Manitoba's array of post-secondary educational institutions to whom funding is allocated by the Council on Post-Secondary Education—the financing of those other inner city institutions which, in their expanded form, would constitute the backbone of an anti-poverty strategy in Winnipeg's inner city requires a new funding mechanism.

One option that deserves serious consideration is the establishment of an inner city fund or funds which would exist at arm's length from the provincial government, which would have the responsibility of allocating funds to inner city institutions which meet certain criteria and standards, and the majority of whose decision-making body would be comprised of people drawn from and with experience in and a committment to the inner city. A variant of this approach was advanced in the Community Plan for Winnipeg's Inner City, prepared in 1991 in the wake of the 1990 Community Inquiry into Inner City Revitalization, which in turn was organized in response to the then imminent demise of the Core Area Initiative.

The Community Plan included a decentralized program delivery system consistent with the observations made repeatedly in submissions to the Community Inquiry. Neighbourhood development funds would be allocated by local resident groups, to which support staff, themselves inner city people, would be attached. Such a decentralized mechanism could be a part of the proposed inner city fund. This body, or these neighbourhood-based bodies, in conjunction with the provincial government, would establish the criteria on the basis of which funds would be allocated to inner city institutions, would set the standards according to which such institutions would operate, and would create the reporting and accountability mechanisms needed to ensure that public money is being spent as intended.

One of the essential criteria—perhaps the most essential—would be that any inner city institution to which money is to be allocated would have to be a genuinely community-based project. This would mean asking such questions as: who designed the project; does it meet needs identified by the community; are community members involved on an on-going basis in making the decisions? Even the evaluation process works best if it involves the active participation of the community. As the Social Planning Council recently observed:

> The review and assessment process is most effective when residents/participants are directly involved. Alternately termed participatory evaluations, or social action research, this mechanism facilitates greater understanding of why certain project activities are more effective than others, and assists in charting directions for the future (Social Planning Council, May 1998, p. 25).

The inner city fund would constitute a pool of capital which might ultimately become the basis for an integrated set of community-based institutions offering training and education, delivering needed services and creating jobs for inner city residents.

Some of the institutions which are essential elements of a workable model are in place and need only the long-term funding commitments that would provide the stability and the scale demanded by the tasks to which they are directed. Other institutions would emerge in response to community needs. They should be funded cautiously at first, to ensure not only that they are genuinely community based, but also that they can demonstrate the organizational skills to achieve stated goals.

But even with a long-term funding mechanism in place, patience would still be necessary. Community economic development takes time. "There are no quick fixes here," Lucille Bruce emphasizes. But in time the opportunity structure in the inner city would begin to open up, significantly greater numbers of people would be gainfully employed, home lives would become more settled and stable, the healing of damaged people would accelerate, and the change would gradually become tangible.

(ix) The Importance of Housing

It would be advantageous to allocate a significant proportion of an inner city fund to housing needs, since an effective inner city housing strategy would be an essential element in an overall strategy targeted at inner city poverty. Several inner city organizations are currently involved in developing non-profit housing. These include Just Housing—a project which emerged out of the Community Education Development Association—two member groups of the West Broadway Alliance, and the newly-established Inner City Housing Coalition. Although such organizations have proved to be skilled and innovative, they do not have sufficient resources to achieve the scale that is needed to begin to have a significant impact. The cost of achieving a more significant scale is not exorbitant, and is certainly less than the benefits it would generate. These benefits would include, among others: job creation, the rehabilitation of valuable housing stock, and a serious attempt at halting rapidly declining inner city property values and thus the rapidly eroding inner city property tax base. The market value of inner city housing is declining dramatically, from an average of $40,000 in 1988 to $22,000 in 1998 in Winnipeg's north end (Aboriginal Council of Winnipeg and Inner City Housing Coalition, December 1998), a measure in itself of the decay of Winnipeg's inner city. The decay has reached the point, as predicted in a 1998 paper by the Canadian Centre for Policy Alternatives-Manitoba (Leo and Shaw, 1998, pp. 6-7), that fires are ravaging the many boarded-up and abandoned inner city houses and buildings. A housing renovation strategy is desperately needed.

The Aboriginal Council of Winnipeg and the Inner City Housing Coalition have developed just such a strategy—a practical, affordable and well-conceived plan that emerges out of their considerable community-based experience with inner city housing renovation. It calls for the establishment of an Inner City Home Ownership Co-operative Investment Fund, financed by a partnership of the voluntary, public and private sectors. The Fund would finance 250 home renovations per year for five years, a total of 1250 homes, and create 100 jobs for unemployed inner city women and men (Aboriginal Council of Winnipeg and Inner City Housing Coalition, December 1998). It is likely that the financial costs incurred would be significantly less than the many benefits that would result. This proposed initiative is yet another example of the many practical solutions to poverty that emerge out of the real-life experiences of those who live and work in the inner city.

(x) Economic Development Corporations

An important recent initiative is the emergence in the inner city of community-based economic development corporations. In 1997 the West Broadway Development Corporation was formed, followed by the North End Community Renewal Corporation in late 1998. They will be involved in a range of activities: upgrading and counselling individuals for job preparedness; business planning, training, financing assistance and on-going management advice and support for those who want to start their own businesses; building links between job seekers and local employers. The community development corporation becomes, in effect, a community-based "entrepreneur," identifying and promoting and facilitating locally-based opportunities. These development corporations share several important characteristics: they are structured in a non-profit, independent, non-governmental fashion; they are democratically controlled by the community; and they promote strategies that arise from local leadership in the community, rather than strategies that are a function of profit-seeking or are devised and delivered in a top-down, outside-in fashion. As Tom Simms commented:

> The "trickle down" economic development approach never seems to reach the residents of the inner city. In contrast, community economic development is a "trickle up" strategy that focuses on growing democratic, social and economic development at the grassroots level in order to ensure that inner city residents are the primary beneficiaries of the approach (Simms, June 27, 1998).

The community development corporation model has the added benefit of being the organizational means by which a variety of inner city community organizations can be loosely brought together—Aboriginal organizations, local businesses, religious and educational institutions, labour unions—and by which partnerships can be fashioned with the public and private sectors and philanthropic agencies in order to assemble significant financial resources for community development.

Community development corporations not only identify and nurture community-based initiatives, they also challenge the local business community to move beyond the charity model and, to the extent financially feasible, to re-orient their efforts to meet local needs. Community development corporations can sit down with Winnipeg businesses to determine the needs of those businesses and to consider how the community might meet those needs. The results might include, for example, the development of particular job preparation strategies to facilitate increased inner city hiring or the local provision of supplies previously purchased elsewhere. Similar arrangements might usefully be negotiated with educational and social agencies operating in the inner city (Hunter, Chapter Six). Given the size of these institutions, an increased proportion of inner city hiring and purchasing would provide a significant economic benefit to the inner city. This is consistent with the "convergence" approach discussed earlier. Community development corporations are the means by which such economic re-configuring, such convergence, might be negotiated.

The community development corporation approach, of course, has its difficulties. How, for example, can genuine community involvement be mobilized and sustained, particularly in communities ravaged by the effects of poverty? If such involvement cannot be sustained, would the result not simply be the emergence of yet another top-down, bureaucratic organization, delivering programs to and for inner city residents? These are difficult problems for which there are no easy solutions. Yet participatory institutions are operating in the inner city; highly skilled inner city administrators and organizers are already working effectively, despite the lack of resources, in the inner city; and a great wealth of energy and talent awaits only the opportunities and supports to begin to contribute to the process of inner city revitalization. The entire process would be advanced if, as suggested earlier, the Winnipeg Education Centre were to add to its program a community economic development stream.

(xi) A Widely-Held Philosophy

The philosophy which underpins the kind of strategy being described here is widely-held by those inner city administrators and organizers who were interviewed. It is the philosophy which guides the innovative, community-based work being done at the William Whyte Community School; which drives the organizational restructuring—the shift away from a "clinical" approach to childcare and towards a community development and preventative approach—currently underway at Ma Mawi Wi Chi Itata; which is the basis of a decade of work at Neechi Foods Community Store and of the recently-formed Aboriginal Ganootamaage Justice Services of Winnipeg; which provides the intellectual foundation for the new North End Community Renewal Corporation and the Inner City Housing Coalition; which is the basis for the North End Womens' Centre's Northern Star Collection; which characterizes the work being done at the Andrews Street Family Centre and the West Broadway Alliance and many other community-based organizations discussed here. This is consistent with the finding of Mike Maunder and Virginia Maracle, two writers who have produced an excellent series of press reports based on close observation of Winnipeg's inner city, and who conclude: "In a year of covering Winnipeg's inner city, by far the brightest lights we've seen are the dozens of programs that are being developed by inner city people themselves to tackle their own problems" (Maunder and Maracle, May 17, 1998). The same philosophy shapes many of the briefs presented to the Inner City Revitalization hearings. It is even found in *Winnipeg's Core Area*, the 1975 study co-authored by Lloyd Axworthy, who referred to innovative initiatives which provided "... clues about the future direction that social service programs might take to change from a remedial passive role to more of a self-help, social entrepreneurship function" (Axworthy and Christie, 1975, pp. 48-49).

These ideas constitute a culture—a widely-held, do-it-yourself culture. People living and working in the inner city see the needs of their communities, develop innovative ideas to meet those needs, and design and implement community-based responses. The pervasiveness of this energetic culture generates a creativity and a form of what, in another context, would be considered "entrepreneurship"— the identification, conceptualization and implementation of (non-profit) organizational responses to community (rather than market) needs. This philosophy holds that smaller is better and that better is also local, flexible, personal, and culturally sensitive. To date, most of these innovative inner city organizations have emerged independently of each other, just "bubbling up from the bottom," as Wayne Helgason puts it, as an expression of the energy and creativity of the inner city. Each embodies to a considerable extent this same philosophy and culture. It is a culture profoundly different from either the profit-oriented and individualistic neoliberalism of recent times or the top-down, bureaucratic culture by which outsiders deliver programs to and for the people of the inner city. Indeed, there is some evidence that bureaucratic social service agencies themselves see the virtues of this locally-based, community development approach. Child and Family Services, for example, is now launching all its new programs in partnership with community organizations, and its Executive Director speaks in glowing terms of the work being done by these community organizations (Maunder and Maracle, July 26, 1998). An adequate funding base, as would be possible with the establishment of an inner city fund, would result in the generation of a myriad of practical, community-based solutions. Indeed, a government inclined to promote this type of inner city economic development strategy could convene a group of experienced inner city administrators/organizers from Winnipeg and beyond and ask them what ought to be and can be done in the inner city. A weekend brainstorming session would generate a wealth of ideas for tangible and workable community-based solutions to inner city problems (Loewen, May 20, 1998; Riley, May 21, 1998).

Causation and Community-Based Solutions

Winnipeg's recent experience is consistent with a broader, global phenomenon: a growing proportion of urban populations is excluded from the formal economy—less exploited than excluded—and is concentrated spatially and ethnically, sometimes in inner cities as in the case not only of Winnipeg but also of many urban centres in the U.S. and Canada, and sometimes in outer peripheries as in many European cities. In these spatially and ethnically concentrated zones of intensified poverty, malign circuits of cumulative disadvantage are set in motion. These generate anti-social forms of behaviour which serve to accelerate and deepen the malign circuits, which in turn justify and accentuate the exclusion. Poverty feeds upon and reproduces itself. The high levels of unemployment and single parenthood, the high incidence of inadequate housing and low levels of educational attainment, the violence and discrimination—all become part of a self-reinforcing process by which the conditions reproduce themselves and the exclusion and structured disadvantage intensifies (Gans, 1996; Marcuse, 1996; Mingione, 1996; Wacquant, 1996). The evidence presented earlier suggests that such a process has been set in motion in Winnipeg. How we respond to it depends in large part on how we think about its causes—about what explains inner city poverty.

Broadly speaking, there are two types of explanations for the phenomenon, not only in Winnipeg but elsewhere as well, of growing inner city poverty: one is structural, the other cultural.

Structural explanations find causes for increased inner city poverty in changes in the structure of the economy. There are a variety of structural explanations, but they have in common the observation that the structure of the economy—at a national and even international or global level, as well as at the local level—has undergone significant changes in the past thirty years, and especially during the 1980s and 1990s. One result has been that the location and the types of jobs have changed to the disadvantage of inner city residents. Companies have closed their plants and shifted the physical location of their productive activities, in some cases to other countries and in other cases to different parts of the country or continent—to wherever lower costs prevail. Many of these mostly mass production industries employed large numbers of people with relatively low levels of skill, paid a living wage and were often located in urban areas. Their closure and/or relocation has had particularly adverse consequences for inner city residents. One version of this explanation holds that the labour market has been split into two tiers: a highly-paid upper tier of managers, lawyers, bankers, accountants and technically-trained people; and a poorly-paid lower tier of urban residents who do a variety of low-wage service sector jobs (Bluestone and Harrison, 1988). Another related explanation, the "urban mismatch" theory, argues that mass production industries which once employed inner city residents have relocated to suburban and exurban sites and have been replaced by service industries, especially so-called information-based industries, for which most inner city residents do not have the skills and which in any event pay lower wages (see for example: Kain, 1992; Kasarda, 1988; Wilson, 1987).

Cultural explanations, by contrast, find the causes for increased inner city poverty in the cultural attributes of inner city residents—their attitudes, values and beliefs, and their consequent behaviour. There are a variety of cultural explanations (see for example: Banfield, 1968; Lewis, 1968; Mead, 1986; Moynihan, 1965; Murray, 1984; Peterson, 1991), but each holds that the high rates of poverty, unemployment and single-parenthood that characterize inner cities are a function not of exogenous structural factors, but of the cultural attributes of inner city residents themselves. The poor respond to their circumstances by developing their own, separate set of—often pathological—beliefs, which in turn are passed along to succeeding generations, instilling in them a variety of economically dysfunctional values. Their values, in short, prevent them from seizing the opportunities available to them. These cultural forms of explanation and the policy responses that follow from them, have become particularly popular in the past fifteen to twenty years, fuelled by the growth not only in Winnipeg but in much of the industrialized world of geographically-concentrated urban poverty.

The argument advanced in this chapter, an argument based in large part on the real-life experiences of those working in the inner city, is that the explanation for increased inner city poverty is multifaceted and the various causes are both structural and cultural. Although poor people develop cultural responses to their circumstances and these cultural attributes—which on occasion include seemingly pathological behaviour—are significant factors in describing and explaining inner city poverty, cultural attributes themselves do not explain or cause poverty. Nor is it the case—as expressed especially clearly in the "culture of poverty" approach—that the resulting cultural attributes lock people into poverty (Lewis, 1968). A more fruitful and nuanced interpretation has been advanced by William Julius Wilson, whose analysis of inner city poverty in the U.S. is applicable to Winnipeg and other Canadian urban centres. Wilson argues that:

> ... cultural values emerge from specific social circumstances and life chances and reflect one's class and racial position. Thus, if underclass blacks have limited aspirations or fail to plan for the future, it is not ultimately the product of different cultural norms but the consequence of restricted opportunities, a bleak future, and feelings of resignation resulting from bitter personal experiences. Accordingly, behaviour described as socially pathological and associated with the ghetto underclass should be analyzed not as a cultural aberration but as a symptom of class and racial inequality. As economic and social opportunities change, new behavioural solutions originate and develop into patterns, later to be complemented and upheld by norms. If new situations appear, both the patterns of behaviour and the norms eventually undergo change. "Some behavioural norms are more persistent than others," wrote Herbert Gans in 1968, "but over the long run, all of the norms and aspirations by which people live are nonpersistent; they rise and fall with changes in situations" (Wilson, 1987. p. 14).

Culture matters, in other words, but it is not fixed. It does not lock people into an inevitable and unbreakable cycle of poverty. Change the opportunity structure, and people will respond, and as they do their cultural norms will, in time, be modified. However, this can best be done by those who are "culturally competent," by those who are sensitive to the cultural circumstances of people in poverty. So for example, even though job creation must be at the heart of any anti-poverty strategy—jobs generate not only income but also family stability and hope for the future, which affects children's educational attainment, which in turn affects their job prospects, thus setting in motion a positive cycle—such a strategy cannot just create jobs and expect all those in poverty simply to join the ranks of the employed. Many poor people lack not only educational/technical skills, but also the social/personal skills needed for most service sector jobs, and they also lack self-confidence, and a sense of self-worth or self-esteem. Poverty has ground them down, has affected how they think, and how they think about themselves, and how they think about their futures and their children's futures and their hopes and aspirations and what might and what might not be possible for them. People in these circumstances need more than simply jobs. They need preparation for jobs, along with a variety of supports to enable them to succeed.

This is best done—given the importance of cultural attributes—through culturally-appropriate, community-based organizations, staffed not by government officials nor corporate employees but by people who have lived in and are intimately familiar with the inner city and what it does to people who are poor—by people who have experiential knowledge of inner city circumstances. This is a community development approach. Community development is an essential part of an anti-poverty strategy because the cultural consequences of poverty have to be taken seriously, just as public investment in people and in job creation are an essential part of an anti-poverty strategy because structural explanations of poverty have to be taken seriously. Structure and culture are closely interconnected in complex and often hard to discern ways.

Conclusion

Winnipeg has a serious problem of inner city poverty. It appears to be worsening. Neither market-based solutions nor bureaucratic solutions have worked. There is, however, a community-based solution that has emerged spontaneously from the inner city itself. This community-based approach is practical and innovative. It is tailored to the needs and circumstances of, and it is built upon the full involvement of, inner city residents themselves. It builds community and in the process repairs shattered lives. It creates hope and pride while producing tangible and useful outcomes. It operates on a small-scale, is attentive to the cultural and personal needs and circumstances of individual people, and it meets real needs. It works, and there is a wealth of evidence that it works. It is the basis of a lasting solution to poverty in Winnipeg's inner city.

The necessary complement to this community-based strategy is a different governmental approach to inner city poverty. The role of the state, of government, is not to promote profit-making opportunities for corporations, nor to "deliver programs" to and for inner city residents. It is to facilitate the process by which inner city people themselves rebuild their communities. An active government role is still needed, but the role is to respond to and assist the practical efforts, the creativity and innovativeness, that characterize so many community-based, inner city initiatives.

This approach is a necessary complement to a broader government investment in people. Throughout the 1990s the provincial government's investment in education, for example, has declined significantly, despite the strong evidence that levels of educational attainment are strongly correlated with success in finding a job and with lifetime earnings. The evidence is strong that public investment in early childhood education produces a financial return far beyond the level of the initial investment (Schweinhart et al, 1993). Investment to increase the availability and accessibility of childcare facilities would create significantly improved opportunities for young parents, especially young women. The evidence is clear that a higher minimum wage would reduce income inequalities, and the evidence is also clear that income inequalities correlate with ill health, which adds to the cost to society of health care. Indeed, the evidence is clear that poverty is the greatest causal factor in adding to health care costs. It follows that increased public investment of these kinds—public investment in people—is needed, is cost effective, and is a necessary complement to the community-based approach to inner city poverty that is described in this chapter and elsewhere in this volume and that is being put into practice in Winnipeg's inner city.

This will cost money. Those who say, "you can't solve problems by throwing money at them," are wrong. Or at least, they are partly wrong. We cannot solve a problem like inner city poverty unless we throw money at it. That is a necessary condition. But it is not a sufficient condition. The question is, how is the money to be spent, to be invested? The evidence suggests that the mechanism ought to be a community-based fund or funds, on whose decision-making board the community is strongly represented, which makes money available to well-conceived and well-managed community-run projects—projects which reflect the widely-held philosophy described in this chapter—and which ensures that the money is spent productively.

Those who argue that we cannot afford such expenditures are completely wrong. If the money is not invested so as to begin to address the problem, the problem will get steadily worse and the total cost to society—in the form of rapidly growing expenditures on child and family services, health care, policing, penal institutions—will escalate and is likely to out-strip any temporary savings achieved by not investing to solve the problem. By contrast, public investment in a community-based anti-poverty strategy will, in the course of time, reverse this process, leading to reduced levels of public expenditures on child and family services, health care, policing and penal institutions. We all benefit from such an investment. It is a flawed form of accounting which advises us that we cannot "afford" to spend money on poverty. The truth is, we cannot afford not to.

If this is a reasonable conclusion, it is outrageous that poverty and all its associated problems are allowed to continue to grow in Winnipeg's inner city, and elsewhere in Canada. The increasing severity of the problems and their consequences and the number of past studies documenting these are now such that it is impossible that governments are unaware of their existence. Yet still they fail to respond adequately. Those initiatives that have been taken invariably fall well short of what is needed. Too little money is invested, for too short a time, with too much control from the top, and as often as not in bricks and mortar rather than in people. Not only is this morally wrong; it is also economically short-sighted. There is simply no defensible reason for the continued failure of governments to invest in an inner city anti-poverty strategy. There are many good reasons—including the well-being of society as a whole—for government to invest in an anti-poverty strategy that works.

What is being advanced here is an anti-poverty strategy rooted in the observation that the solutions to the problems of inner city poverty are already there, being put into practice by inner city people themselves, hard at work within their communities. There is plenty of empirical evidence to support this observation. What is needed now is the political will to take steps to fully support these locally-based initiatives at community-building. These are solutions that work.

Interviews

Bruce, Lucille. Native Women's Transition Centre. June 4, 1998.
Champagne, Louise. Neechi Foods Community Store. February 24, 1999.
Chorney, Paul. West Broadway Alliance. May 22, 1998.
Goodman, Janice. Andrews Street Family Centre. January 26, 1999.
Guiboche, Audrey. Niji Mahkwa School. June 23, 1998.
Hammond, Barry. Point Douglas Residents' Association. May 21, 1998.
Helgason, Wayne. Social Planning Council of Winnipeg. June 5, 1998.

Hill, Josie. Ma Mawi Wi Chi Itata. June 17, 1998.
Hunter, Heather. William Whyte Community School. May 20, 1998.
Knol, Dilly. Andrews Street Family Centre. January 26, 1999.
Loewen, Gary. SEED Winnipeg. May 20, 1998.
Laramee, Myra. Niji Mahkwa School. June 23, 1998.
Mallett, Kathy. Aboriginal Ganootamaage Justice Services of Winnipeg. June 15, 1998.
Maracle, Virginia. Winnipeg Free Press. June 9, 1998.
Maunder, Mike. Winnipeg Free Press. June 9, 1998.
Northcott, David. Winnipeg Harvest. June 4, 1998.
Riley, Pauline. Manitoba Action Committee on the Status of Women. May 21, 1998.
Sacouman, Sister Lesley. Rossbrook House. February 15, 1999.
Selinger, Greg. Winnipeg Education Centre. June 3, 1998.
Simbandumwe, Louise. SEED Winnipeg. May 29, 1998.
Simms, Tom. Community Education Development Association. May 25, 1998.
Spillett, Leslie. New Directions for Children, Youth and Families. February 5, 1999.
Tetlock, Chris. North End Women's Centre. January 21, 1999.
White, Leroy. Northern Star Collection. January 21, 1999.
Wiebe, Erika. *West Central Streets.* May 27, 1998.

References

Aboriginal Council of Winnipeg and Inner City Housing Coalition. *Inner City Home Ownership Cooperative Investment Fund: Concept Paper* (Winnipeg, December 1998).

Axworthy, Lloyd, and Pat Christie. *Winnipeg's Core Area: An Assessment of Conditions Affecting Law Enforcement* (Winnipeg: Institute of Urban Studies, October, 1975).

Banfield, Edward. *The Unheavenly City* (Boston: Little Brown, 1968).

Black, Errol, and Jim Silver. *A Flawed Economic Experiment: The New Political Economy of Manitoba* (Winnipeg: Canadian Centre for Policy Alternatives-Manitoba, 1999).

Campaign 2000. *Child Poverty in Canada: Report Card 1998* (Toronto: Campaign 2000, 1998).

Canadian School Boards Association. *Students in Poverty* (Ottawa: Canadian School Boards Association, 1997).

Canadian Union of Public Employees (CUPE). *What We Owe to our Families: A Brief on Child Welfare in Manitoba* (Winnipeg: Canadian Union of Public Employees, 1996).

Carter, Tom. "Community Inquiry into Inner City Revitalization: What Should be the Focus of Future Initiatives?" *Institute of Urban Studies Newsletter*, 33, January 1991.

Cho!ces and Canadian Centre for Policy Alternatives. *Alternative Budgets*, various years.

Clatworthy, Stewart. *Final Evaluation of the Winnipeg Core Area Agreement Housing and Community Improvement Area Programs* (Winnipeg: Winnipeg Core Area Initiative, September 1987).

Community Inquiry into Inner City Revitalization. *Final Report* (Winnipeg, June 25, 1990).

_____ . *Community Plan For Winnipeg's Inner City* (Winnipeg: 1991).

Community Welfare Planning Council. *Social Service Audit* (Winnipeg, 1969.)

Durkheim, Emile. *Suicide* (New York: Free Press, 1951).

Decter, Michael and Jeffrey A. Kowall. *The Winnipeg Core Area Initiative: A Case Study* (Ottawa: Economic Council of Canada, Local Development Paper No. 24, April, 1990).

Esman, Milton J., and Norman T. Uphoff. *Local Organizations: Intermediaries in Rural Development* (Ithaca, New York: Cornell University Press, 1984).

Falconer, Patrick. "The Overlooked of the Neglected: Native Single Mothers in Major Cities on the Prairies," in Silver and Hull, 1990.

Filmon, Premier Gary. "State of the Province Address," Winnipeg Chamber of Commerce, December 3, 1998.

Gans, Herbert. "From 'Underclass' to 'Undercaste': Some Observations About the Future of the Post-Industrial Economy and its Major Victims," in Mingione, 1996.

Greenstein, Robert. "Universal and Targeted Approaches to Relieving Poverty: An Alternative View," in Jencks and Peterson (eds.), 1991.

Harrison, Bennett, and Barry Bluestone. *The Great U-Turn: Corporate Restructuring and the Polarizing of America* (New York: Basic Books, 1988).

Jargowsky, Paul A. *Poverty and Place: Ghettos, Barrios, and the American City* (New York: Russell Sage Foundation, 1997).

Jencks, Christopher, and Paul Peterson(eds.). *The Urban Underclass* (Washington, D.C.: The Brookings Institution, 1991).

Johnston, Frank. *Core Area Report: A Reassessment of Conditions in Inner City Winnipeg* (Winnipeg: Institute of Urban Studies, 1979).

Kain, J.F. "The Spatial Mismatch Hypothesis: Three Decades Later," *Housing Policy Debate*, 3, 1992.

Kasarda, John. "Jobs, Migration and Emerging Urban Mismatches," in Michael G.H. McGeary and Lawrence E. Lynn Jr. (eds.), *Urban Change and Poverty* (Washington, D.C.: Academy Press, 1988).

Kiernan, Matthew J. "Intergovernmental Innovation: Winnipeg's Core Area Initiative," *Plan Canada*, 27, 1, March 1987.

Kubiski, Walter. *Citizen Participation in the '90s: Realities, Challenges and Opportunities* (Winnipeg: Institute of Urban Studies, Occasional Paper No. 30, 1992).

Kuyak, Joan Newman. *Fighting for Hope: Organizing to Realize our Dreams* (Montreal: Black Rose Books, 1990).

Kyle, Irene and Maureen Kellerman. *Andrews Street Family Centre* (Ottawa: Canadian Association of Family Resource Programs, 1998).

Leo, Christopher, and Lisa Shaw. *Inner City Decay in Winnipeg: Causes and Remedies* (Winnipeg: Canadian Centre for Policy Alternatives-Manitoba, October, 1998).

Lett, Dan. "All agree childcare in turmoil: Fix elusive," *Winnipeg Free Press*, June 3, 1998.

Lewis, Oscar. " The Culture of Poverty," in Daniel p. Moynihan (ed.), *On Understanding Poverty* (New York: Basic Books, 1968).

Lindberg Consulting. *Students at Risk Project, Focus Groups, Executive Summary* (Winnipeg: Manitoba Education and Training, 1998).

Loxley, John. *Childcare Arrangements and the Aboriginal Community in Winnipeg: A Report Prepared for the Royal Commission on Aboriginal Peoples* (Winnipeg, November 1993).

Lyon, Deborah, and Lynda H. Newman. *The Neighbourhood Improvement Program, 1973-1983: A National Review of an Intergovernmental Initiative* (Winnipeg: Institute of Urban Studies, Research and Working Paper No. 15, 1986).

Manitoba. *Report of the Aboriginal Justice Inquiry of Manitoba* (Winnipeg: Queens Printer, 1991).

———. *Report of the Independent Review of the Circumstances Surrounding the April 25-26, 1996 Riot at the Headingly Correctional Institute* (Winnipeg: Manitoba Justice, 1996).

Manitoba Association of Social Workers (MASW). *Submission to the Community Inquiry Into Inner City Revitalization* (Winnipeg, 1990).

Manitoba Children and Youth Secretariat. *Strategy Considerations for Developing Services for Children and Youth* (Winnipeg, March 1997).

Manitoba Family Services. Annual Reports of the Childrens' Advocate (Winnipeg: Queens Printer, various years).

Manitoba Health. *The Health of Manitoba's Children*, by Brian Postl (Winnipeg: Queens Printer, 1995).

Maunder, Mike and Virginia Maracle. "Fixing the City," *Winnipeg Free Press*, May 17, 1998.

——————."Getting at the Roots," *Winnipeg Free Press*, July 26, 1998.

Marcuse, Peter. "Space and Race in the Post-Fordist City: The Outcast Ghetto and Advanced Homelessness in the United States Today," in Mingione (ed.), 1996,.

Mead, Lawrence. *Beyond Entitlement: The Social Obligations of Citizenship* (New York: Free Press, 1986).

Medoff, Peter and Holly Sklar. *Streets of Hope: The Fall and Rise of an Urban Neighbourhood* (Boston: South End Press, 1994).

Mingione, Enzo (ed.). *Urban Poverty and the Underclass* (Cambridge, MA: Blackwell Publishers, 1996).

Moynihan, Daniel p. *The Negro Family: The Case For National Action* (Washington, D.C.: U.S. Department of Labor, Office of Family Planning and Research, 1965).

Muldrew, Fiona, and Louise Simbandumwe. *Final Report on the Lord Selkirk Park Community Economic Development Project*, Presented to the Winnipeg Community Economic Development Resource Group, September 1997.

Murray, Charles. *Losing Ground* (New York: Basic Books, 1984).

Nozick, Marcia. *No Place Like Home: Building Sustainable Communities* (Ottawa: CCSD, 1992).

Peterson, Paul. "The Urban Underclass and the Poverty Paradox," in Jencks and Peterson (eds.), 1991.

Prairie Research Associates, Inc. *Operational Review of the Winnipeg Child and Family Services Agency* (Winnipeg: Department of Family Services, March 26, 1997).

Putnam, Robert. *Making Democracy Work: Civic Traditions in Modern Italy* (Princeton, New Jersey: Princeton University Press, 1993).

Rebick, Judy. "Kick 'Em Again," *Elm Street*, September 1998.

Rothney, Russ. *Neechi Foods Co-op Limited: Lessons in Community Development* (Winnipeg: Winnipeg Native Family Economic Development, Inc., July 1992).

Russell, Frances. "Free Market Fails Poor," *Winnipeg Free Press*, March 31, 1997.

Santin, Aldo. "Big Bucks, Vague Impact," *Winnipeg Free Press*, December 5, 1999.

Schellenberg, Grant and David p. Ross. *Left Poor by the Market: A Look at Family Poverty and Earnings* (Ottawa: CCSD, 1997).

Schumpeter, Joseph. *The Theory of Economic Development* (Cambridge, MA: Harvard University Press, 1936).

Schweinhart, Lawrence J., Helen V. Barnes and David p. Weikart. *Significant Benefits: The High/Scope Perry Pre-School Study Through Age 27* (Ypsilanti, Michigan: The High/Scope Press, 1993).

Silver, Hilary. "Culture, Politics and National Discourses of the New Urban Poverty," in Mingione (ed.), 1996.

Silver, Jim. *The Cost of Privatization: Olsten Corporation and the Crisis in American For-Profit Home Care* (Winnipeg: Canadian Centre for Policy Alternatives-Manitoba, 1997).

——————. *Thin Ice: Money, Politics and the Demise of an NHL Franchise* (Halifax: Fernwood Publishing, 1996).

———. and Errol Black. "Business Leadership and Urban Economic Development: The Case of Winnipeg 2000," *Prairie Forum*, Vol. 22, No. 2 (Fall) 1997.

———. and Errol Black. "A Perverse Economic Strategy," *Winnipeg Free Press*, December 30, 1998.

———. and Jeremy Hull (eds). *The Political Economy of Manitoba* (Regina: Canadian Plains Research Centre, 1990).

Simms, Tom. "Preschool a Crucial Time," *Winnipeg Free Press*, March 7, 1997.

———. " Inner City Housing Needs Boost," *Winnipeg Free Press*, January 19, 1999.

Skocpol, Theda. "Targeting within Universalism: Politically Viable Policies to Combat Poverty in the United States," in Jencks and Peterson (eds.), 1991.

Smith, Bev. "They're Ba—ack! Ma Mawi Returns to Neighbourhood," *West Central Streets*, January-February, 1999.

Social Planning Council of Winnipeg. *Winnipeg's Downtown: A Comparative Demographic Analysis* (Winnipeg: Social Planning Council of Winnipeg, September 1996).

———. *An Integrated Community Approach to Health Action: Evaluation Findings and Lessons Learned* (Winnipeg: Social Planning Council of Winnipeg, May 1998).

———. *Child Poverty in Manitoba: 1998 Report Card* (Winnipeg: Social Planning Council of Winnipeg, 1998).

———. and Winnipeg Harvest. *Acceptable Living Level*, Winnipeg, September 1997.

Toronto Food Policy Council. *If the Health Care System Believed 'You Are What You Eat': Strategies to Integrate our Food and Health System* (Toronto: Toronto Food Policy Council, Discussion Paper # 3, October 1997).

United Way of Winnipeg. *Trends, Issues and Innovations in Winnipeg's Human Care Services: A Report on Discussions amongst United Way of Winnipeg Member Agencies* (Winnipeg, February, 1997).

Wacquant, Lois J.D. "Red Belt, Black Belt: Racial Division, Class Inequality and the State in the French Urban Periphery and the American Ghetto," in Mingione (ed.), 1996.

Wilkinson, Richard. *Unhealthy Societies: The Affliction of Inequality* (London: Routledge, 1996).

Wilson, William Julius. "Social Policy and Minority Groups," in Gary D. Sandefur and Marta Tienda (eds.). *Divided Opportunities: Minorities, Poverty and Social Policy* (New York: Plenum Press, 1988).

———. *The Truly Disadvantaged: The Inner City, The Underclass and Public Policy* (Chicago and London: The University of Chicago Press, 1987).

Winnipeg Child and Family Services. Annual Reports, various years.

Winnipeg Core Area Initiative. *Partnerships for Renewal* (Winnipeg: Winnipeg Core Area Initiative, 1992).

Winnipeg Harvest. *Fact Sheets*, various years.

Winnipeg Native Family Economic Development Inc. *It's Up To All Of Us: A Guide to Community Economic Development in Winnipeg's Inner City* (Winnipeg, February 1993).

Winnipeg School Division Number One. *School Demographics Reports*, various years.

Yalnizyan, Armine. *The Growing Gap: A Report on Growing Inequality Between the Rich and Poor in Canada* (Toronto: Centre for Social Policy, 1998).